CREATING
THEATER

CREATING THEATER

The Professionals'
Approach to New Plays

LEE ALAN MORROW
and
FRANK PIKE

Vintage Books

A DIVISION OF RANDOM HOUSE
NEW YORK

A VINTAGE ORIGINAL,
FIRST EDITION
November 1986

Library of Congress Cataloging-in-Publication Data

Morrow, Lee Alan.
Creating theater.
1. Theater—Production and direction.   I. Pike,
Frank.   II. Title.
PN2053.M64   1986   792′.02   86-40149
ISBN 0-394-74279-6

Manufactured in the United States of America

10 9 8 7 6 5 4 3 2 1

Book design by Andrew Roberts

To our parents

Acknowledgments

In order to successfully complete this book, and to arrange so many personal interviews, we came to rely on the kindnesses of many friends and strangers.

We extend our heartfelt thanks to Actors Equity, Bridget Aschenberg, David Ascher, Spencer Beckwith, Lois Berman, John Breglio, Allison Burnett, Reva Cooper, Mitch Douglas, the Dramatists Guild, Sherry Eaker, Judy Fish, Elan Garonzik, Milton Goldman, Peter Hagen, Liz Holloway, Jeff Hunter, Trent Jenkins, Sue King, Marion Koltun, Richard Kornberg, George Lane, Robert Lantz, David LeVine, Biff Liff, Glenn Ligon, William MacDuff, Sandra Manley, Debbie McGee, Helen Merrill, Meg Mortimer, Gilbert Parker, Claudia Reilly, Flora Roberts, Howard Rosenstone, Katie Rothiker, Luis Sanjuro, Leah Schmidt, Lee Silver, Monty Silver, Leslie Spawn, Clifford Stevens, the Society of Stage Directors and Choreographers, Bob Ullman, United Scenic Artists, Georgianne Walken, Ronnie Yeskel, and our editor at Random House, Derek Johns.

Finally, through her unwavering devotion to this project, and her place in our lives as a friend, Eileen Fallon has proved to be that one person "without whom this book would not have been possible."

CONTENTS

INTRODUCTION

American theater is experiencing a renaissance. This renewal, this revitalization, is what we have set out to explore in *Creating Theater*.

In the great moments of theatrical activity—the golden age of Greece, the Elizabethan era in England, the period between the world wars in America—it has been the living playwright who has reawakened and re-created the theater. Today in America, such writers as Lanford Wilson and Marsha Norman, Wendy Wasserstein and Christopher Durang, Charles Fuller and Maria Irene Fornes ask probing questions of, make startling revelations to, and forge intellectual and emotional alliances with their audiences. They hold up mirrors to America and their own experience, and we discover ourselves in the reflections.

Throughout the first half of the twentieth century, the primary platform for new plays was the commercial Broadway stage. Then, as production costs continually rose and film and television became important media for serious drama, Broadway producers showed increasing reluctance to risk money on untested plays and playwrights. The result was that new play production declined drastically in the United States from the early fifties to the late sixties.

The revival of new play production began in earnest in the early seventies in small, not-for-profit theater companies, such as Circle Repertory and Playwrights Horizons, peopled by "graduates" from the early experimental theaters, Cafe Cino and La MaMa, and the leading professional training schools, Yale and Juilliard. At the heart of this renaissance was a revolutionary means of developing new plays and encouraging new playwrights: the workshop approach.

The overwhelming and continuing success of workshop-developed plays and musicals compelled more and more theater companies to attempt workshops. The technique was simple: often starting with an early draft, the script of a new play was taken through a series of unrehearsed or minimally rehearsed sit-down readings. The playwright, actors, and maybe a director gathered in someone's living room or a company's rehearsal space. The evolving script was read, the reading discussed, and the playwright inspired to return to the typewriter for further writing and rewriting.

When everything a playwright could learn through sit-down readings was exhausted, the evolving play was often put through a more formal, staged reading. By getting the actors up on their feet, even with scripts still in hand, the playwright, as well as an interested director and producer, is given a sense of the physical relationships in the play, a suggestion of performance, an experience closer to production. For the director and the actors, a staged reading simulates the dynamics of actual rehearsals without the pressures of an impending opening night.

Constant feedback from directors, actors, designers, and invited audiences, along with relatively unhurried rewriting between steps, results in a more substantial product, created in a more sane environment. The workshop approach of testing, shaping, and perfecting a script before a final commitment of funds and energies enables more new playwrights to develop and achieve their potential, and more new plays to reach production successfully.

Since the early eighties, the workshop approach to developing new plays and playwrights is no longer considered experimental and vaguely avant-garde. Commercial producers have assimilated the workshop into the standard rehearsal process as a means not only of developing a script, but also of reducing the risks of producing new plays, an economic necessity in these financially tight times. Each theater company using workshops has created its own variations: Some use readings to determine the extent of their escalating involvement; others develop new plays but do not produce them commercially.

Creating Theater examines the workshop approach to the development of new plays and the collaborative effort that is its foundation. Today's plays are created through the collaboration of a new breed of directors, actors, designers, and theater companies, who, like the playwrights, have grown up with the workshop approach.

New plays are usually produced in an improvisatory atmosphere, without a safety net of tradition—there is no production history to fall back on. Everything involved in doing a new play is done from scratch, without acting versions of the script telling the director exactly how each scene was originally staged; without the template of film versions of the play; without reviews of the New York production; without set, lighting, and costume designs copied from publicity photos and so on. Every member of the production team—the theater producing the play, the playwright, the director, each actor, and each designer—depends on his or her own imagination and ingenuity and that of the production team as a whole. The success of a new play is invariably founded on the successful collaboration of the artists involved.

Putting up a new play can be an overwhelming experience. To begin with, it must be selected from hundreds or thousands that a theater might receive during a year. Can a script's potential be accurately judged? If the new play is to be produced in workshop, the production team has to figure out how best to use the workshop approach. Should there be a series of sit-down readings, then rehearsal, or a nonperformance workshop first? Also, the play may change drastically between the first reading and production. Roles may be reduced, expanded, or even cut completely. Sets, lighting, and costume designs completed before the start of rehearsals may have to be rethought in a matter of days or even hours as the script continues to evolve. Decisions made spontaneously become a part of the text forever.

In preparing *Creating Theater* we spoke with some of today's most important playwrights, directors, actors, designers, producers, theater companies, and critics—seventy-five people in all. The conversations, lasting anywhere from forty-five minutes to several hours, took place in restaurants, offices, theaters, homes, over the telephone, over drinks. With an eye toward presenting a wide range of theatrical experience, we chose a variety of artists—seasoned veterans and relative newcomers, people from Broadway, Off- and Off Off-Broadway, and regional theater. We ended up with hours and hours of tape-recorded opinions, prejudices, insights, and advice. The conversations have been edited, but we have let the artists speak for themselves with a minimum of commentary or editorializing on our part.

Through the arrangement of responses, we have created a mock round table discussion, providing the reader with a range of perspectives. The reader is invited to compare and contrast the opinions, insights, and advice, not only within a chapter, but from chapter to chapter. Much can be learned from the answers of a director, a designer, and an actor to the question, "What do you look for in choosing a new play?" In addition, it is possible to view a particular play or production from multiple viewpoints. For instance, the reader can find comments on Lanford Wilson's *Fifth of July* from the play's director, set designer, lighting designer, and one of the actresses, as well as the playwright himself.

An actor, for example, can gain valuable perspectives on the craft of acting by turning to the chapter "Actors and Actresses," and then add to those insights by reading in other chapters what playwrights, directors, designers, and *other* actors have to say about working with actors. By looking at a production of a new play from all sides, the reader—whatever his or her interest in theater—will gain a more complete understanding of the collaborative process. It is important to know each artist's process, especially with new plays. While the goal is the same, the artists advance at different speeds. The vast majority of the playwright's work is usually completed before the actor learns his lines; the director's approach or concept is usually finalized before the designer begins sketching.

Working on *Creating Theater* taught us that there is no single "right" way to develop new plays. As many playwrights hate staged readings as love them. As many actors memorize their lines before rehearsal as go in absolutely cold. Some directors prepare blocking in advance, some do not. Almost any path can lead to success on a new play, but perhaps the only trait inherent in all successful collaborations is the willingness to let the play be the focal point of the reading, the workshop, the rehearsals, and the performance. As Marsha Norman puts it, new plays do not succeed "when they are statues raised to the ego of any of the artists involved." Even the playwright must eventually bow to the supremacy of his or her work.

There is great comfort and a certain familiarity in staging a revival. We know the story, the characters, and the emotional and intellectual demands that will be made on us. Staging a new play, on the other hand, is an experience as potently "religious" and transforming as was ancient theater—itself the expression of a religion. At its finest, the new play experience acknowledges the communion of the audience and performers with their greater society, their greater world.

Theater persists because of new plays. Those who love theater go to be challenged, infuriated, taught, and transported. There is a profound and basic joy in seeing something for the first time, learning something previously untaught, knowing something that moments before was unknown.

LEE ALAN MORROW

FRANK PIKE

CREATING
THEATER

PLAYWRIGHTS

The playwright's process is longer than that of any other collaborator responsible for bringing a new play to life. Directors, actors, and designers are often involved with a script for only a few months before moving on to another play, another production. But a playwright lives with a script for years, from the initial image or idea, through successive drafts, to the casting, rehearsing, and shaping of the premiere production.

The first part of this chapter explores the writer's private self, the solitary artist molding language to fit a certain vision, arranging the hundreds of imagined and autobiographical details. When the script—a blueprint for performance—is more or less complete, the playwright's public self emerges to work with the director, actors, and designers who will interpret the play and give the playwright's words life.

In this chapter, playwrights discuss the dynamics between the private and public self. They also talk about their backgrounds and training, the influences on their work, and the process of pulling together raw material, drafting, and rewriting. They discuss how they collaborate in workshops and in rehearsals with other theater artists. They offer advice to writers just starting out and ponder the essential elements of good playwriting and exciting theater.

The twenty playwrights we interviewed represent all regions of the United States, all ages and all levels of experience. One thing they all share is a commitment to their craft and their art; they are long-distance runners.

Lee Blessing has had numerous productions in regional theaters. *Independence, The Old Timers' Game*, and *War of the Roses* were produced at the Humana New Play Festival of the Actors Theatre of Louisville. He has received National Endowment for the Arts (NEA), McKnight, Jerome, Schubert, and Wurlitzer playwriting grants. He lives in Minneapolis, where he is a member of the Midwest Playwrights' Center.

Bill C. Davis lives in Los Angeles and Connecticut. His Broadway play, *Mass Appeal*, was later produced as a film starring Jack Lemmon and Željko Ivanek. His other plays include *Dancing in the End Zone* and *Wrestlers*. Davis is also an actor.

Christopher Durang has written the following plays: *Sister Mary Ignatius Explains It All for You, Beyond Therapy, The Baby with the Bathwater, The History of American Film,* and *The Marriage of Bette and Boo*. He received Obie Awards for *Sister Mary* and *Bette and Boo*, in which he also acted. Durang wrote *The Idiots Karamazov* with Albert Innaurato, and *The Luisitania Songspiel* with Sigourney Weaver.

Maria Irene Fornes came to the United States from her native Cuba in 1945. Fornes has won more Obie Awards than any other living playwright except Samuel Beckett and Sam Shepard. She also received a special Obie for "sustained achievement." Fornes's many plays include *Fefu and her Friends*, *The Conduct of Life*, *Molly's Dream*, *The Successful Life of 3*, and *Promenade*.

Charles Fuller won a Pulitzer Prize for *A Soldier's Play*, which was originally produced by the Negro Ensemble Company. His adaptation of this play for the film *A Soldier's Story* received an Oscar nomination. Fuller has received an Obie Award and Guggenheim, NEA, and Creative Artists Public Service program (CAPS) grants. He was born and continues to live part of the time in Philadelphia.

A. R. Gurney, Jr. was born in Buffalo, New York, and currently divides his time between New York and Massachusetts, where he teaches literature at M.I.T. *The Dining Room*, originally produced at Playwrights Horizons, has become a staple of regional and community theaters. His other plays include *Scenes from American Life*, *The Middle Ages*, *The Perfect Party*, and *Children*. Gurney is also a novelist.

Beth Henley, born in Mississippi, won a Pulitzer Prize for her Southern gothic comedy, *Crimes of the Heart*. Her other plays—*The Wake of Jamie Foster*, *The Miss Firecracker Contest*, *The Debutante Ball*, and *Am I Blue?*—also reflect her Southern upbringing.

Tina Howe began writing plays when she was teaching high school in Maine and Wisconsin. Her best-known work, *Painting Churches*, produced by New York's Second Stage theater company, won an Obie Award. Her other plays include *The Art of Dining*, co-produced by the Kennedy Center and the New York Shakespeare Festival, and *Museum*, which premiered at the Los Angeles Actors Theatre.

David Hwang is the recipient of an Obie Award, a Drama Desk nomination, a Chinese-American Arts Council Award, and Rockefeller, Guggenheim, and NEA fellowhips. His plays, which explore Asian-American society, include *The Dance and the Railroad*, *FOB*, and *Family Devotions*.

Corinne Jacker comes from Chicago. Her best-known work, *Bits and Pieces*, premiered at the Manhattan Theatre Club. *Harry Outside* and *My Life* were originally produced at Circle Repertory, where Jacker is a member of the playwrights' lab. Jacker has written several screenplays and served as head writer for a major soap opera. She also writes science texts on such topics as cybernetics.

Heather McDonald has just begun her career as a playwright. *Faulkner's Bicycle* was given a production in the Yale Repertory Theatre's Winterfest and at the Joyce Theater in New York. Another play, *Available Light*, was first produced at the Humana New Plays Festival of the Actors Theatre of Louisville.

Emily Mann won Obie Awards for writing and directing *Still Life*. *Execution of Justice*, her play about the assassination of gay activist Harvey Milk, has been produced on Broadway and in many regional theaters, such as San Francisco's Eureka Theatre, the Arena Stage in Washington, D.C., Actors Theatre of Louisville, and the Guthrie Theater in Minneapolis. Mann has received Guggenheim, NEA, and CAPS grants.

Stephen Metcalfe was commissioned by the Manhattan Theatre Club to write *Vikings* and *Strange Show*. His other works include *Half a Lifetime* and *The Incredibly Famous Willy Rivers*. He has received NEA and CAPS grants.

Marsha Norman was a book critic and the children's page editor of the *Louisville Times* when Jon Jory, artistic director of the Actors Theatre of Louisville, encouraged her to write plays. Her Pulitzer Prize-winning play, *'night, Mother*, premiered at the American Repertory Theatre in Cambridge, Massachusetts. Her other plays include *Getting Out*, *Circus Valentine*, *Traveler in the Dark*, and *The Laundromat*, which was televised in a production starring Carol Burnett and directed by Robert Altman.

Eric Overmyer received national recognition with his fantasy play, *On the Verge*, in which three Victorian travelers set off on a voyage through time. Overmyer has served as the literary manager of Playwrights Horizons, and is the recipient of a McKnight Fellowship. His plays, including *Native Speech*, have been performed in New York, Seattle, Los Angeles, Baltimore, and Denver.

Peter Parnell lives in New York and has written such plays as *The Sorrows of Stephen*, originally produced by Joseph Papp's Public Theater, and *Romance Language*, produced at Playwrights Horizons. His play *The Rise and Rise of Daniel Rocket* was shown on Public Television's "Theatre in America" series in a production starring Tom Hulce and Valerie Mahaffey.

John Pielmeier is a member of New Dramatists. His play, *Agnes of God*, was originally produced at the Actors Theatre of Louisville, and later made into a film starring Jane Fonda, Meg Tilly, and Anne Bancroft. His other plays include: *The Boys of Winter*, produced on Broadway with Matt Dillon and D. W. Moffett, *Jass* and *Sleight of Hand*, both of which received Honorable Mentions in *Playbill* competitions. Pielmeier won a Christopher Award for his teleplay of *Choices of the Heart*.

Ted Tally was born in North Carolina. After completing his MFA in playwriting at the Yale School of Drama, he became a resident writer of Playwrights Horizons. *Terra Nova* has become one of the most produced plays in the country. His other plays include *Little Footsteps*, *Coming Attractions*, and *Hooters*. He has received NEA, CAPS, and CBS Foundation grants.

Wendy Wasserstein is a resident writer of Playwrights Horizons. *Uncommon Women and Others*, her first hit, produced at the Phoenix Theatre, was subsequently televised with Meryl Streep and Swoosie Kurtz. Her play *Isn't It Romantic* has had great popular success throughout the country.

Lanford Wilson was born in Lebanon, Missouri, the setting of his cycle of Talley plays—including *Fifth of July*, the Pulitzer Prize-winning *Talley's Folly*, and *Talley and Son*. His other works include *The Hot l Baltimore, Lemon Sky, Angels Fall, Serenading Louie, The Mound Builders, Balm in Gilead,* and *The Rimers of Eldritch.* He is a co-founder of the Circle Repertory Company, an Off-Broadway theater dedicated to creating new plays through an ensemble of playwrights, directors, actors, and designers.

How did you become a playwright?

CORINNE JACKER: I wrote my first full-length play when I was eleven—it was an adaptation of *The Seagull*. In college, I took one playwriting course at Northwestern University, got a *C* in it and was told I deserved less, but they didn't want to ruin my chances for graduate school.

MARIA IRENE FORNES: I have no formal training as a playwright. I just started writing.

TINA HOWE: I was never stagestruck. My husband really is. When we go to the theater, I'm always surprised at how starry-eyed he gets—sweaty palms, fibrillations of the heart. My tug toward being a writer is more literary.

CHARLES FULLER: I was working in Philadelphia as a housing inspector. Some friends and I formed a group and used part of a church as a theater. I wrote little skits—things that would reduce the tension between the blacks and the Puerto Ricans in the community. I learned theatricality from those skits. We staged gun battles in the streets and had the actors run down to the door of the theater. People followed to see what was going on, and then the play started. We learned how to make things happen in the theater.

MARSHA NORMAN: I believe my sense of craft comes from my music background. In music you can't simply play something louder in order for it to have more impact. There is a real sense of drive in music, of continuing and returning to themes, the difference it makes when a new instrument comes in, the care that has to be taken so the listener is carried along.

I'd been a lifelong fan of the theater and I'd seen an awful lot of theater. I would sit there and think, "I could do that." That thought was a constant companion for years. What kept me from doing theater was my knowledge, even then, that you couldn't earn a living in theater, and the assumption that writers in the theater don't come from families like mine and from my part of the country. I grew up with the assumption that writers came from wealthy East Coast families that sat around the dinner table talking about Shaw. My parents had never heard of the Pulitzer Prize until I won it.

Playwrights have a particular point of view, an instinct. It's a feeling for drama, a preference for one-to-one confrontation. I come from a family where silence was perceived as the best way to spend a dinner, and if you broke that silence it was only to say something "cheery." I grew up thinking of what I *might* be saying and was not allowed to say. My plays are constantly about the saying of the unsayable thing.

LANFORD WILSON: When I moved to Chicago from San Diego, I was working for an advertising agency, but thinking of being an artist, an editorial illustrator. I was writing stories, and began one that didn't really sound like a story; it sounded like a play. I was not two pages into it when I said, "I'm a playwright." If anyone had asked me that night what I did, I would have said, "I write plays." It didn't matter that I didn't know a damned thing about plays.

The University of Chicago had an adult education play-writing class. I took twelve sessions. The professor would say, "A play must have conflict. Here is an example of conflict. Now that everyone understands what conflict is, go home and write a scene with conflict and bring it in typed next week." The next week, four actors from the Goodman Theatre would come and read the scenes, sight unseen. There we were, sitting and hearing real, professional actors reading our work. It was absolutely thrilling, just thrilling.

A. R. GURNEY, JR.: I became a writer because I had an old-fashioned private school education where the standard procedure was to write a composition a week. You had to produce something each week. I got into the habit of writing. I've never learned any real rules of playwriting. You learn by constantly doing your work, reading it out loud, having it read out loud. I'm not sure the stuff about exposition, turning points, and obligatory scenes is that helpful. Schools provide opportunities—no matter how limited the scale—to have your work done. That's the best training for a playwright.

PETER PARNELL: The stuff I wrote at Dartmouth didn't necessarily appeal to my teacher or to the department, but they did it. What I learned in school was that in great plays, everything—every single moment—is where it is for a specific purpose. From looking at the great plays you can learn the nuts and bolts of form.

TED TALLY: My training really started in graduate school. In the mid-seventies, Yale had a grant from CBS to bring in professional writers as tutors. I worked with David Mamet, Terence McNally, and Arthur Kopit. Writing took on a whole new professionalism. It didn't seem so ivory-tower.

Suddenly there were living, breathing people who made their living writing plays—something I had only imagined. They made playwriting seem like a realistic mission for the first time.

Who has influenced your work? Which writers do you consider to be role models?

LEE BLESSING: The writers who influence me most—Mamet, Shepard, Churchill, and Norman, among others—seem to be those I don't write like. But they are all excellent and they make me challenge myself to try to pursue excellence in my work. The best kind of influence, I think, is excellence, of whatever sort, attained.

A. R. GURNEY, JR.: Because I've been in school, as a student or as a teacher, for a good part of my life, I've constantly been reading plays, teaching them, talking about them, thinking about them. The great playwrights have been my role models.

JOHN PIELMEIER: My truly favorite writer is J. M. Barrie. I think he had an innate understanding of the theater that no other writer in the twentieth century really has, with the exception of Thornton Wilder. Barrie really knew what made terrific theater. Anybody who can write a play in which the main character flies is just amazing.

TINA HOWE: I had grown up going to Marx Brothers movies and loving chaos unleashed, but I'd never seen it live on the stage. Seeing a production of *The Bald Soprano* when I was in Paris was a revelation. All these crazy people running around, speaking French and dropping from the ceiling. To me it was like real life! It wasn't absurd. It was this tremendous shock of recognition. I went haywire. I realized I wanted to put a beautiful kind of madness on the stage. I saw this as a mission, somehow.

BETH HENLEY: I remember reading *Waiting for Godot* while I was in high school. It blew my mind. It was so funny and so out there.

CHRISTOPHER DURANG: When I was growing up, I watched old movies all the time. Fellini and screwball comedies influenced me, but not consciously.

EMILY MANN: When I first started working at the Guthrie Theater on a fellowship I coached Shakespeare. I worked with actors on making the monologues into a true *dialogue* with the audience. I think Shakespeare was amazingly showbiz and theatrical and knew a monologue was the best way to reach out to an audience intellectually and emotionally. Take "To be or not to be. . . ." Hamlet is including the audience, asking them to be part of his decision: "You've seen what I've seen. If you were me, what would you do?" I've brought the theatricality of Shakespeare's monologues directly to my work.

TED TALLY: I had so many influences on my work that they all sort of mushed together. I never sat down and said, "I want to be Sam Shepard." I might want a play of mine to have the vividness of language that Sam Shepard's have, but perhaps a better sense of structure. I always look for what is best in a writer. You take what you can learn, from as many people as you can.

LANFORD WILSON: John Guare and Sam Shepard write wonderful plays, but they sure didn't influence me any. We were all extremely different, original, working from our own experiences and ideas. From the first stroke, we all knew exactly who we were.

Traditional American theater was all I knew: Arthur Miller and Tennessee Williams. I hadn't read Strindberg, Shaw, Chekhov, and Ibsen, or seen them. I'd seen Shakespeare, but try to be influenced by him!

Years later, I'd been called "Chekhovian" so many times, I wanted to see what the fuck that was. I bought four of Chekhov's plays, read them, and was blown, of course, utterly out of the water. He's probably been an influence since then.

What do you want to say through your plays? Why is playwriting a better medium for expressing what you have to say than fiction or poetry?

EMILY MANN: I'm not a novelist or a poet. I'm a playwright, so I do my damnedest to make my material into a play. I didn't become involved in theater because of the show business—though I love it—but because theater is where you can battle out big ideas.

I've always had a love affair with ancient Greece. The people got together once a year to watch a communal story, to laugh and cry. They then had a year to think about what they had experienced. Theater was a civic event, so it had to deal with larger issues. I think our theater can still do that.

DAVID HWANG: Every once in a while I ponder what my plays are about, but I never come up with a good answer. I seem preoccupied with our collective past, and our individual pasts—things that have happened to us at an earlier point of life which may have a bearing on what we do now.

LEE BLESSING: I like playwriting because it forces us to realize something together, in a group. Neither fiction nor poetry really does this. Also, playwriting has a much greater component of emotion than is generally found in these other genres. I am always trying to move an audience toward a group discovery: of humor, of tragedy, of an idea, of an emotion.

TED TALLY: If there is a recurring theme in my work it is the theme of competition and failure—striving for a goal, reaching it, and finding it isn't that important.

CORINNE JACKER: I'm interested in finding a way to go on, finding a positive something to hold out. Choosing the present and not the past, sanity and not insanity.

TINA HOWE: More than anything, I want to make people laugh. I was always a clown as a little girl, so tall and funny looking. I sound pompous when I talk about the *craft* of writing plays or the *importance* of moving an audience, but to be absolutely honest, what I'm really after are those laughs.

Where do you find material—characters, relationships, situations, conflicts—for your plays?

LEE BLESSING: In a world as woefully arranged as this, it's easy to find material. Everyone's life holds the potential for tragedy or comedy on the personal or political level. I happen to live and work in the Midwest, but the same spiritual defeats and efforts against hopelessness can be found anywhere. My characters are the same as anyone else's, except perhaps for occasional mannerisms of speech.

MARIA IRENE FORNES: Plays are limited by using real people as character models. When you are writing purely from imagination, you let the characters move and behave as *they* want; they find their own parameters, their own lives.

When you deal with situations you have witnessed or experienced, you know exactly what happened. If you decide that actuality doesn't work for the play and something has to be changed, what do you follow? When you follow the characters in your imagination there is not one truth, but a number of possibilities, all of which are true.

The character that is completely imagined comes out of myself. Every character I imagine is part of me. I'm not embarrassed to put myself onstage. The sadistic captain in *The Conduct of Life*, and the victim of that sadistic captain—you can't *write* them unless you *are* them. If a character is brutal, it is because I am brutal. I take the blame and the credit. No writer can write a character unless she understands it thoroughly inside herself.

TINA HOWE: I think it's true of most playwrights that their characters—male and female, young and old—are just aspects of themselves. When I people the stage with all these souls, what I do is split myself up. I implode and all these little fragments tear around inside me like crazy and become the characters.

LANFORD WILSON: I deliberately look for colorful people. They're very right for theater. Theater has to be theatrical. If you can get color into the accountant, you've got something. Write the whole thing first and then say he's an accountant. That's a very wacky accountant, but so what? Theatricality feeds and challenges the actor, the director, and the designers.

Just before I started working on *Hot l Baltimore*, I read

Dickens's *Our Mutual Friend*. I had just done *Lemon Sky* and *Serenading Louie*, and they seemed pale and quaint compared to Dickens. I knew I had to goose my work. I knew I had to have characters that were more far-out. Your characters have to have some magic.

CORINNE JACKER: Like every writer, I'm a magpie. I pull material from everywhere. I read a lot of novels and non-fiction. And, of course, material comes from my own life. Like every playwright, I write plays that are autobiographical and yet not.

PETER PARNELL: Finding material takes a long time. If I research some area knowing there is a story I am interested in, then that becomes several months of reading, taking notes, and wandering around a lot in bookstores and museums. In the reading I do, character, metaphor, and other aspects of the play somehow coalesce. You don't know where you're going to end up, but you sort of do.

A. R. GURNEY, JR.: In the past ten years I've drawn characters more from my life. There's a time for everybody when they want to write about themselves. While I have always been interested in the gap between the world I grew up in and the world that exists today, I don't think I really probed or explored it until the past ten years. There were people alive I didn't want to hurt.

DAVID HWANG: I'm quite aware of the extent to which my own life is embedded in the things I write. I'd like to think it's not obvious to the casual observer. Essentially, what I do is take the essence of an experience and transmute it into a form where the specifics are different. Take *Dance and the Railroad*, for instance. I've never worked on a railroad, but I have understood what it is like to be at war with yourself over your own artistic impulses, in the battle between commerce and art.

HEATHER MCDONALD: Writing is a tool for dealing with the world. No matter what, everything you write is inevitably going to be filtered through you. It is a great exercise to start out with the intent to explore something more than yourself because what you write is eventually about yourself anyway.

JOHN PIELMEIER: Everyone says, "Write what you know." Of course that's true, but I think we all know everything, in a sense. I think I'm one of the few writers around today who doesn't have a play that I'm aware of with any remote resemblance to my own life, to autobiography. All of my plays come from my head, my imagination.

TED TALLY: I had a sense my own history was not that interesting. I grew up in a suburb—it happened to be in North Carolina but could have been anywhere in the country—with middle-class parents, and a safe, protected, normal background. I thought, "I didn't go to Vietnam. I've never been in prison. I'm not homosexual. I don't have this great burning anger against society. Nobody cares what I have to say." I am beginning to realize that I do have some things to say, and I can trust in them.

Some French writer said, "All fiction is imaginative autobiography." I never used to believe that, but maybe now I do.

Do you follow some sort of writing routine?

TED TALLY: I'm horribly lazy, self-indulgent, and sloppy. The great bane of my existence is that I don't have better discipline. That said . . . I get up in the morning, have breakfast with my wife; she goes off to work, I sit down at the typewriter at nine o'clock, and work until I feel burned out. It might be two hours or it might be six or seven. I work until I get a bad headache or feel I'm not really making progress. In the afternoons I will usually read over what I wrote and make changes, or go to a movie.

Sometimes it is astonishing how little gets done for the amount of time that goes into it. I have a tendency to rewrite the same page fifty-seven times—changing the same two lines over and over. It all varies from one play to the next. Every play seems to demand to be written in its own way.

CHRISTOPHER DURANG: I don't work every day. The Protestant work ethic is something Catholics don't have.

BILL C. DAVIS: I feel guilty about not writing. If there is something I am ready to start writing then my writing schedule starts, but I don't write every single day. I alternate writing indoors with milking my goats outdoors.

I live on a farm in Connecticut. The farm is more of this world than Broadway is. I have to milk the goats twice a day. It's relaxing and you don't know you're thinking about problems while you're milking. A few nights or a week later a solution hits you. Milking goats absorbs a lot of the tension. There is a logic to it; it's a different clock to live by.

BETH HENLEY: A lot of times I'm in my office just picking lint off the carpet, or calling my mother, or writing birthday cards. If I'm working on something, or if I have a deadline, I work.

JOHN PIELMEIER: I don't write every day. When I'm working on a specific project, I will try to write as often as I can. Before I start a project, it is very important for me to have everything else in my life straightened out—answer all the correspondence, clean the house. I'll start around ten in the morning, write until I'm hungry, eat, and then go back to work until I'm tired. Sometimes I'll work all day, even in the evening. I will often give myself a deadline (which I am constantly readjusting) as a goal.

LEE BLESSING: I write longhand, from late morning on. I even recopy in longhand. I like playwriting, because the product is short enough that I don't *absolutely* have to compose on a typewriter. That's something I find hard to do. I can't afford a word processor.

HEATHER MCDONALD: My daily writing schedule depends on how broke I am, what kind of job I've got. Whatever the current limits or restrictions on my time, I try to make a schedule and then stick to half of it.

The thing I most enjoy about writing is finishing, because then I can go and do something else. People have this romantic idea about writing, but it's so goddamned tedious. Within a four-hour stretch I will probably get in about an hour's work. I sit there and gnaw on things. I never have been struck with brilliance when I'm taking a shower. Any good writing I've done comes from sitting and mulling over everything and finally grunting it out a bit at a time.

EMILY MANN: I'm now a mother, and it's amazing how that focuses me. I used to wait all day and when it was right I would dash in and write in a white heat. I can't do that anymore. I have three to five hours in the day when I can write with no distractions. I carve out that time and all my mind focuses on getting there. There is no ritual at all. I either do it or don't that day, and too bad for me if I mess up.

TINA HOWE: I think that if you're a mommy you learn very quickly how to use your time. When the kids go off to school, that's it. You have four hours, so you go tearing into your room and you are very purposeful and disciplined. I think that even for women who don't have kids, there is some clock. Sometimes I envy those men who write for two weeks and then go on a bender. I think men have that luxury.

A. R. GURNEY, JR.: Because of the school compositions I had to write in the thirties and forties, I *have* to write the first draft with a fountain pen. If it were in pencil, it would be just a sketch or a doodle. I've tried ballpoint pen, but it seems too modern, unreal. I don't turn to a typewriter until I've got almost a complete, full-length draft. It's a lot of starting, stopping, beginning again.

I start, write about four pages, throw it away, start again. The first line and the second line have to be absolutely right before I can get any sort of a run at it. Once I think I've got a run on a play I just write along, even if it is terrible, because I know I've got a good start back there at the first line.

When I have a feeling I've come to an end, then I type on an old mechanical typewriter in which I only use cheap, cheap, cheap yellow filler paper. The typewriter means it is a little more serious now, and I've got to call the thing to account.

As I go over this draft, typing, the discoveries are interesting. I have no idea I wrote some of it. The writing process makes you forget even as you are writing. They say women in childbirth forget the pain almost immediately afterwards. For me, I'm writing along, and it seems okay at the time, but I seldom remember what it says. Typing on this yellow paper is always exciting and surprising. Some of it is not that good, of course, but I rewrite along the way.

Finally I type the thing on white paper, what I call—absolutely foolishly—"the final draft." We're nowhere near the final draft, but this is the draft I will let sit for five days to a week. I go over it again, make corrections in pencil and in ink, and have it typed up by somebody else. That draft, typed by somebody else, is the first draft I will show anyone. None of this goes out of this apartment, or wherever it is I'm working, until then. A work doesn't seem showable until it has a finished, semiprofessional look.

TINA HOWE: I am a rabid fan of the late Glenn Gould and I have been writing plays since 1957 to his Bach recordings. All of my plays are Glenn Gould's inventions, partitas, suites, *The Well-Tempered Clavier* and the *Goldberg Variations*, over and over, over and over. I think through the years that baroque fugal structure has crept into my writing. Invariably musicians comment on the musicality of the rhythms of the language in my plays.

DAVID HWANG: I usually write in longhand in a reclining position—virtually half-awake, half-asleep. I work either early in the morning or late at night. I'll keep a pad near the bed, wake up, open the pad, and start scratching. I will also scratch before I go to bed. When I'm working, and into it, I will work three or four hours in the morning and then three or four hours before I go to bed.

MARIA IRENE FORNES: I would never sit in front of a blank page and try to write a play. I would, in the past, if an idea came to me, write it down. It might be a page, two pages. Then when I was ready to write a play, I would go through the various scraps of paper I had saved and see if there was anything interesting.

Since I have been teaching, my writing class is where I write. We all write there. I am much more disciplined.

I now write whether I'm inspired or not, and have written six plays since my workshop began three years ago. When I am in my house I don't sit down punctually at any time. I procrastinate and have many reasons why I can't write.

Each day I read everything I have written, make corrections, move forward to the point where I had stopped, and go on. I would never start in the middle of a race, so I start always at the beginning, running to my last stopping point, and then continue. Since I make changes as I go along, the first parts are always on the fifth or sixth rewrite, while I am just writing the end.

PETER PARNELL: I don't spend more than four or five hours a day actually writing, but I don't focus on a lot of things other than writing during the rest of the day. I use a typewriter. I type with one finger. I love making corrections. I love the mess.

MARSHA NORMAN: When I first got my computer I was a real disciple. I went around giving lectures and seminars, telling people we couldn't go on anymore without these machines. After a year of feeling that way, I discovered I was having conversations with the screen. I was beginning to write for the screen.

The screen is fond of a different kind of writing than the paper is. The screen is real interested in long, complex sentences: dazzling, showy work. Paper is interested in poetry: single words and short phrases.

What I do now is to use the computer like a refrigerator. I do the work on yellow paper, store it in the computer, and use it for editing. Paper has restored the sensual pleasure of writing—the actual choosing of the pen and ink, and that walk across the page. It's been a real interesting journey back to where I began.

CHRISTOPHER DURANG: I used to write in longhand and then type it over. I had this hideous typewriter from high school and finally the *T* broke off and there was no way of fixing it. I got a word processor, went to a seminar Marsha Norman gave, and asked many a question. Now I find it hard not to write with the word processor.

WENDY WASSERSTEIN: I can spend a day reading the paper, returning phone calls, seeing who's around for lunch, wandering around in the afternoon, having anxiety for an hour about why I'm not writing, going to the theater. I can figure out ways to let months and months go by without writing.

When I am writing, I have to get up in the mornings. I don't really write all that well in the afternoons. I work best under a deadline, under pressure. I become compulsive. When I'm really on it, I write in the mornings, go out for a grinder, and then write again in the afternoons. It's kind of exciting, those times, but it's not a great way to live.

Do you find outlines useful in gathering your thoughts? Do you do any research?

BETH HENLEY: I carry a notebook around so that I can write down notes. I'll write down images I see, what some character might be wearing, a piece of furniture I think of for the set, some dialogue somebody might say. Once I get the characters, I make long lists for each one. One character would say this, this, this, and this. Another character would wear this. Somebody carries a shotgun—who would that be?

I'll write a list of scenes: Who is onstage first? Who joins him or her? Who leaves? Who arrives? Whatever character is onstage first—if she's alone—obviously can't say anything, so what is she going to do? I go back to my charts. I wanted somebody to light candles on a cookie? Well, *she* can do that.

JOHN PIELMEIER: On my latest play I worked from an outline. I made a character sheet for each character. I kept a very thick notebook of my research. Once I had it all down, it took me only about six weeks to write the play. I also think about the play thematically before I write. If I don't do that, I tend to get sidetracked. I end up with a first draft that is a lot cleaner than if I hadn't used an outline.

The outline is very general. It's usually simply a matter of saying that such-and-such happens in a scene. A lot of things creep into scenes that don't show up in the outline. There is inspiration involved. Sometimes I shift scenes around. I'm very free. The outline helps me to know the general arc of the piece.

TINA HOWE: I make a lot of outlines—scene by scene. I find it very dangerous for me to be just writing cold, because I then go off on these little baroque bits about all sorts of arcane things which have nothing to do with the play. The whole enterprise can evaporate. I have to tie myself down as best I can to whatever plot I have. On each scene of the outline I will write one sentence to say what happens in that scene, how it advances the story.

TED TALLY: I found when I began with a strong sense of structure—outlines and such—it was constricting. The writing would come out sort of canned. It's the easiest thing in the world for a playwright to come up with a kind of arithmetic to make the sums come out. I think that is a hollow victory. The best plays are the ones where the writer himself doesn't know everything that's going to happen. If you are continually surprising yourself as a writer, you will surprise and hold your audience.

LANFORD WILSON: I've found when I know the end of the play at the start, it's really not fun to write. It doesn't surprise me nearly as much. Since I want the play to seem largely spontaneous, I'm in real trouble when I know too much.

HEATHER MCDONALD: When I'm in the early stages of writing, I can spend a lot of time going to the library—where at least the wheels are turning—instead of sitting at the typewriter, moaning. I enjoy having to find out about things I don't know. I like to amass this mound of notes and then carve out of it. By the time I get to writing I'm fairly sure of what I want to do.

Let's explore your writing process. How do you begin turning your ideas into plays?

LANFORD WILSON: I wander around for at least six months, disturbing everyone I know, saying, "I have nothing to say. I should never have been a writer. I don't know how a play is written. I don't know what a play is. I haven't an idea in my head, so what is the point of pretending? Well, there is that idea I had. . . . If I *were* going to write it, what would it be like?" So then one character or the other starts talking. I write that. Suddenly one of them says, "Oh, shut up!" and I have a point of view.

CORINNE JACKER: Gradually I turn into a bitch. I know now when I get really hostile I am "with play" and it's time to drop that play. Of course I have a hard time sitting down to write. I have all sorts of disguises, tricks, and games. I trick myself sometimes with knitting. I will knit on a very complicated project. I'll start knitting in the morning and tell myself I won't be able to start writing until I finish this many rows, or this particular part of the pattern—that kind of frippery. I really don't know what I'm doing when I start. You start with instinct. You start with a particular moment.

BETH HENLEY: It's time to begin writing when you hate yourself and want to commit suicide because you haven't written your play. When I start thinking that if I don't finish my play I'm going to die, nobody will know what it was, and somebody else is going to say what the end of it would have been. . . . I start writing like a mad person trying to finish it.

TED TALLY: You let your idea for a play nag at you and get under your skin, then you write. You might have half a dozen ideas and only one is built around and built around like a grain of sand in an oyster shell. You become obsessive. You walk around all day dreaming about your idea. It comes up in conversation with friends. You know your idea is the real thing if it insists on being written. If writing about this idea becomes almost a matter of life and death, then you know you are on the right subject.

LEE BLESSING: When I have a good idea for a play—something that can *sometimes* be summoned by rigorous, analytical thinking—I tend to let it recline in the living room of my mind for a month or more. If at that point it still looks attractive to me, I invite it into the bedroom. Later, I take it for long walks and get to know it. I plan the play fairly completely before I write any of it.

WENDY WASSERSTEIN: I don't think visually all that much, but I will have a final image that makes me want to write a play. With *Isn't It Romantic* I didn't have an image at first, but as soon as I got it—the girl dancing alone—I could finish the play.

TED TALLY: A play very often occurs to me as an image, a sense of place. I have to really know what the environment of the play is. In the case of *Terra Nova*, it started from seeing a photograph of Perry's expedition in Antarctica. I wondered who these men were and what they were doing there. What could make somebody do something so crazy?

BETH HENLEY: I usually get a situation in my mind first. With *Crimes of the Heart* I wanted to write about some catastrophe in a family and the family having to come back home to face it. Then, from the situation, I thought of the characters and invented the story.

With *Miss Firecracker* I knew somebody was going to be on the roof at the end of the play watching fireworks. I didn't really know which character or characters it would be, how they would get up there, what they would be doing. I work from feelings, intuition.

HEATHER MCDONALD: Everything I've written has begun with a picture that won't go away. *Faulkner's Bicycle* came from an image of someone building sailboats in an attic, building so many that finally the attic was filled with sailboats and she had to leave. The image kept coming back, so I began to write a play about sailboats.

JOHN PIELMEIER: Most ideas for me really begin years before I ever put anything on paper. I'll think of an idea. I'll maybe sketch something very briefly and put it in a drawer. I let it go at that. Then, at some point, I know it's time to write, and I sit down and write it.

A lot of times I'll write a scene with a fabulous twist, look in an old notebook three weeks later, and see that I had the same idea three or four years ago. I'm sure my unconscious had been working on that idea for a long time. Plays evolve gradually from their inception to their conception. It's not a conscious evolution.

CHRISTOPHER DURANG: The initial impulse for a play varies. *Sister Mary* is a good example. My mother was dying of cancer, and it was a long death. When somebody is dying there isn't much you can offer them except the comforts of religion. I got to remembering some of the things I was taught and no longer believed. I was really struck by the notion of being six or seven years old and having intricate knowledge of what acts sent you to hell and what acts didn't. The Catholic church didn't leave much to the imagination.

I wanted this nun character to be onstage giving a lecture in which she explained *everything*. The emphasis on "everything" was the important part. She covered everything in the universe. The Catholic church did—and, frankly, still does in a way—cover everything. If push comes to shove on a particular issue, the answer will be, "Well, we don't know the answer. It's a mystery, but we'll know after death." What a nice comfort it must be to have an answer for everything was the impulse for *Sister Mary*.

A. R. GURNEY, JR.: Sometimes things find you. A phrase might just keep repeating in my head. I'll drop this phrase into my head and the play will begin to crystallize around it. I'll just write a scene which that phrase seems to want to be in. Other times, I will fabricate an idea intellectually and hope something happens: "What if I wrote a play that took place entirely in a dining room?"

I'm kind of old-fashioned in that I'm really not happy unless I've accomplished something in my day's work. I don't think reading—as much as I like to read—is legitimate. I find it very hard to read unless I've earned that right by writing. I sit there and confront a piece of paper: "What am I going to do today to earn my afternoon's enjoyment?" Sometimes I do what is called "free writing"— just sit there and write. Maybe nothing happens, but then one or two little images or phrases emerge, and something begins to happen.

How do you put together a first draft?

BETH HENLEY: I don't know how my plays are going to end. I don't know about the end of the first act before I get to the middle. I'm real unspecific about the second act until I get to the end of the first. You want to leave yourself open for surprises that are going to happen when the characters begin interacting. I don't really have it all plotted out, though I have pages and pages of notes of things they *could* say and things they *could* do.

EMILY MANN: Since I work from transcripts of interviews, I have a different process from most writers. Most writers sit at their word processors or yellow pad and when their stack of paper gets higher and higher they know they're making progress. For me, it's when the stack gets smaller and smaller. It's more like sculpting than painting. I start with a big square of clay or stone and chip away to find the image underneath. I have transcripts of interviews, notes. They all get put into a huge pile, which then gets distilled and distilled and distilled. I'm looking for the purest form of the truth, the simplest means of expression.

WENDY WASSERSTEIN: I generally start by writing a few scenes which aren't that good. Then I'll rewrite one, and rewrite it again and again until there is a real scene there.

I have to find the voices of the characters. I write a lot of scenes to find their voices.

TED TALLY: It's happened several times that I've written fifty, sixty, seventy pages, following a thread, before I realized what the play really was, and then I had to go back and rewrite everything.

STEPHEN METCALFE: Writing, for me, is almost like an actor's doing an improv. I give myself very specific objectives, a place to go; then I start working toward that place. It is almost as if all the characters are improvising as they go along.

LANFORD WILSON: I write in longhand in a notebook and when things seem to be going well I'll begin to type it out. I'll pull from my notes scenes, characters, conflicts. Out of that will come a structure.

I ordered the scenes of *Fifth of July* to educate the central character—letting him see his fear, learning the necessity of facing that fear, showing him the strength his family and lover provided. *Fifth of July* was originally set in an advertising agency in Chicago. Then I moved it to Long Island, and finally to Missouri. It wasn't until I thought of setting the play in this old house in Missouri that the structure of the play's scenes came together. The house served as a metaphor for the central character.

TINA HOWE: It takes me an enormous amount of time to realize what I'm after. I start with a remarkable setting and a cataclysmic event—a sweep of red on a white canvas. Then, suddenly in the middle of the first act, I have a revelation of what the play is about. I then start all over again and have more revelations. Usually they're so major

I have to start the whole play yet again, because each revelation affects everything.

For three years, *Painting Churches* was about a girl coming home and having her mother make a dress for her debut as a pianist. For three years I struggled and struggled, writing eight drafts which weren't bad, but they didn't work. Finally I got the idea that the girl would be a portrait painter and was coming home to paint her parents' portrait. It was a moment of blinding awareness, an epiphany. And everything fell together. That's how we playwrights work.

DAVID HWANG: In the beginning, when my impulses were more pure, I was just writing for the sake of writing. Things seemed to come very easily. It is something I pine for now. The temptation is to fall back on your old tricks, to take a way out you've taken before, and not try anything new or risky. Writing is a juggling act made more difficult the longer you've been at it.

CHARLES FULLER: Most important to me is the first scene. If in the first five minutes I can't interest you and keep you in your seat, I'm lost. When I rewrite, I always go back to the very beginning and work my way forward to the newest section so that, by the end, I've done those first pages thirty or more times. I have to be certain I can't open the play in any other way. The rest of the play proceeds out of that. Everything you'll need to know about what you are going to see comes in those first five or ten minutes.

CORINNE JACKER: I'm not in any way aware of the audience when writing the first draft. I usually write as many drafts of a scene as there are characters, plus one more. The one extra is the audience draft. The long shot, so to speak, is the audience version. I will try in the first draft not to think at all; to sit down, and, somewhere between six and ten days, as fast as my fingers can type and my brain can go, write. Almost all of it disappears later on, but I'll do that first.

PETER PARNELL: The best time is the first draft. It's very exhilarating. It's very private. Nobody knows what I'm writing. Friends know I'm "in" writing a new play. I never, ever show people work while I'm working on the first draft, but I've gotten to the point where, if I'm feeling confident or having trouble, I will talk to friends. My first drafts tend to be very strong. My instincts are good, and that's something I'm learning to trust more and more.

When will you first show someone a draft of a new play? What do you hope to learn?

CHRISTOPHER DURANG: I always like to have a completed draft, or at least one act completed, before I show the play to anybody. Early criticism can be too discouraging. It almost always degenerates into "Well, this is how I'd do it."

PETER PARNELL: I don't deliver a first draft until I'm very clear about what I don't like. I'm in a vulnerable place, but it's not that vulnerable because I've lived with the play and have a greater degree of objectivity. When the first draft is finished I won't look at it for three weeks or a month.

BILL C. DAVIS: First thing I want is an actor's perspective. Actors are trained to make everything logical for the character—how to get from point *A* to point *B*. The script should also be doing that. Collaboration allows the actors, director, and playwright to show each other the transitions between those points.

EMILY MANN: I have a small group of very close friends—some writers themselves—and my husband, to whom I give an early draft. I listen to them and their responses very carefully. I may also give a script to someone who might be interested in that particular idea or subject. It might not be someone I give every script to, only this particular one. I show a draft when there is a shape and a form, and I think I'm telling the story I want to tell. It's usually before I ever have a reading of it. If the comments I hear really strike a bell, I might do more work before I have a reading.

LANFORD WILSON: I work for Circle Rep. That's my theater. I'll show my director, Marshall [Mason], the first *paragraph* of a draft. I'll read it to anyone passing in the hall. If I'm writing for specific actors, I'll have them read a scene even if it's the only thing I've written so far.

Eveyone is told when they join Circle Rep that until a draft of a play is finished, whatever they think, they must say the pieces I show them are wonderful and great. I was stopped in mid-flight on three plays by having someone say, "Well, that isn't such a great idea." Now they've learned. It's "wonderful and great" until it's finished, and then they can ask, "What is this piece of shit?"

BETH HENLEY: As soon as I get the first act typed up, I show it to a real close friend, to somebody I really trust. But my first draft is basically like a third or fourth draft.

I write the dialogue in longhand real haphazardly in one notebook. I go over that and make changes. I copy that haphazard version into another notebook in neat handwriting. I then go over the neat handwriting and make changes before I turn the play over to the typist. So, in a sense, anything that is typed up isn't really a first draft.

CHARLES FULLER: The first person who sees my work is usually a director. I find the creative energies are better when I keep plays to myself until I'm almost done. If it is something I'm really not sure of, then I don't want to talk about it and get any opinions that blur my focus. I'll tell people the title of the work, or the general area I'm working in, but what it is finally going to be, I'm really not sure myself.

TINA HOWE: No one makes me more nervous reading my stuff than Norman, my husband. When I give him a new script I have to leave the house. I usually go on a wild shopping binge so I can forget everything.

Norman's tough because he's very different from me. He's honest, has a lot of integrity, and I'm—what's the word?—impressionistic, crazy, all over the place. I tend to go for the baroque. I go for excess and Norman goes to the heart of things.

JOHN PIELMEIER: The first time through, I call it my *rough* draft. Then I go through that, revise it, type it up clean, and call that my *first* draft. I'll show that to my wife and then get some actors whom I know and have worked with before to read it. Out of that I will make a *second* draft.

What about rewriting once you've finished the first draft?

TINA HOWE: Rewriting is like watching a Polaroid print develop: the man's face is yellow, his hair is red, and the grass is blue. Everyone is standing in the right place and you realize you have to make certain adjustments.

JOHN PIELMEIER: I try to stick with the initial impulse. I think the danger of doing a lot of rewriting is that you often get away from your initial impulse. Sometimes your initial impulse is not always right, but more often it is. In general, initial impulses are to be trusted.

WENDY WASSERSTEIN: When you go through many drafts you continually have to go back to your first instincts.

PETER PARNELL: You have to learn to preserve what makes you excited about a piece and not ruin that. I hold up my first draft for comparison against later changes. I make a lot of changes, but I don't want to stray from the initial impulse that got me excited.

BILL C. DAVIS: Ultimately, the script has to answer the questions the actors have. If the answer is not in the script, then something has to be done. Rewriting *Mass Appeal* was educational. I learned a lot about writing, getting the point down to the bone, making the line as spare and right as possible.

LEE BLESSING: As I've gone on, I seem to be doing a little less rewriting—which is either a very good sign or a very bad one. If it's good, it means my initial conceptions for plays are getting clearer and perhaps potentially richer. If it's bad, it means my inherent laziness will soon win the battle to dominate my life for good. When I do rewrite, I'm always looking for a way to make the play's action clearer and more compelling.

ERIC OVERMYER: In rewrites I look for where I haven't quite realized the language or imagined something suffi- ciently. I overwrite, so I cut a lot. You tend to under-explain at first, then you have readings and all the advice you get pushes you in the direction of over-explaining. You have to resist that. You can't clarify everything; some of the play has to remain ambiguous.

When do you know it's time to stop working on a play?

A. R. GURNEY, JR.: At a certain point you say "That's it" to a play. You work as hard as you can to make it as good as you can. I have occasionally—after a play has opened—gone back to it. If it got bad press, I may try to rehabilitate it; but normally your head isn't in the same place when you go back. Those rewrites you might do may be well crafted, but they're not felt. The love affair is over.

MARSHA NORMAN: A moment comes when you must move on. I can't take any more time because I'm living a finite life. Plays are like children: the same growth process can't be expected of all of them. They're quite different creatures and must be treated that way. A certain kind of respect must be paid to them after they're written, and sometimes that involves saying, "Okay, go, I'll see you later."

JOHN PIELMEIER: The hardest decision a writer has to come to is when to shelve a play. I've put away everything I wrote before *Agnes of God*. It's writing that was very important for my development as a writer, but I'm not going to show it to anybody. It's not interesting to anyone other than myself.

TED TALLY: I read somewhere that Tom Stoppard once said, "A play is never finished; it's abandoned." I think that's basically true. You must reach a point where you know—better than any critic—there are still problems with it, because you've lived with it for so long, but your energy would be better spent on a new play.

CORINNE JACKER: I accept opening night as a reasonable end to the writing of the play.

LEE BLESSING: The play is finished when it's published and/or no one wants to produce it anymore.

Let's focus on the informal sit-down reading, where a group of actors, with little or no preparation, read a draft of your play. What do you try to get out of a sit-down reading?

EMILY MANN: I like the honesty of sit-down readings. I like to get the actors around a table from noon to five, tell them everything I can about how to make the play work, tell them what I know, and then let them fly with their own strong choices two hours later in front of an audience.

You find out the big stuff: whether the story's being told, where you've got and lost your audience, where the laughs are, if you've cast it right, if the characterizations are telling the story, and how the audience is responding to those characters. You learn about the outlines of your play.

JOHN PIELMEIER: I think all playwriting is essentially map making. Readings really clarify that map. A play is never completed until it is performed. Theater is entirely a collaborative process. Not only do actors and directors help me write my play, but I help them in the performing of it. I think a sit-down reading or a workshop is very much in the spirit of collaboration.

TED TALLY: My first goal in a reading is to see if the play is coherent, if it holds up, makes sense. Even an around-the-table reading can tell you if the play basically is saying what you thought it was saying. Just let the actors read it and see what sort of sense they make of it based only on the evidence of the written page, without cueing them as to what you want.

CHRISTOPHER DURANG: I find actors reading a play aloud extremely helpful. If you know enough actors to cast approximately well (it doesn't help if someone is totally miscast), hearing the play read aloud makes issues and problems immediately clear. We had an early reading of *Sister Mary*, and there were ten minutes that screamed out, "Cut me. Cut me."

ERIC OVERMYER: I think readings are very misleading. People who expect writers to rewrite on the basis of readings are being a bit unfair. You're getting a lot of information, but it's not necessarily accurate. A reading can help you sort out what is happening, but playwrights who rewrite extensively from readings are, I think, deluded.

A. R. GURNEY, JR.: There is a false sense of completion before you have actors read your play. You think it is done, but in your heart's core you know it's not. At a reading I listen for that wonderful hush when a play is working, that laughter, that suspense, that sense of relief at the end.

I listen for those moments when the air seems to go out of the room, moments when you can palpably feel no one is liking the play. That's instinct. Even in a small reading I want the play to be perfect, watertight. I don't take notes. I can go back over the script two weeks later and remember exactly the reactions during the reading.

You have to learn who to listen to and what to listen for. There are certain criticisms—those that feel truthful and right—that hang in the air long after everyone has gone. The best insights will stay with you, they will naturally accrue to the play. The trivial ones, the personal ones, the faulty ones will fall away like chaff.

BETH HENLEY: The way I like to do readings is real low-key: at my house, with just my friends; no producers or hotshots. I ask actors who I think are really, really good and right for the part. I want them to show me what they think about it, without my saying anything. I just want to hear it real spontaneous. My goal is not to get so drunk that I pass out before we reach the intermission. I am too paralyzed to take notes, but basically the problem points stick in my mind so much that I don't need to write them down. The next time I go over the script I'll remember what struck me during the reading.

CHARLES FULLER: I don't do readings of plays. I hear it all in my head. If the characters aren't people to me, then they won't be to the actors or the audience.

HEATHER MCDONALD: I don't find around-the-table readings that useful. A play is people in action. Around-the-table readings are very static. If a play is fairly hot off the press, just hearing it read is very valuable. But after a certain point, you need to see the bodies pushing and pulling each other in order to get a sense of the play's action.

TED TALLY: You should have a few people hear your early drafts, but they have to be highly trustworthy. The equation is not completed without an audience. After the reading, canvass them over the phone or over lunch one at a time, but not in a group, when people feel they have to be witty. If it seems to go over well, and the basic truth is what you intend—never mind the details—then it's time to think about some kind of staged reading.

What about staged readings? Are they helpful?

BETH HENLEY: For *The Debutante Ball* we did a sit-down reading at my house and then had four days of rehearsal before a staged reading. The staged reading really helped because it was closer to a performance than a sit-down reading. I tried to look at the reading not for the performances, but for the technical problems in the script—how it moved and built. I made a lot of good changes after I saw it.

TED TALLY: Problems that are purely technical—How is this set going to work? Is the first act too long? How is this going to be costumed?—are all solvable in rehearsals for a full production. In a staged reading we're really talking about the essence of the script—Does it hold an audience? You need to feel as secure as you can going into rehearsals because, once you are in the center of that maelstrom, it's too late to turn back.

JOHN PIELMEIER: Staged readings offer the advantage of some rehearsal: The playwright and director can steer the actors onto the right path. Also, in a staged reading you can do away with someone reading the stage directions aloud. That, in itself, can help to clarify things. An action that takes twenty seconds to perform might take three minutes to read in stage direction.

I never think of staged readings as auditions for producers. Any reading I do is for me to hear the play.

DAVID HWANG: My goal in a staged reading is to get a full production. Usually, when you do a staged reading it means someone is interested in your play but is not quite sure yet. You want to get the script presented in such a way that whoever is interested will want to do your play. On top of that, you want to see that they will produce the play in line with your vision.

CHRISTOPHER DURANG: I tend not to be drawn to staged readings. However, if you haven't had production experience, I think staged readings are exciting because any little bit of production is more fun and instructive than none.

The director shouldn't overdo the staging. I once saw a staged reading—a woman was talking to her son while she was moving out of the apartment—where this poor actress was carrying folding chairs across the stage, one after another. All this time she was carrying her script. It was so distracting. You couldn't understand a single word the actress was saying. It was pointless. Who needs to know that carrying a chair is what moving looks like?

ERIC OVERMYER: I think a staged reading is neither fish nor fowl. I don't think it's a helpful middle place between a reading and a production. It gives the playwright a superficial rehearsal process that seems more exhaustive than it is. When you see actors up and moving you think you're watching the play come to life when, in fact, they're just skimming the surface.

CORINNE JACKER: I almost never do staged readings. It's one of the things I'm quite antagonistic about. It's a bastard art that just isn't true. Either you want to work with actors and find out what they have to contribute to the play, or you don't. If you do, you should let them rehearse; if you don't, then you shouldn't.

BETH HENLEY: I would prefer to do several sit-down readings and then have a really, really long—six- or seven-week—rehearsal period for the play.

Do you like feedback after a reading? Do you like having an audience present?

JOHN PIELMEIER: It's very dangerous to have an open forum with a bunch of strangers. You can never say, "Well, tell me about it." You've got to ask very specific questions. I used to do coding for market research and I learned two important points that I've adapted to audiences. You have to find out what parts of the play the audience found *unbelievable*, and what parts they found *confusing*.

It's very important to isolate the problems, not to try to find solutions. You can't let anyone tell you how to fix your play. The important thing is to define the problem specifically; the solution will then be obvious.

LEE BLESSING: I don't much like public audience responses after readings of my plays (though I occasionally must endure them). It seems to me that suddenly the very people who came to witness something *collectively* are being asked for *individual* opinions of what just happened. This is hard on the audience and even harder on the author. No one audience member has the whole experience in his head. He can't honestly speak for the group or for the author. He can only speak for himself, for a *fraction* of the experience, not the whole of it. Yet too many people come on like major New York reviewers, and truly do seek to package everyone else's experience.

On the other hand, I do at times hear useful reactions in that setting, both positive and negative. I suppose what I've reacted against most in public discussions are direct questions put to the playwright. This is a most destructive practice, and should *never* be allowed.

One-on-one response is a totally different matter. Panels,

too, can be very frank and mutually useful, at times. I have had some good times at those, especially when they take place in bars. Seriously. Criticism received in such a manner is always gratefully accepted. It is then sorted into two piles: the total malarkey and the probably right. I pick up the latter pile and tote it home.

BETH HENLEY: I would never go through another discussion again. At one discussion people asked me, "Does this play have a meaning, and if so, what?" That isn't helpful. If people go to see my play and don't get it, fine. But I don't want to have to stand there and defend what I've written.

LANFORD WILSON: From the response at a reading you basically learn you haven't done at all what you intended to do. My ideal workshop situation is the Circle Rep workshop. During the discussion after the reading the author is not asked questions. The audience doesn't ask, "What did you intend by that?" They just say what struck them, their impressions. They say where they didn't like the play, what they thought it was going to be, and where in the play they weren't satisfied. Sometimes they don't get something you wanted them to get. Sometimes they get something so different from what you intended that you don't know where to go. You try to see if the audience's description of the play they saw in any way coincides with what you wanted to write.

Then the writer asks specific questions: Did you like so-and-so? Did you understand that he felt this, or that he had been there? Sometimes the audience has no idea about something you thought you had laid in so obviously. It is a great help to know when you haven't communicated something.

EMILY MANN: If a moment that, at the typewriter, I thought would work wonderfully is not working in at least two sit-down readings in a row, chances are the problem is in the writing. If the problem is not the writing, I have to figure out what to tell an actor to make this work. If there is nothing I can come up with, then the problem *is* the writing. I try to fix it. I've learned that when it's an important moment to you, and it's clear that it went past *every* person sitting in the room, your writing is not connecting.

A. R. GURNEY, JR.: The first time a public audience hears a reading of one of my plays I want more of the same thing I got at the first reading in my apartment—that sense of the play not working, getting out of focus, the air going out of the play. Problems seem magnified tenfold when you get into a more public situation. I sit on the side, and, since I know the lines and have seen the actors go through the play already, I normally watch the audience, their expressions, their shifting in their seats.

DAVID HWANG: Early on in my career I thought other people knew more about playwriting than I, and therefore I incorporated everything they said during critiques. I would do a lot of rewriting, almost all of which I would later throw out. Doing all that unnecessary work taught me about filtering criticism. All these people said what they believed—I'm sure that they were interested in the good of the play—but in the end it's my play.

ERIC OVERMYER: In a reading the actors are getting a very quick take on the material. They're just reacting to it. You don't really know what's their problem and what's your problem. To solicit opinions is not helpful. It's my experience that the kind of criticism you get in readings is, "If I had written this play, it would be like this. . . ." You don't get informed criticism that's trying to see through the text to what the writer is trying to do. People aren't shy about offering advice about plays. Anyone on earth will tell you what's "wrong" with your play.

STEPHEN METCALFE: I don't like getting into situations where people tell me what they didn't like. In the early readings especially, I like to see where things get murky. I like hearing the actors say where they got thrown off. I like hearing what people like. Positive reinforcement is something I need to get off, boom, working on the next draft.

I rarely take many notes at readings. Cuts I mark, zip-zip, as the actors read through the play. If I can come out of a reading with two or three very specific things to work on, then I feel very good about the reading.

BETH HENLEY: After a reading either I will go up to the actors or they'll come up to me. I ask, "What did you think? Does this work for you?" That sort of thing. It won't be, "Let's sit around and discuss this." That gets people into feeling they have to have an opinion, and I feel like I'm on trial.

MARSHA NORMAN: I have done readings at home to find out if the thing is playable. Is it well balanced? I have benefited greatly from staged readings in front of audiences, though you have to be very careful to come in knowing the questions you want to ask. You have to have the strength to disregard eighty percent of what you hear. People are so eager to say, "You know, if that one character were a man instead of a woman, it would work much better."

CORINNE JACKER: I think the workshop process can go on too long. You can lose the energy of the play. There comes a time when a risk has to be taken. If the risk is put off too long the play can become an "in joke," so to speak.

TINA HOWE: I hate readings. I feel actors and directors do their best work when they have a finished play. I feel it is my responsibility to finish the play and make it clear. I don't want to confuse anybody by giving them work that isn't thought out. I hand the play in under the assumption that I have given it my best and have answered in the script every possible question one could have.

What do you feel is the playwright's role in rehearsals? How do you give and receive suggestions from the director and actors?

BETH HENLEY: I go to all the rehearsals, except when I completely lose my mind. I can't stay away. I just love rehearsals. I love being in the theater. I love watching people discover something. It's really fun for me. If I make one little change a day, I feel as though I've done something.

MARSHA NORMAN: In those early rehearsal days, you are confronted with the necessity of turning your play over to people who know nothing about it. It is jarring because you've been hearing the play in a very specific way, knowing exactly how it should sound.

Playwrights, if they are not experienced, can get in the way early in rehearsals. The actors are beginning their process. They can't have answers given them too soon. Quite often, the playwright will sit there in rehearsal and have to say, "I don't know," to a question he or she absolutely knows the answer to. Of course you know. You have to determine if you are helping the actors or not.

HEATHER MCDONALD: I go to rehearsals all the time because, after three hours of working on a scene with an actor who is bitching about it, suddenly you realize that you've written something impossible to perform. You learn from sitting and hearing your work over and over.

I hear a lot of writers say, "*They* did this. *They* did that. I got fucked over." If *you* are there every day and fight to be a part of all the decisions along the way, in the end, you were a part of the process. It's about being an adult and taking responsibility for the process.

TED TALLY: I go to all rehearsals. I wonder sometimes if I should begin cutting back to only going at the beginning and at the end. Maybe I'll try that next time. My tendency has always been to want to be at every rehearsal. You do lose objectivity that way, I suppose, over the long haul.

DAVID HWANG: In the past I would be at rehearsals and be very attentive to the demands of the text, but I wouldn't be very attentive to the direction and the technical stuff. I would work very hard writing the thing, but once it was out of my hands, my mind wasn't really engaged in the production process. I think certain of my plays in production have suffered because of that. I've learned to be more active on all fronts during production.

TED TALLY: I'm never really happy when I'm at the typewriter. I'm only happy when I'm in rehearsals. Until the play's tangible, I'm always very unsure.

TINA HOWE: I know that rehearsals are the most exciting time for the actors and certainly the most exciting time for the director, but for me, it varies. Sometimes it's a revelation.

PETER PARNELL: I get bored in rehearsals. I shove off with them, and then I usually disappear for long periods of time. I don't like to disappear for too long because I'm never able to work on anything else while rehearsals are on. Basically, all I do is wander around and get bored or nervous.

CHARLES FULLER: Watching the actors do it over and over again doesn't thrill me. I will watch it in bits and pieces for the first couple of weeks. I try to write in such a way that, if too much were done to it, the whole play would be destroyed. I try to create a character so true that it is difficult for an actor to go wrong. I don't like to leave that sort of thing to chance.

JOHN PIELMEIER: I was an actor, so I think I'm sensitive to actors and their confrontations with writers. I remember how much I would hate writers who came in and did things behind the director's back, but not know what they were talking about. I say everything I want to say through the director. I'm certainly not quiet if something is bothering me. I think it's my duty to explain, to clarify. I can save everyone time.

A. R. GURNEY, JR.: Rehearsals can be very painful, not because of any sense that "they're ruining my play," but the reverse. A community is being formed and I'm not part of it. They're the ones who go out for coffee together. The playwright can't say things because he'll mess up the whole process. Many directors are extremely sensitive and want you only to talk to the actors in the most general terms. The best directors invite you into the rehearsal process as a full collaborator.

HEATHER MCDONALD: I've noticed that there is a certain stage of rehearsals in which the actors love the director and hate the playwright. You're the enemy; you've written some impossible scenes. At another point, they hate the director and not the playwright, because the director is Dad and asking them to do impossible, horrible things.

STEPHEN METCALFE: I've been lucky: I've worked with directors who like having me there, like my being a part of their discussions, like my being an extra pair of eyes. I have a very hard time with a director who wants me to sit in the corner.

You have to let the director do his job. It would be a mistake to jump up and say, "I disagree." You can talk with the director, and through him to the actors. There has to be only one mouthpiece. The director is also your protection in many ways: He's there to make sure the actors don't run up asking you to change things.

Ultimately, rehearsal is breaking the play down into the smallest possible pieces and asking the most fundamental questions about those pieces. Then it is up to everyone— director, actors, playwright—to answer any questions and put the pieces back together. If the playwright can't answer a question, then it's time to rewrite.

ERIC OVERMYER: Watching good actors perform will also suggest possibilities; they'll throw out sparks. Just the sound of their voices, their intonations, some physical thing they do, shows you your play. For instance, they'll give a line reading you haven't heard before that gives a moment resonances you had no idea were there. On the other hand, inadequate actors can obscure a play.

BETH HENLEY: If you have bad actors, you just want to pull out your hair every second. If you've got good actors, it's fun watching them discover things, taking things in directions you might not have expected, expanding things you didn't see that big, or focusing in on different colors. I want actors to make my material look better than it is, or at least as good—certainly not worse.

What about rewriting during rehearsals?

HEATHER MCDONALD: During rehearsals you learn the most about your work. I tend to do a lot of rewriting during the first weeks of rehearsal. You suddenly hear things you'd never heard at your typewriter.

I would rather have rehearsals four hours a day for six weeks than eight hours a day for four weeks. Then you could go in, see things, have that information, and still have time in the day to write, and give the actors time to deal with revisions.

JOHN PIELMEIER: I love to do a lot of rewriting and cutting in rehearsal. Of course, I want things to work immediately. Once we go into rehearsal the play has already had an opening night in my head. It's played beautifully, tremendously, in my brain, and I find it frustrating to see these human beings kind of staggering around trying to figure this play out. Watching them you realize that the play isn't perfect; it needs work.

LEE BLESSING: Any play that needs extensive revision during the rehearsal period was not ready for production in the first place. To put it up is playing Russian roulette. Small revisions are no problem, but no writer should revise anything in a play against his better judgment.

CHRISTOPHER DURANG: I don't like to do a lot of rewriting during rehearsals. It means something was wrong with the script before you started. If you must rewrite, you have to try to cope with it. It's an unhappy situation and very hard on actors. As they get closer to opening night, they want the security of knowing what they're doing.

I'm usually pretty flexible about minor rewriting. If an actor requests a line change that doesn't matter one way or another to me, but makes the actor happy, I'll go along with it. Every so often someone will have a problem with a line I happen to be enamored of, and then I usually try to win them over by convincing them to see my point of view.

MARSHA NORMAN: I don't like to rework much in rehearsal. If I am absolutely positive the actress is right to play this role and she keeps having trouble with lines, remembering them or something, then I know something is the matter and am willing to take a look at it. Rewriting big sections can be devastating.

It is very easy, with the prevailing winds of the commercial theater, for writers to be coerced into making changes that don't need to be made. The rehearsal process can be too tense, and quite often you find yourself making revisions because the playwright is the one who can change the easiest. Everyone would like it to be your problem instead of theirs, so they can go home and have a barbecue while you go home and rewrite the play.

What happens to writers, young writers especially, is that they rewrite under pressure and then get blamed in reviews for what is on the stage. The writer thinks, "That wasn't my idea. The director wanted that." You should never rewrite anything unless you are willing to take full responsibility.

BETH HENLEY: I'm more cooperative about making changes than some of the actors. The actors get real married to some of their lines, and if you cut they feel it's because *they* are bad. Or they "need" this line, they've "just got" to have it—that sort of thing.

MARIA IRENE FORNES: Usually when I take a play into rehearsal, the play is not finished. I am inspired by everything the actors do. I like the deadline pressure of four weeks of rehearsal. After rehearsal I go home and write.

STEPHEN METCALFE: I like the pressure of the performance deadline and I think the performers do too. That's what it's all about. I feel very strongly that in the theater it is Us (all of us who work in the theater), and Them (those who come to see our work). It's important to work up to Them, when They come in.

> *Playwriting is different from other kinds of writing because it's ultimately a collaborative effort. How do you make the process work best for you?*

ERIC OVERMYER: The whole sense of how the collaboration works is very skewed right now. A lot of people feel they can participate in the actual writing when in fact they can't, and shouldn't. You have actors, directors, and designers all wanting to be co-writers. I think that's very damaging and accounts for a lot of the homogeneous, mediocre product in the theater today.

LEE BLESSING: Directors, designers, and actors consider themselves theater people. They do not generally consider playwrights theater people. Therefore, they do not often listen to playwrights during a high-pressure time like the production period. To avoid this, the playwright must know people he can work with (people who are genuinely interested in his opinion) and try very hard to get them.

Directors say selecting the right cast is ninety percent of their job. Selecting the right artistic team for a production is ninety percent of a playwright's job in production. It may be an unfamiliar duty, but it is vital.

The playwright's role in rehearsal is to have already made sure he has chosen the right director, designer, and cast for the show. If he hasn't taken the responsibility for making these choices—even if he's had to fight for them— then he has no role in the rehearsal.

Once in rehearsal, assuming one has the people one wants, it's best to let the director direct, the actors act and the designers design—and to comment and complain *immediately* about anything one does not like. It's most useful to complain only to the director since it is his job to fix it.

TED TALLY: One of the hardest things for a playwright is to be patient. The playwright would love to walk in after a week of rehearsals and see the whole thing up there on its feet. The problem is that if the production is perfect after a week of rehearsals it will be stale after three weeks. Letting the production and the rhythm of the process build from first reading to opening night is something a good director can control. Let the play be clumsy, awkward, stupid in rehearsal. These are the play's labor pains.

TINA HOWE: I'm embarrassed at rehearsals to see people struggling over something I've written.

WENDY WASSERSTEIN: It's so exciting to go out with people, figure out what you're going to do, and then get up in the morning and rewrite. Once you understand what you've got to do, that's exciting.

MARSHA NORMAN: I don't say what comes out of my pen is perfect. Theater is collaborative. Quite often, the writer is better served by and learns more from a wonderful production of a flawed piece—a very deliberate, honest, sensitive production with all the play's flaws intact.

What do you look for when choosing a director for your play?

LEE BLESSING: No play should be directed by someone with whom the playwright hasn't had a *long* talk about every aspect of the production. Preferably, this should happen before the director is hired. Directors tend not to like this because they think it pins them down too early. But they get to direct six plays a year. Playwrights write only one. It's important to get a director who treats the playwright like a partner and a peer. When this does happen, it can be very satisfying for both parties. Besides, it's honest.

TED TALLY: In the early stages of a first collaboration between a playwright and a director there is a kind of delicate sparring back and forth: "Who is this guy? Can I trust him?"

I wouldn't want to work with a director whose work I had not seen. I would call actors and producers he worked with. You send him a script, he reads it. You meet, have a drink, talk about the script, and find out if you're both talking about the same play. You want to make sure he's not thinking about doing some vast number on it. It's such a delicate relationship: You have to make sure he wants to make your play come alive.

BETH HENLEY: When I first started out, I didn't know any directors. The directors I've worked best with are those I felt most comfortable with when I first met them. There was some spark there. I know they're good by the way they talk about the material, the way we relate to each other, their sense of humor.

MARSHA NORMAN: You want to find in a director someone you can be with for a while as a person. I'm always looking for a certain kind of person where, if all else fails, at least we'll enjoy having dinner together.

What I always ask directors when I don't know them—and ask in a more subtle way when I do know them—is, "What do you *like* about this play?" So often directors come in with the attitude that something has to be changed. What I want to try to determine is if we are working by the same guiding principles, basically responding to the same strengths in the play.

It can be very dangerous for young writers to come in contact with a director who wants to "save" the piece. There are a number of directors who take on what they see as "flawed" pieces in order to save them.

In the best possible situation, everyone has a sense of service: the writer feels he serves the story and the characters; the actors feel they serve the play; the director feels he serves the actors and the play. The writer also feels that he is there to do whatever he can to make things smoother for the actors and the director. Basically, all are pursuing a single goal which is not the raising up of a statue to a singular ego.

PETER PARNELL: As Tom Babe says about working with directors, "If you have to explain point A, you're in trouble." You must have an understanding with a director that A is A and won't change, or else your collaboration won't work out.

STEPHEN METCALFE: I can't imagine working with a director I hadn't really sat down with and talked to at great length. There should be a strong personal connection. I feel I have a lot of directorial instincts, and so I've got to have a director who, if he doesn't welcome that, can at least put up with it, and isn't threatened by it.

TED TALLY: I don't know how anyone can be a director. That's such a difficult job. It requires an enormous amount of ego to be at the center of this vast, unwieldy apparatus. The buck stops with him. And yet, a good director is constantly subverting his own ego so that the play can come forward. It is a difficult balance.

PETER PARNELL: Directors have certain strengths. Some are good with actors but not with design. Others achieve visually stunning effects, but are not good with actors. It's rare to get someone good at everything. The director also has to be the one who gets your vision, your language, your world, right. Some writers, because they've been burnt, turn to directing their own plays.

How do you work with a director?

JOHN PIELMEIER: Working with the director is an ongoing discussion.

HEATHER MCDONALD: Theater is a collaborative form, but if too many people shape the vision it becomes diluted. I have had to fight to get *my* vision of my plays on stage.

BILL C. DAVIS: Being an author is difficult because it means authority. I feel I will be resented if I exercise the rights I have as author. Consequently, I don't assert the authority I have. But I need a certain authority and strength to achieve my play's maximum potential.

My first dealings with directors were based on deferring. They did nothing wrong; it was my own natural insecurity. There is more pain in continual deferring than in one short "No!"

PETER PARNELL: You've got this play that's being done one way—directors have their vision of the play and how it can be made better—but you have to know what *you* want to say. Some writers are strong and say, "No, this is what I want." I tend to get excited by what people say and I try it. You have to learn to stick with what you want.

TINA HOWE: A good director feels it is her job to serve the play, so if something isn't working, she asks what you had in mind rather than yells at you. If something wasn't clear in the script, you need to explain what you had in mind.

MARSHA NORMAN: It takes a long time to see enough of a director's work to know the range of his or her work, the reasons he or she may or may not be good for your play. Young writers don't have a real choice of directors. The thing for young writers to do is to simply sit and learn. It's school here.

LANFORD WILSON: Marshall [Mason] and I look at each other in rehearsal, silently saying, "Is that clear to you? Do you know what they're talking about? Is that repetitious? Do we really need that?"

One reason our productions look so good is that when Marshall and I agree someone is off the mark, I'll say, "Well, I'll tell him *that*, if you tell her to do *this* so that he doesn't have to do it all himself." It's as though one and a half persons are the director.

Marshall will tell me if it is *very* important to him whether something is cut or stays. If a line's construction really bothers him and I like it, I'll tell him that I *really* do like it and he'll have to find a way to do it. It is consensus. I understand that rehearsals are Marshall's time to work and I'm there to support him. I'm good at that. We are always helping each other help the others.

Many playwrights have lately turned to directing their own plays. How do you feel about directing your work?

EMILY MANN: If playwrights are good directors they should direct their own plays. Definitely. At some point. If they have enough distance on their work, then no one knows the work better. This horrible myth that good writers don't know what they've written has got to end. Good writers know what they've written. Good writers who are also good directors can implement the writing through the production.

As a director working with other writers, I know all too well how often writers know their words but fail to see the play as a piece of theater. Writer-directors not only know the words on the page but see and know absolutely what they wrote in its *theatrical* entirety.

DAVID HWANG: I think it helps you as a playwright to direct, because the more you know about the medium the better equipped you are to use it. But I also find directing really exhausting, because you have to be all things to all people.

MARIA IRENE FORNES: I always direct my own plays. When I first started doing plays, I wanted to direct them because I thought it would be fun, but I encountered the traditional feeling in theater that playwrights can't direct. Outside of one occasion, I was never delighted with what the director had chosen to do. No one is perfect, but I was not allowed to offer suggestions or alternatives. I think that is outrageous.

People who say playwrights can't be objective about their own scripts seem to think playwrights have some sort of mental defect. Your point of view might be different from someone else's, but that doesn't mean you are not objective about your work. Who says directors are objective? Directors bring their own biases and beliefs to the work. I don't want to be objective. I want to be as blind as my passion would have me be.

How involved are you in the casting of your play?

BILL C. DAVIS: I never realized how important casting was. There is a certain kind of hubris: "As long as they get the words out, we'll be fine." That's not the case. Certain actors or actresses just connect to a character, embody that character. Then your play is really happening rather than being recited. It's a magical moment when the actor defines the role and the role defines the actor.

All the actors seriously being considered for a role can, technically, do it. It's something extra that you go for. The first time you do the play you must be very specific and very obvious about how it should be cast. In my mind I might be thinking it would be interesting to cast it *another* way, but the play has never been done before. *This* is the first time. There's no *other* way yet.

LEE BLESSING: The playwright should learn everything possible about casting, since it is crucial and hard to do, and if the playwright doesn't cast the show, someone else will—sometimes badly. Playwrights should get to know actors in workshops so they can make intelligent casting choices in productions. Everyone has his own agenda for casting plays. As much as possible the playwright should strive to get *his* agenda adopted.

STEPHEN METCALFE: When you see a performance that doesn't work you can do one of two things: Either say, "Well, it's not going to be here this time," or fire the actor. That's why the playwright should always be part of the casting process. He's got to be satisfied the actor has the instincts and is in touch with the character, so he's not stuck with someone who doesn't know what's going on and cannot relate to the character or the world of that character.

BETH HENLEY: Some actors come on real slow—they know not to put on the gas until previews, and then they really blow you out of the saddle. Of course, there are the actors who don't put up anything and then you are stuck with a dead duck on your hands.

You make mistakes with casting and you're often stuck with them. It's hard.

MARSHA NORMAN: Writers are usually charmed at hearing their words said. You'll sit there and think, "That's the right feeling. That actor understands." It is imperative for writers to be with directors who have a true feeling for casting.

To be cast in my plays, people must have a natural sense of humor; they must be naturally funny by themselves. Cast the dark sufferers in my plays and my plays go right down the drain. If you cast people who are eager to go out there and feel the pain, you haven't a chance. My plays are not written that way; they are written in constant conflict against the pain. If you have somebody who is not fighting it, where's the struggle?

How involved with the actors are you in rehearsals?

WENDY WASSERSTEIN: I used to think you wrote a play, gave it to a director, who gave it to actors, and it had a life of its own. A good actor can add a great deal, give it a life. It's almost a silent collaboration.

TED TALLY: The playwright must not undercut the authority of the director. I tend to smile and nod to actors and say, "Work on it," rather than tell them how I would do it. They must arrive at some sort of solution themselves.

CHARLES FULLER: I hardly ever answer questions at rehearsal. Anything I say tends to confuse the actors because the director is also talking to them. I'm not so sure I'm the best person to talk to actors. I tend to tell the actor things about the character I didn't even put on the page. Pretty soon you're confusing yourself. If it's not on the page, it doesn't belong onstage.

JOHN PIELMEIER: I do a lot of talking directly to my actors, but I don't ever go to an actor behind the director's back.

ERIC OVERMYER: I did a lot of acting, and know how actors work, but they're very peculiar creatures, and it's better to trust the director to get your message across.

CORINNE JACKER: If an actor hears too many conflicting statements, or if you are speaking in two different languages, it can confuse the actor. That's not useful.

PETER PARNELL: The writer has to get his comments in and get as close to his vision as he wants. It's through the director that all this happens.

CHRISTOPHER DURANG: Directors are understandably concerned that they remain the voice that sets the tone and the vision.

BETH HENLEY: Actors seem to take it real hard if the playwright says something to them. It scares me to talk to actors because I might make them cry or something.

LANFORD WILSON: Marshall [Mason] and I will talk about how to approach an actor with a certain problem and try to get him over the hump to what we think the character should be in terms of rhythm and general attitude. You take the actor aside and be supportive, make a few suggestions. Most actors will pick up on those suggestions. The next time through you correct the next little moment you don't like. Over the course of a month's rehearsal period, you set up signposts to lead the actor to the kind of character you want.

TED TALLY: I talk to the actors less and less, because they are out there scared, and they're looking for shortcuts. They're looking to skip the first awkward stages of the process and get right to the answers and solutions. If they can't, they'll try to get those answers and solutions from the playwright or anyone they can. They'll get direction from their girlfriend, their agent, the guy who brings in the coffee: "Am I doing that right?" I understand that; I used to be an actor.

LANFORD WILSON: Actors come over to me in rehearsal all the time asking if they can change a word because it gets in the way. I say "yes" three-quarters of the time. Other times I say, "No, I really like this and you'll just have to get this jaggy rhythm." Sometimes it doesn't matter, and other times it matters a lot. If it is for clarity or ease, that's fine.

Say the line is, "He comes home, you're going to get it." The actor might put in a "when" at the beginning. I'll say, "No, I want that skip-jump sort of rhythm." You'll never get the rhythm of the play if you don't correct the actors on those things.

I'm writing a sort of chorale, and I am concerned with the rhythm and sound of the play. All good actors understand that.

A. R. GURNEY, JR.: I don't usually trust actors' first impressions. They tend to respond intuitively, "I can't say this line. It doesn't feel right," when you are absolutely certain the line works. So you say, "I'll think about it." Other times they're right. Every time they come to that line, there will be a hitch, and you have to change it. You have to trust your own work so that the initial impressions of actors won't force you into compromising unnecessarily. At the same time you had better listen, because they are the ones going out there onstage.

TED TALLY: Another thing to learn is not to react too hastily to the process. While the actors are feeling their way through the play, you're going to see a lot of things happen to your material that would make you tear your hair out. If you're satisfied that you have the right director and if you're satisfied you have the right actors—two very big ifs—then a problem they can't solve will become evident in time. You have to let them try to solve it first.

Actors are the best gauge: An actor might not be able to verbalize what he thinks the problem is, but if a good actor can't make something work, and you see him working hard at it, trying different things, then it's not the actor's problem—it's yours.

TINA HOWE: I really respect actors. I really admire them. I'm amazed at how they can just get up and show their feelings. I know a lot of writers sort of resent actors, because they can do what playwrights can't do, but I tend to fall all over myself about actors.

LANFORD WILSON: I'm really crazy about actors. I've almost always written roles with specific actors in mind. You see something in an actor—a quirky movement, a turn of phrase—that suggests a whole character. Trish Hawkins had a sense of curiosity, an inquiring energy which I used as the model for the "train freak" character she played in *Hot l Baltimore.*

MARSHA NORMAN: Actors are interested in how much fun it is to be onstage. Playwrights are not interested in that at all. When you have actors helping you, some of the "what fun it is to be onstage" can creep into the script, and that's a violation. That doesn't belong. I have a very specific and, perhaps, peculiar point of view about the theater. I know what is satisfying to me and I know what I like.

Marvelous contributions are made by actors. Plays live because of actors. But the basic framework of the piece has to be there and be there from the beginning, and that has to come from one person, the playwright.

How closely do you feel the playwright should work with the production's designers?

LEE BLESSING: If the playwright can choose a designer he knows and trusts, he should. If not, he should learn about the designer in question, ask to see the designs as soon as possible, and *voice objections early* when and where necessary. Bad design, like bad direction or a bad cast, can and will sink a show.

PETER PARNELL: A designer will let you know in a hurry if you've asked for something that can't be created. You say, "Can I go from this to that?" They either say, "Yes," or "No, that can only happen in a movie." You don't want to be told too early that something can't work—which puts all the more emphasis on selecting the right designers. You don't ever want a problem to be a failure of that person's imagination.

HEATHER MCDONALD: If allowed, I have a lot to say about how a production of my play should look. I will fight for that, to the death of a lot of relationships, because the play is my vision.

DAVID HWANG: The designer for one of my plays brought a model to a production meeting. We all looked at it. I didn't say much, and I later heard he wished I had said more. There is a point where the playwright can become obnoxious and you want to lock him out of the room, but I've gone too much to the other extreme. The whole design process could stand a little more input from me.

BETH HENLEY: I'd like to get more involved with designers. I feel as though I don't want to hurt their feelings when they bring in their drawings; they're always real happy with them. With costumes, I'm better at saying what I like and don't like. With sets and lights I'm a total disaster.

CORINNE JACKER: We playwrights don't talk to designers enough. I like hearing what designers have to say. We rarely have that dream situation where, before a play goes into production, we all—designers, director, writer—sit around a table and talk to make sure that everyone has the same concept in mind. That should happen more.

CHRISTOPHER DURANG: I used to let the director go off alone to the design meetings. Now I don't. A set that ends up being wrong for a production can genuinely harm a play as much as miscasting can. I find design interesting, but I know that some playwrights don't.

William Ivey Long wanted Bette in full bridal regalia in *The Marriage of Bette and Boo.* We wondered what would happen if she stayed in that for the entire play. It would make thematic sense, but would be an awfully strong statement. It might also be terribly pretentious and problematic.

William told me about women in the past being encouraged to shorten their wedding dresses into party dresses. We had Bette come on in Scene Five wearing a shortened dress. I thought the audience might not get the connection, and so I added the line, "At the suggestion of *Redbook,* Bette refashions her wedding gown into a cocktail dress."

Part of the enormous laugh the line got came from the fact that the audience must have known we wanted to get her out of that wedding dress, and instead of pretending it didn't happen, we turned a spotlight on it. I like that kind of thing.

TINA HOWE: For me design is crucial because my plays are so visual. I'm now much more conscious of the kinds of choices you can make just in terms of design.

I think part of the reason *The Art of Dining* never quite worked is because we did it in a realistic setting—and God knows that that play is not a realistic one. *Dining* may take place in a restaurant, but the actions in the play are bigger than real life. I feel we made an error going for such a realistically dead-on set. Had we been a little more expressionistic, I think the whole thing would have taken off.

LANFORD WILSON: I was working on *Talley's Folly* and imagined a set on the order of a small garage beside a river, with a couple of boats turned upside-down on sawhorses, and a lot of windows through which the sun could shine. The river was supposed to be out in the audience, so one side of the garage was open to the river. But in my mind it really had a fourth wall. *Talley's Folly* was a nice play with good possibilities for a set designer.

Our designer, John Lee Beatty, came to a meeting, pulled out his design, and I said, "You son of a bitch." His design was so much more wonderful than I had ever imagined, and absolutely right for the play. Real water so the boat would rock! Who would have dreamed of that? All of this came from the line, "Whistler Talley built outrageous things; outrageous, wonderful, magical things." It was perfect, of course. The most extraordinarily perfect set design I'd ever seen.

How do you deal with reviews? Are they helpful or harmful?

CHRISTOPHER DURANG: Criticism is an impossible task.

TED TALLY: My reaction to newspaper criticism: screaming, jumping, throwing things. I write angry letters I never send. I always vow I'm never going to read the reviews because, after all, I'm above that kind of thing and what are they going to tell me that I don't already know? You can't resist.

I've had critics see the same performance and write diametrically opposed reviews. With *Terra Nova*, one critic said the play wasn't "moving." Another critic thought it was the most moving play she'd seen in her life. It's so subjective. You have to hope you are getting through to some-body. And if you are getting some encouragement, go on.

STEPHEN METCALFE: It's like having apples and oranges: The critic comes in and says he likes oranges; if you have apples, it's "bad." Not that he "doesn't care" for apples, but they are "bad."

ERIC OVERMYER: The worst kind of reviewer is the one who says very proudly that he wants to be an *un*informed audience member. He doesn't want to read the play, doesn't want to know anything about it. That's a consumer reporter.

PETER PARNELL: I don't know how you deal with criticism. As I get older I want to be taken seriously on some level. The child in me screams out that I am doing good work and I want to be recognized for it. When the critics do that, even if they don't quite understand what I'm trying to do, I'm grateful. When they don't, I get angry and hurt.

BETH HENLEY: I don't read reviews because it's like getting a shot of Pentothal: Your blood turns to ice when you hear bad reviews. It's humiliating and horrible. I don't read them because I don't want what they say to stick in my mind and make me miserable for years to come.

If it's an unqualified good press, I'll read it; otherwise I won't. I'll have friends read the reviews and tell me if I can read them or not. You don't take the good ones too seriously because you always think it's the bad ones that are true.

EMILY MANN: I think I'm quoting my husband when I say, "If you don't believe the bad reviews, you can't believe the good ones." It takes incredible discipline to deal with what is thrown at you, good or bad. It can take years to figure out the truth about a play. I don't think criticism ever gets easier, but I think you get smarter.

A. R. GURNEY, JR.: I read all the reviews. The reviews which determine if a play is going to run I read carefully. I read them now more as a businessman. A bad review is just as painful now as it was on my first play. The difference is that the pain doesn't last as long. I know there are those points when you walk outside and the world isn't that bad. I know those postpartum moments come.

CORINNE JACKER: I've found that about ninety percent of the time, the point chosen by the reviewer as being "wrong" is never where the problem is. What I've learned is to look at what people *say* the problem is and go back from that point to what the real problem is. It is often something they weren't properly prepared for.

I now believe that criticism is neither as stupid nor as ill intentioned as it seemed when I was younger.

TINA HOWE: I can't handle reviews. I suppose it's because I got good ones for the first time in my life for *Painting Churches,* and I'm so aware of how much of a roll of the dice it is. For me there is a capriciousness there which I find just terrifying.

HEATHER MCDONALD: If someone says in print that this is the worst play ever written, it's hard not to lie down and weep, gnash your teeth, and eat a lot of chocolate.

The best thing I've ever heard [about playwrights and critics] is that, after Clive Barnes wrote in his review of *The Art of Dining* that Tina Howe should stop writing plays and go home and cook her husband a good meal, she—

since she lived on the same block as he—trained her children to throw rocks at him.

MARSHA NORMAN: I think we in the American theatrical community are really in trouble because of the importance currently given to critics. As a group, critics know very little about the process of theater.

Critics have basically given themselves over to writing consumer criticism. We don't have great criticism; we have reviewers now, not people who love the theater and know it well. We have people who are merely saying whether or not you should spend forty dollars to see this thing. The real problem in the commercial theater is that the audience is letting the critics make the decision for it.

The critics here in New York are not allowing writers to have careers. In England it is expected that playwrights will have failures, and English audiences know a playwright can't do it "right" each time.

BILL C. DAVIS: Why is it set up as a game? I think critics are part of the whole process of getting a play on. Critics are like federal inspectors for meat—they put "Grade A" on plays. A lot of the public will like what they are told is good. The laughs for *Mass Appeal* at the Manhattan Theatre Club were tripled after the reviews came out and said the show was funny. I got sick. All of those things were there before. I think it is a self-fulfilling prophecy.

WENDY WASSERSTEIN: I read all the reviews. If a problem is consistently pointed out, then it is something that has to be addressed. Sometimes you can't write because of the bad reviews you remember. I don't pick up the newspapers myself. I have someone else pick them up, read the reviews, and then tell me what they're like.

It never gets easier. Even if I write fifty-six plays, that

moment of going to get the paper to read the review is still terrible. With a play, there is no way you can just say, "So what, I got a *C*," as you would with a college essay.

A. R. GURNEY, JR.: The *New York Times*—whoever its drama critic is—determines our fate. That leads to all sorts of terrible problems for people who want to write for the theater. What the *Times* critics in other fields have to say is not of quite such importance. If they don't like a novel or a building it still survives, but a play can't if the *Times* critic says it's terrible.

The *Times* is the equivalent of Louis XV, who, when Molière was writing, said, "I don't like *Tartuffe*." Well then, it's not performed.

JOHN PIELMEIER: Criticism is very hard. It's one thing to deal with criticism on a one-to-one basis, but it's hard to deal with negative criticism that is in print. I think any kind of constructive criticism has to be made in a give-and-take situation. What is so irritating about criticism in newspapers is that it automatically shuts off a give-and-take. A writer cannot sit down with the critic and explain himself. Consequently, and very unfortunately, critics allow themselves to say things they would never say to a person's face. That's downright rude.

Today, there is too much reviewing going on and not enough criticism. I think a truly insightful piece of criticism should have neither a negative nor a positive tone. Too many reviewers take everything personally. They write a review as if your play was written to personally give them a bad time. Instead of disagreeing with a writer's decisions and choices in a play, they end up trying to destroy the play, the impulses that fed into the play, and the writer. Everything is so askew. I believe intelligent criticism isn't going to offend anyone.

*Do you feel critics are capable of separating a new play from
its production?*

MARSHA NORMAN: They cannot distinguish between the
production and the play. They have not educated today's
audience about the difference. The theater has not yet developed a system of selling copies of plays in the lobby so
that people can go home and make up their own minds
about what was on the page and what was on the stage.

LEE BLESSING: Reviewers are almost never capable of separating a new play from its production, nor would they want
to bother. They obviously consider it the playwright's responsibility not only to write a play well, but also to see
that the production of it is excellent. Therefore, the playwright had better get used to the idea of exercising, as
much as possible, his influence over a production. In the
case of a new script with a bad production, the playwright
is almost inevitably blamed.

TED TALLY: I honestly don't believe critics can separate the
production from the script itself, though they pride themselves that they can. Even those connected with the production can't separate what was an actor's inspiration of the
moment, or what was the director's contribution in some
quiet conversation.

A. R. GURNEY, JR.: I don't think critics can adequately tell
the difference between the play and the production. But a
production should be a coherent whole: We don't want a
double vision; we want it all to work together.

ERIC OVERMYER: Critics can't separate the play from the
production. It's obvious they don't know anything about

the way actors or directors work. They especially don't know what a director does. And on a new play the writer always takes the blame.

MARSHA NORMAN: Plays are puzzles to be solved. You create the puzzle and people all over the world, for hundreds of years, speaking all kinds of languages, have to put the very same puzzle together again. If the play is what they call "actor proof," the chances are you will get something that looks pretty much the same—there is only one way to put that puzzle together.

From time to time you will see puzzles that are either fabulous or are absolute trash, depending on who puts them together. You are constantly seeing your play put on by different people, but your name is always on it, and, as a general rule, critics don't do a good job of distinguishing between the play itself and the people doing it.

How do you feel you've grown as a playwright? Where do you think your writing is heading?

TINA HOWE: *Museum* and *The Art of Dining* go to great lengths to hide the ache underneath. I think the reason *Painting Churches* was successful was that I was finally opening up; just opening up and standing my ground.

I am a very buried kind of person. I realized, when I watched an audience watching *Painting Churches*, that audiences want to be moved. They want to go through something. To lead them through something, you, the writer, have to expose a piece of yourself. That's what I'm slowly beginning to do.

WENDY WASSERSTEIN: I see myself moving a little bit away from myself, but not a great deal. You've got to write things that are difficult for you. You've got to want to write it enough to spend three years on it, until it is read, produced, and done right.

TED TALLY: What I have begun to realize is that a play doesn't have to be about five guys trying to reach the South Pole in order to be of interest. The writers whom I admire are able to make enormous capital out of seemingly small means. I'm trusting a bit more that I will also be able to do that. I am only now reaching a point where I trust that my own experiences are worth something.

DAVID HWANG: The Asian-American subject matter I've dealt with, being relatively unique, has given me a certain leg up. I think I am a good writer, but when I get off that subject matter I'm really up against everybody else, without the advantage of writing about something different. It's a challenge to see how my writing stacks up as just pure writing.

MARSHA NORMAN: I'm up against this series of expectations about what my work sounds like, what sorts of issues it addresses, what particular theater pleasures it provides. To write in another direction brings outrage. The thing about the theater is that you must do your practicing in public to learn your lessons. What baby writers have to learn is that you can't let anything stop the natural process. I can't stop myself from going in another direction just because everybody loves *'night, Mother*. That would be to betray everything I know about working as a writer.

CHRISTOPHER DURANG: I don't think writers need to be, or should be, obsessed with "breaking new ground." One of the things that rankles me about critics' reviews of my plays is that they tend to say I've "done" such-and-such before. When the critics say I've done something before, I think, "When?" It comes from what people expect of you. They do try to pigeonhole. If Chekhov's plays were done now, would they say, "Oh, he's done this before"?

BETH HENLEY: My newer plays are maybe not better than *Crimes of the Heart*, maybe just different. You keep growing because you keep living.

What makes for good playwriting?

ERIC OVERMYER: Good writing just jumps off the page. Anything that is in a true voice, an original voice, really leaps off the page. Good theater is what made good theater for the Greeks and the Elizabethans.

One of the litmus tests of a good play is that it is not a television script in disguise. I think, "Could this only work in the theater? Could this be better done as a movie with close-ups and angles, or not?"

I think theater should stick with what it and nothing else can provide: language, imagination, dream.

MARSHA NORMAN: When I began to write I was at the point where writing was the only thing that would save my life. I discovered that only writing will take care of my problems. God knows I've tried every other way. I must deal with this drive, this sense of imperative, and the feeling that something has to happen, that things simply cannot go on in the way they have. This, to me, is what theater is all about—a critical moment in a life, a moment where it is just not possible to go on in the same way. That's the only kind of theater I want to be in. I'm not interested in another ordinary day, which, quite frankly, television does better. We are at a moment in the American theater where we have to think of what the theater does better than other forms.

TED TALLY: What makes exciting theater is when it's very, very important. Every play has to be a matter of life and death for the writer and for the audience.

TINA HOWE: A writer knows that what is most private in her heart of hearts is also the most astonishing.

STEPHEN METCALFE: I like my "kitchen sink" plays and I'm very proud of them. I find I'm more moved by kitchen sink drama than by a lot of other things. I like writing about people in situations where they are confronted with an event that makes them reevaluate life.

In New York City, where we are all so obsessed with our careers and our lives, we sometimes forget that for the majority of people out there, their families, friends, and kitchens are the most important things in life.

CORINNE JACKER: Edith Oliver made me promise very early on in my writing life that I would never write about an artist. I promised her, and I think I've kept that promise. She's right. We have all kinds of plays about actors, directors, writers, painters, poets, but not about steamfitters and contractors. For me the most important thing is that plays have to be about people in the real world. I think we tend to write about people who are sealed in vacuum-packed environments. That's quite dangerous.

BILL C. DAVIS: I try to get down to the most basic things, to bear witness to my experience of the world and bring it to the stage, give it life, show it.

EMILY MANN: Beside the obvious elements of a good story and craft, good theater to me is the unshakable engagement of actor and audience, the dialogue between actor and audience.

A. R. GURNEY, JR.: We Americans are not people who stay in one space for too long. One can write plays about trapped people—trapped in junk shops or in kitchens—but my vision of what is dramatic about our country is that we are engaged with other people at a number of different places and times. To accommodate even a small part of the breadth of this country, I've found I've got to move my plays around a bit.

In *The Dining Room,* there is one dining room, but I try to suggest that it is many dining rooms. Half the problem for me, at least for a while, was to find a form that would accommodate the variety, diversity and different spatial relationships in this country, rather than to settle for a realistic frame. Writing in scenes has been my attempt to find this form.

MARIA IRENE FORNES: I don't miss popular success. I think popular success puts a kind of obligation on the artist. I think the longevity of an artist depends on always being willing, able, and unafraid to step into unknown territory. Success tends to make people afraid to try. Something inside you shrinks at the thought of doing bad work. When you are not famous and no one really cares much what you do, you are not afraid to fail.

What is beautiful about my art is the adventure of the work, not success, money, and people recognizing me in the street. When I enter the work, by myself or in a room with my colleagues, that is the supreme adventure—the adventure of putting the play on the stage and seeing if it works. That is the greatest riches one could want.

What's your advice to a playwright just starting out?

A. R. GURNEY, JR.: If you want to be a playwright, that in itself is a choice. You can publish a book for five or six thousand dollars, but even the smallest production costs twenty-five thousand. If you are interested in live theater— the collaboration you can have with a live audience—then be a playwright. You have to recognize that the odds are against you. We have very little theater tradition in this country; our theater really started with O'Neill. Know what you're getting into when you write plays. It's a tough, special kind of craft.

Put yourself in a position where you can get your plays made public. Not that they'll always be fully performed, but at least done in classes where they'll be read out loud. Go public as soon as you can. Don't turn up your nose at coffeehouse productions or high-school readings. Get it out there and get it done. Don't harbor plays in your trunk; doing them whets your appetite.

BETH HENLEY: The best advice I've got is to finish your play. Stop talking about it. Stay home and finish your play. Just get to "The End." Don't try to make every line and every page perfect.

So many people get a good idea, or a good character, or they *want* to be writers, but they never finish anything. If you finish something, then at least you've got something to work with.

TED TALLY: Hemingway once said you've got to have two things to be a writer: seriousness about the work, and talent. Notice that he listed seriousness first.

Stubbornness is extremely important to writing success and almost as important as talent. The world is not waiting for anyone to write a new play and the world will not stop if you don't write that play. The play has got to be very, very important to you if you expect it to be important to anyone else.

CHARLES FULLER: You must write a play from the seats, otherwise you are always inside it and never see it. Don't lose the perspective of the spectator.

TINA HOWE: I tell my students not to be afraid of their vision. I think it's funny that young playwrights tend to be rather tentative and fearful and to second-guess themselves. So my advice is to go for broke. If there is some impulse that makes you want to write a play, you've just got to put everything you have into it and let out all the stops. I think that the only way theater is going to be exciting again is if the next generation will be braver and more audacious.

BILL C. DAVIS: Don't be afraid of real-life experiences. Listen to people. That is basically the core responsibility of all artists, to listen deeply and be a witness to life. The urge to write is a deep, psychological response to feeling at odds with the world.

EMILY MANN: I break form a lot, so I can't advise others to "know your craft." If you have something to say, find a way to say it that is alive. Who knows where that will take you, or us?

WENDY WASSERSTEIN: The best plays are written by the individual who has enough confidence not to be frightened. Then you need craft. Talent alone will not win out.

CORINNE JACKER: Don't study playwriting in college. Don't take courses about it. Do it.

ERIC OVERMYER: You have to trust your own best instincts. Don't listen to too much advice. Find a place—any place—that'll do your work. Plays don't do you any good in a drawer: You can't work on them or learn anything from them then.

PETER PARNELL: I think you can only keep learning by writing. Don't be afraid of thinking dangerously. After a while, you are what you write. Just do it. Know that you are going in for the long haul. You should be writing at the top of your powers as you get older, but so much depends on the collaboration, the time of year you open, the reviews you get. The rewards are always out of proportion. The pressure can kill you. None of this is good for the long haul. What writer can we name who has aged gracefully?

DAVID HWANG: You have to take the long view in this. My big thing right now is: Am I going to be happy when I'm sixty with the decision I'm making now? You don't know. If you decide to make the theater your life, you have to realize that you may work for twenty or thirty years, and at the end of that time you may be a *somewhat* better writer, reaching a *somewhat* larger group of people, and making a *somewhat* larger amount of money. That may be it. You have to be willing to say, "That's enough for me."

It's a question of perspective. Do you want the life of a playwright? For their own sake, young people have to search their souls very rigorously to answer that question truthfully.

JOHN PIELMEIER: I think the most important thing to find is a mentor—someone who's older and has experience in the field, someone who can really inspire you and connect with you, and feed some of his or her personal fire into your soul.

LEE BLESSING: Learn everything you can about theater, because it is in productions that your plays live or die. Get into workshop situations with people before you use them in productions. The more good (*your* definition of good) actors, directors, and designers you know, the more power you'll have. Be ready to sacrifice your first three or four plays to experience. Write at least one new, *good* play a year.

Be positive with everyone you meet in theater, even the assholes. They are only doing their job—sometimes well, sometimes badly.

TINA HOWE: Be obsessed. It's awful when I'm in the thrall of a new play: I'm just berserk. People used to ask, "Oh, how do you manage to be a writer and have a family?" My family keeps me sane; its hands hold me down to earth. If I didn't have them I'm convinced I would be on the street speaking in tongues. I would be right out there on the street, walking in the middle of the traffic, talking to the cars. A new play completely takes over my life. You must think of nothing else.

MARSHA NORMAN: Playwrights who truly do not have any other choices survive. Most of us who continue to write need it in some central, absolutely critical way. If it were against the law to write plays, if people were put in prison for writing plays, I would still do it. You must arrive at that moment of understanding the relationship between you and the writing. If it is not that central, then there is nothing in the world that justifies doing it. It's too hard, too brutal. The system as it exists now—especially the commercial theater—makes writing a play practically an act of desperation, an act of insanity.

What is required is a faith that is strong enough to sustain you. You can't love the accomplishment the most. You can't love anything better than the making of it. You have to remember that you love the doing of it, and keep yourself doing it in spite of what you know is going to happen along the way.

DIRECTORS

The director is the playwright's closest collaborator. Work with a playwright starts weeks, months, even years before opening night. Long-term, sometimes lifelong, relationships often develop. The director and the playwright may build a mutual trust, a shared instinct, and develop the technical and emotional shorthand of two people who thoroughly understand each other. The result may well be increasingly rich, more assured work from both collaborators. Consider such successful director-playwright teams as Marshall W. Mason and Lanford Wilson, Jerry Zaks and Christopher Durang, Carole Rothman and Tina Howe, Gerald Gutierrez and Wendy Wasserstein, Gregory Mosher and David Mamet.

The director must be all things to all people: counselor to the playwright, inspiration to the actors, adviser to the designers.

Most important and, perhaps, critical to the success of any theatrical enterprise is the understanding among all collaborators that the director's word is final, that the production is his or her vision of the play.

In this chapter directors talk about all aspects of their profession, including their training, influences, and what qualities in a new play are attractive to them. They take us through the workshops and rehearsals of a new play. They discuss critics, give advice to directors just starting out, and offer ideas on what is good directing and good theater.

Melvin Bernhardt directed the premieres of such plays as Beth Henley's *Crimes of the Heart*, Paul Zindel's *The Effect of Gamma Rays on Man-in-the-Moon Marigolds*, and A. R. Gurney, Jr.'s *The Middle Ages*. He received a Tony Award, and Drama Desk and Outer Critics Circle awards for his direction of *Da*.

Arvin Brown is the artistic director of the Long Wharf Theatre in New Haven, Connecticut. He directed *A View from the Bridge*, *American Buffalo* starring Al Pacino, *The Glass Menagerie* with Jessica Tandy and Amanda Plummer, and *Joe Egg* with Stockard Channing and Jim Dale. He has received two Tony Award nominations and a Vernon Rice Award.

Pat Brown is the artistic director of the Alley Theatre in Houston, Texas. She founded the Magnolia Theatre in Long Beach, California, and was later named the first director of the Theatre Communications Group. Closely identified with the plays of Alan Ayckbourn, Brown directed the American premiere of *Season's Greetings*.

Gerald Gutierrez was trained as a pianist and an actor at Juilliard. He directed the premiere of David Mamet's *A Life in the Theatre*, and later directed and adapted the play for PBS-TV's "Great Performances." His other premiere productions include Wendy Wasserstein's *Isn't it Romantic*, Jonathan Reynolds's

Geniuses, Peter Parnell's *The Rise and Rise of Daniel Rocket,* and Albert Innaurato's *Gemini.*

Emily Mann began her professional career as a Bush Fellow at the Guthrie Theater in Minneapolis; she was the youngest director and first woman to direct on the Guthrie's main stage. She is a playwright and has directed her own plays *Still Life* and *Execution of Justice.* She staged the New York production of *A Weekend Near Madison* and has directed at regional theaters across the country.

Marshall W. Mason is cofounder and artistic director of Circle Repertory in New York. Mason has won six Obie Awards and has been nominated for four Tony Awards. He is the recipient of Drama Desk, Outer Critics Circle, Margo Jones, and Shubert Foundation awards. Mason is most known for his work with Lanford Wilson, having directed Wilson's *Fifth of July, Talley's Folly, Talley and Son, The Mound Builders,* and *Hot l Baltimore.*

Tom Moore is the director of *Grease, 'night, Mother,* and *Traveler in the Dark.* He is a resident director at the American Conservatory Theatre in San Francisco and has directed extensively at the Old Globe Theatre in San Diego, the Mark Taper Forum in Los Angeles, and the Guthrie Theater in Minneapolis.

Gregory Mosher is the former artistic director of the Goodman Theatre in Chicago and currently the artistic director of the Lincoln Center Stage Company. During his close association with David Mamet he has directed the premieres of *American Buffalo, Edmond,* and the Pulitzer Prize-winning *Glengarry Glen Ross.* He has also directed new works by John Guare, Emily Mann, David Rabe, Michael Weller, and Tennessee Williams, among others.

Lloyd Richards is the artistic director of the Eugene O'Neill Theatre Center's National Playwrights Conference. Richards is also the Dean of the Yale School of Drama and the artistic director of the Yale Repertory Theatre. His directing credits include

Fences, Ma Rainey's Black Bottom, A Raisin in the Sun, Paul Robeson, The Yearling, I Had a Ball, The Moon Besieged, and *The Long Dream.*

Carole Rothman is a cofounder of the Second Stage Theatre in New York, a theater dedicated to giving contemporary plays a second chance. She has directed *Painting Churches, How I Got That Story, My Sister in This House,* and *Minnesota Moon.* Rothman has directed for the Manhattan Theatre Club, The Mark Taper Forum, Circle Rep, and the Kennedy Center.

Douglas Turner Ward is the artistic director of the Negro Ensemble Company, for which he has directed Charles Fuller's *A Soldier's Play, Ceremonies in Dark Old Men,* and *The River Niger,* also starring in the latter two. Ward has received Vernon Rice, Drama Desk, and Obie awards.

Jerry Zaks was originally an actor and founding member of the Ensemble Studio Theatre. His direction of Christopher Durang's *Sister Mary Ignatius Explains It All for You* at Ensemble Studio has led to a long collaboration with Durang. Zaks subsequently directed Durang's *Baby with the Bathwater, Beyond Therapy,* and *The Marriage of Bette and Boo.* He also directed Larry Shue's *The Foreigner* and the Broadway revival of John Guare's *The House of Blue Leaves,* for which he received a Tony Award.

H*ow did you come to choose directing as a profession?*

GERALD GUTIERREZ: When I was in sixth grade my mother took me to see *Fiorello!* When the siren went off in the overture I knew I wouldn't be practicing piano for long.

As I was finishing high school Juilliard was starting its drama division. I auditioned for the acting program and got in. The day I had to tell my parents—who had dreams of my being a concert pianist—that I wanted to be an actor wasn't pleasant. In my second year at Juilliard, John Houseman, the head of the drama division, kept urging me to try directing. I thought he was pushing me into directing because he hated the way I acted, so to shut him up I tried directing.

I did the first act of *The Apple Tree* with Patti Lupone as Eve, Kevin Kline as Adam, and John Houseman as God. We put it on for the rest of the school. I stood in the back of the theater shaking. It was unbelievably thrilling when the audience laughed exactly when I thought they'd laugh. I knew I was a director. It was like *Fiorello!* all over again.

MELVIN BERNHARDT: I was eleven or twelve when I saw a summer stock production of *Watch on the Rhine*. I wanted to be in the theater from that point on. I did some acting, but quite soon discovered I wanted to be a director. I was always more interested in the whole play than just my role.

The appeal of directing was getting what I saw in my head onto the stage.

MARSHALL W. MASON: I wanted to be an actor all my life—beginning with a childhood performance in a play in church.

Alvina Krause, my acting teacher at Northwestern, took her best students to her summer repertory theater in Pennsylvania. She turned me down the first time I asked to go. I realized then I wasn't going to be the greatest actor in the world—a crushing blow.

Miss Krause's associate asked if I had ever thought about directing. I replied that I wanted to direct *Cat on a Hot Tin Roof* because I really felt it deeply, felt as though it were a play I had written. So, at the age of nineteen I directed *Cat on a Hot Tin Roof*. The production received a standing ovation and I realized that perhaps I was a director.

ARVIN BROWN: I got into directing by fluke. The school I was attending on a writing fellowship in England had an evening every year of one-acts directed by graduate students. This particular year they didn't have enough graduate students in theater to go around, and they asked me to step in. I knew nothing about directing, had no background, no experience other than my love of text.

I discovered that the impulses that led me into writing were realized, in a sense, by directing. The director's impulse to create a world, people it with characters, see it come out of his or her own understanding of human nature, is similar to a writer's, except that the original vision is someone else's.

CAROLE ROTHMAN: I started directing when I was in high school. It's somewhat fluky for someone to decide to be a director that early, but I just didn't want to be an actor.

JERRY ZAKS: I came to New York to be an actor. I was very lucky; I got a job on my first audition and worked steadily after that.

As a charter member of the Ensemble Studio Theatre, I first fell into directing. I directed because one of my fellow actors had suggested it to me. It was wonderful, for the first time, to be able to insist on the things I thought should be done. I discovered directing was a much more involving activity than acting.

GREGORY MOSHER: I started directing plays when I was nineteen because I realized I'd never succeed as a conductor.

What people have been major influences on your development as a director?

MELVIN BERNHARDT: I think my whole generation can call Elia Kazan father. His productions had excitement and theatricality.

TOM MOORE: Bill Ball was a great teacher. I don't think anyone in America has his audacity, his sense of theatricality. If I have a spiritual kinship to particular playwrights it's to Feydeau or Kaufman and Hart.

GREGORY MOSHER: Ingmar Bergman—his simplicity, starkness, and tension. The first books that influenced me were Peter Brook's *The Empty Space* and Jerzy Grotowski's *Towards a Poor Theatre;* they were the bibles of my generation. I learned that all you need is the word and an actor to bring theater alive.

EMILY MANN: We all have to admit we've been influenced

by Peter Brook, though I've learned from a lot of people. I'm influenced by good work.

CAROLE ROTHMAN: I studied with Marshall Mason at Circle Rep for two years. I think Marshall is the best teacher of directing I know, wonderful and inspiring. He is one of the few people who knows how to approach directing practically. He has a system, a style, and he's very perceptive about other directors' work. I took what he taught me and transformed it into my own theories.

ARVIN BROWN: The way I learned to read as a budding writer, before I was even interested in directing, taught me instinctively how to read the dramatic text. I understood about reading for motivation, for undercurrents, for subtext, for language as a reflection of character, for atmosphere.

As far as directors influencing me is concerned, Bill Ball's production of *Six Characters in Search of an Author* was the real beginning of my understanding of how much a director's vision shapes the dramatic spirit. Half the experience of that evening in the theater was Bill Ball and half was Pirandello. I realized directing was the overall sense of the scope of the play being pretended onstage.

What are the differences for you between directing a new play and a revival?

MELVIN BERNHARDT: When directing a revival I've got a lot of leeway. I don't have a responsibility to Luigi Pirandello to present a play of his in the exact way *he* may have seen it. My responsibility to the audience is still to do Pirandello's play, but I may emphasize certain aspects, update it, cut it.

The responsibility and obligation of directing the first production of a play is to get the author's vision onstage. I have to get inside her head. The play didn't come out of nothing. It came out of her life and her experiences— whether or not the material is actually autobiographical. An important part of my job is to get to know the author enough to know how she thinks and feels, why she wrote the play.

GREGORY MOSHER: Whether the playwright is alive or not, the process is the same: You try to fulfill the playwright's intentions. It's often indispensable to be able to talk to the writer. Just the way a writer talks, the way he uses words, can tell you everything about him and his play.

GERALD GUTIERREZ: A revival has a history to it, whether you've seen a production or not. Usually, when you do a revival you're doing it to reignite the initial passion for the play or to redefine, refocus it. A revival is always in reaction to the play itself and the play's history.

A revival tends to focus more on the performance than on the production. On a new play, I work much more with the writer, given the fact that directors are always there to serve the play. In a revival, where all that initial script work has been done, a production is about getting the performances from the assembled cast. Sometimes the reason for doing a revival is to see a certain performer play a certain part. The first time out, it's always about the writer.

EMILY MANN: The premiere of a new play carries an added responsibility, not just to unveil a new interpretation of the play with a group of actors, but to bring out in every detail the author's vision and what the author has to say. The star of the evening is the new play. A living author and a new play in front of its first audience is an event different from a new production of a loved play. It is the director's responsibility to bring the new play into the literature and to establish the unknown writer.

ARVIN BROWN: The difference between directing a revival and a new play is that they each call for a different mindset, but I wouldn't say the difference is qualitative. When you are preparing to do a revival there is a certain protection in that you know you are going to be tackling something that has worked. On the other hand, the director is often competing with someone else's interpretation, and the actors are competing with the original performers. There is a sense that some parts belong to certain actors for all time. No actress will be able to play in *Glass Menagerie* with any real freedom until everyone who saw Laurette Taylor as Amanda Wingfield is dead.

PAT BROWN: I try to approach every play—whether a new play or a revival—with an open and unbiased mind, to let the script speak to me as if I'm hearing it for the first time. It is impossible, however, to clear one's mind completely of past productions of many plays, particularly great contemporary productions. No doubt a director is influenced to some degree by productions that have come before.

MARSHALL W. MASON: You have no idea whether a new script is going to work. The director and the actors approaching a classic carry an assumption that the writing is right. Therefore, it becomes their job to explore the terrain the playwright has suggested, though they have a good sense of their ultimate destination, their final goal. When you are working with a new play, you don't have that Northern Star to begin with; you are sailing uncharted waters. There is constant exploration of the central thrust or question of the play by all the people involved. You don't know what's going to be memorable, bad, essential, what should be cut, and so forth. The script is not inviolable; it is evolving, developing.

DOUGLAS TURNER WARD: I can't stand doing what I did last year. I didn't will it, but the only thing that keeps my creative juices flowing is immersion in the undefined. I like to devote my attention to the new, the most difficult of the new, the experimental. There must be challenges for me.

What attracts you to a new play?

GERALD GUTIERREZ: Talking about what I like in a play makes it all sound more analytical than it is. I really don't have a checklist of things that I like. I don't know why I like some plays and not others.

TOM MOORE: I think choosing a play is instinctive. Something happens to me as I read it. If I don't see it in my head, it means that play is probably not right for me. When I read *'night, Mother,* I knew it was a very important piece of literature and worth doing whether it survived commercially or not.

JERRY ZAKS: I know what I believe when I see it on the stage. I think I'm a real good audience. When I read a play that makes me laugh, I know there is no good reason why it can't do the same thing to an audience.

MELVIN BERNHARDT: I read a lot, and I like certain plays and don't like others. Plays that make me laugh, that touch me, and make me feel good at the end—that's what I like best. I don't have the time to do a play that doesn't passionately move me. I don't want to go to the theater and listen to ordinary language. I don't want reality on the stage. We can't expect people to go to the theater unless the two hours in the theater have more stuff in them than two hours outside the theater.

MARSHALL W. MASON: I look first for believable characters, people who are in a circumstance interesting to me. I'm drawn to a playwright who writes with an elevated sense of language. A certain poetry is a critical aspect of theater's magic.

Ultimately, through the character, the language, and the action, what you're really looking to find out is whether the playwright is saying something that is true and really important. In terms of my own vision of reality, is this play true? I look to see if the play is relevant in some particular way to life as the artist has experienced it. The truth of the vision, the relevance, the excellence of the execution— that's what I want to find.

ARVIN BROWN: The single quality that jumps out of every script I like is honesty. The kind of text that attracts me is one that comes right from the writer's gut. Often that has led me into naturalism. I respond to writing that comes from the heart and isn't essentially literary.

DOUGLAS TURNER WARD: I'm not interested in doing plays just to hand things to the audience on a platter. I don't sit back and apply academic, rule-book ideas about new plays before choosing them. Usually, somewhere in my embrace of a new play, there must be an element of dramatic expression that I perceive as original, vibrant, eye- and ear-catching in its potential impact on an audience.

People think that plays, to be powerful, must be literary in an academic sense. The reason I can commit myself to a work is that I can see it, hear it up there onstage. I can see it moving, see the people, the relationships. If realized, the image that I see is perfection.

It's hard to pinpoint a sure thing that makes a play say, "Do me." Sometimes there will be a signal achievement in dramatic writing, a powerful element in something that otherwise is weak—a character perhaps, distinctive language, a unique conflict.

PAT BROWN: I think all professional directors, if they were honest, would say they have directed many plays in their careers simply because the plays were offered and they needed the work. Ideally, however, I prefer to direct plays to which I have a strong emotional and intellectual response. Our response, as artists, is shaped by our development as individuals, so individual directors respond to different kinds of plays. But I feel a professional director ought to be able to direct *any* play, at least competently.

LLOYD RICHARDS: In the early stages of my career, I sometimes chose to work on plays that I didn't feel strongly about. But never again. I got into a position where I could do plays I really wanted to do. I don't believe in doing a play in which I can't invest myself totally. It takes blood to do a play. You can't make that kind of investment without caring about the work.

As a director, deciding on whether to direct a play, I ask the following questions: Am I engaged by the play? Do I care about what the playwright cares about? Is his way of revealing what we both care about unique? Is his voice a valid one? Is the structure of the play essentially dramatic? Is the spine of the play—a complete story with revelation and conclusion—embedded in the material somehow? Is the playwright someone I want to work with? Can we emerge with something better than either of us can articulate alone?

EMILY MANN: The depth of the ideas and the voice at work capture my attention.

JERRY ZAKS: If I read a script and laugh out loud or cry, I want to do it. A play will either affect people or it won't. I'm not saying a play that makes people think is wrong, but a play that is designed only to get someone thinking, as opposed to making them feel something, is generally not the sort of play that appeals to me. It's probably why I didn't like math.

I want a play to show me part of myself or a part of my experience that I don't want to look at, for whatever reason. I want something that makes me appreciate my own humanity more. We all go through the same things and have the same feelings.

What I loved about *Sister Mary* was that Chris put into words his passionate feelings about something that made me, a Jew, appreciate and be moved by his feelings. I've always responded to the story in the simplest terms: This was a woman of tremendous faith—unreal faith grounded in reality; a woman who would commit murder in defense of her faith, that which she holds most dear. The politics grew up around the play. If I'd been attracted by the politics, I would have gone around discussing the play and not directing it.

GREGORY MOSHER: It's fairly obvious. You're going to live with the play you choose for three months to three years, and you want to be able to live in the world of that play—its ideas, its language, its people—and not get bored. You must always feel that the play is out ahead of you, that it has mysteries. For example, I went to see a performance of *Glengarry Glen Ross* months after directing it. I saw in a particular moment an entirely new meaning, and I thought I knew that play inside out.

*Do you use informal sit-down readings for new plays you're
working on? What do you want to get out of a reading?*

GERALD GUTIERREZ: If what you want to hear is the sound
mosaic of a play, then you do a reading with actors who
are quick, intelligent, and have the necessary technique.

TOM MOORE: What I hear in my head tells me what will
work or not. As soon as an actor reads it, I will forever hear
it in that way. I'm scared of readings and tend not to use them.
I don't even want to do a production of something I've seen
a good reading of. I find the reading is too influential.

JERRY ZAKS: I only use readings when I need them. I was
asked to do a play recently. I read it to myself and had a
very good response. With each subsequent reading I became less enthusiastic. I organized a sit-down reading of
it. Hearing the play read aloud made it very clear that the
play was too verbose. It's very seductive to try to make a
play that isn't perfect work. But if the play is not there in
the words, all the director will do is call attention to his
own work.

ARVIN BROWN: One must never ever compromise on the
quality of the actors. There is no learning from bad actors.

DOUGLAS TURNER WARD: A lot of times you get a grab bag
of actors at a reading. Usually, there is a useless discussion
afterwards, and people very often say what they didn't understand about the play. That's death. It's deadly for the
playwright and deadly for the theatrical experience.

I often test out the viability of a new play through my
own acting. I tape-record the play, reading all the parts.

This gives me a reference by which to hear and see the play better.

People who experience a play by seeing a reading usually don't have the remotest ability to sense the nature of that work put on its feet. They also tend to be literal-minded. Unfortunately, what they don't understand the writer goes and explains in the text. The very thing the writer had left to the audience's imagination is suddenly closed off by too much explanation.

EMILY MANN: You try to get the reading as right as possible so that you can analyze what the play is doing. You get to know the play a little bit better. You get to see the play on a performance level of some sort. You might think about staging when you're listening to it; close your eyes and hear these voices in a three-dimensional space. Basically, you see how much more writing needs to be done.

MELVIN BERNHARDT: I listen for dead spots, breaks in the connections, where the play falters, where the through-line disappears. I look for potential problems that can be addressed before I take the play into rehearsal.

ARVIN BROWN: There are actors who are amazingly adept at picking up a script and activating the right emotions. That's wonderful. For the reading to have any value at all for the writer, there ought to be some rehearsal. Maybe not even a conceptual rehearsal, but just reading through the play a couple of times so you can give the writer some hint of what he has written.

Do you find staged readings useful?

MELVIN BERNHARDT: It's very rare that a play comes my way fully written and ready for production. Too many writers ask us to work on an early draft, expecting that it will be sorted out. Actors can't come in and give first-draft acting. I don't know how to do first-draft directing. It makes no difference if we're in a reading or on Broadway, I direct the same way.

MARSHALL W. MASON: Circle Rep puts actors, a director, and a project together to rehearse for two weeks. The playwright is asked all those difficult questions he or she is going to be asked when the play goes into full rehearsal. It provides an interplay between the various artists in the collaborative effort. The questions that come up in the process of developing a script can be invaluable.

PAT BROWN: A staged reading provides an opportunity for some rehearsal, a chance to explore the script.

LLOYD RICHARDS: By the time I've read through the play a couple of times, I know what I want to find out from a reading and I structure the reading to get that information.

GERALD GUTIERREZ: It's another step. You have the playwright there to test what you felt when reading the script. I don't block staged readings. That would be a waste of time. Who designed the set? Me? For me, doing a staged reading means having the actors on stools and the stage manager sitting on the side and telling the audience what's happening. I prefer to use the rehearsal time to explore the characters and their relationship to the play. There's no question that everyone knows more about the play after a staged reading.

I think the current practice of using staged readings as a substitute for backers' auditions is anti-development. All of the decisions made in rehearsals are based on pleasing the potential producers, not on testing the work, developing the work. You're slamming doors.

EMILY MANN: I do not direct staged readings. Period. The end. It's an exercise that is of no use to me as a writer or as a director. I'm not learning more about the play. I'm getting superficial, idiotic, in-a-clutch acting choices that don't tell me or the writer anything. Staged readings end up being a lot of wasted effort on the part of the actors. It's frustrating for everyone.

ARVIN BROWN: There is a gap between a reading and a fully staged workshop production. The way the staged reading tries to fill that gap is terribly awkward. Many, many scripts really aren't helped by readings. The essence of what is good is in action. I defy anyone to sit down with a copy of *The Changing Room* and find much in it. I can pick up a script that may be very, very terse and understand how it will work onstage. But that isn't going to emerge in a reading. And the chances are that the effect of the play isn't going to emerge in a staged reading either.

In staged readings you get into all kinds of awkward pragmatisms about the actors holding the script: Do you put down the script for the kissing scene, or do you keep it in hand to make it clear you haven't switched from a staged reading into a performance? With all the inherent problems, how can you justify staged readings as a viable technique for developing new plays?

MELVIN BERNHARDT: A staged reading usually has to do with showing how the play could work if you were to give it a production. My goal is to make it clear to the audience.

There is a middle ground in staged readings that can lead to disaster. If you begin to explore the emotional life of the character, you need a full rehearsal period. We cannot actually immerse ourselves in layers of subtext, or the entire emotional life of the play. We are merely presenting the *possibilities* of the play. How can an actor do more when he is sitting on a hard chair, in his own clothes, on some other show's set, with next to no rehearsal? There is a danger of trying to do too much in a staged reading.

Directing a staged reading is like directing a full production, but you are stylizing the action, scaling it differently. Just having an actor put his script down can stand in for a major piece of blocking if the moment were fully produced.

JERRY ZAKS: Staged readings? Oh, I don't know. The actors don't know if they're giving a reading or a performance. It's an identity crisis.

Do you like having an audience present at a reading? What sort of feedback do you look for from the audience? From the actors?

MARSHALL W. MASON: After a reading at Circle Rep, we take comments from all the people who attend. The criticisms are taped, as is the play reading, and the tapes are made available to the playwright to listen to two or three weeks later, when he or she has calmed down a bit from either loving or not loving the reading. The first time a script's read, you can't really hear the specifics. If you go back two or three weeks later, you can dispassionately listen to the reading and the criticism, and revise.

GERALD GUTIERREZ: I'll have friends come listen to a play reading and I'll listen politely to what they have to say, whether or not I agree. My disagreement can solidify my opinions, which leads to further questions for the playwright.

I'm usually not very interested in what actors think about the play. If they excel at talking about plays they should either write or direct. I'm much more interested in seeing what happens when they give me what they're good at, which is acting one part. I think if writers listen too much to actors, they can get into deep trouble. Actors usually look for the minimum amount of work for the most amount of payoff.

ARVIN BROWN: Most audiences at readings tend, if anything, to overpraise rather than underpraise. As long as the writer is able to preserve a troubleshooting approach to the reading, it is more healthy to have people there.

If I am struggling with severe structural problems, I have the script read to a theater-wise audience. If I'm looking to see how much of the story I have managed to convey, or how people feel about the characters, I have the play read before a "general" audience.

EMILY MANN: After *one* reading, who can tell the playwright—who's spent over a year on the play—what's wrong? Beware of knee-jerk reactions.

What sort of work do you do on a script before going into rehearsals?

GREGORY MOSHER: I assume the script is what the writer intended to write. If a character repeats himself, says the same line three times in a row, I don't make a mental note to "fix" that line. I wonder why that character would say the same thing three times in a row. I don't assume it's a "mistake" on the part of the playwright.

You soak in the play until the logic of it becomes apparent. You wonder what story the events tell. Take *Amer-*

ican Buffalo: If this story is about three guys committing a coin theft, then everything in the play must have to do with the coin theft, because nothing should be extraneous. That doesn't make sense when you read the play. So you throw that idea out. Finally, you think the play is the story of a man trying to destroy the relationship between a father and a son. That fits. The play is revealed. You just keep testing hypotheses. Answers come from asking over and over again what the story of the play is.

MELVIN BERNHARDT: I'm not one of those directors who feels you should cross out all the author's stage directions without looking at them. I need to know what the writer wants to happen. The writer's vision of the physical production might be the best way of doing things.

MARSHALL W. MASON: It's impossible to know the play too well. The director has to be in the position where it's as though he or she had written the play. You've got to feel the play as deeply as the writer, which means reading and reading, always carrying the script around with you. You must dwell on it.

The way I begin to interact with the script is by dividing it into small beats, units of action that begin in a certain kind of way and go on until something happens that changes that action. Generally, I can mark beats every three to five pages. Some beats happen in a page; others can go for eight pages or more.

Once I've divided the play into beats, I do a character-scene breakdown in which I represent graphically with *x*'s and *o*'s the exits and entrances of the speaking characters and the silent ones. As I look at the graph, there is a visual image of the play's traffic, the comings and goings of people, the evolution of relationships. A well-written play has a graphic pattern to it, an arc.

CAROLE ROTHMAN: I like to read a play several times and then spend time mulling, letting it sink in. The really talented directors are those people who can be creative and let their imagination flow.

To have a really good concept of how to do a play, you have to know what it's going to look like, how it's going to move, how it's going to affect an audience. When I did *How I Got That Story*, I did a lot of reading about Vietnam, but I also read *Gulliver's Travels* and other satire.

I know a lot of directors who will listen to a piece of music for inspiration. I'm more in tune with something visual than something aural. I remember once clipping a picture out of a magazine because it evoked the world of the play so well.

I break plays down into big beats first. That helps me to get a feeling for the structure, the pacing, and the music of the play—how the rhythms rush over you. I'll say what happens in each scene, name each scene. Otherwise, how can I remember? In rehearsal you sometimes don't remember exactly what a scene is about. I fill the margins of my scripts with notes, anything that comes into my head. I jot down questions to ask the playwright. I may not refer to my notes until well into rehearsal, but they can remind me of things I've forgotten.

GERALD GUTIERREZ: I read a new script a million times. I read it when I don't want to read it. It breaks down as I read it. I tend to be very conscious of when I begin to drift away. I don't do a detailed promptbook for a play. All that analysis, analysis, analysis gets in my way. I do have a notebook for a show, but that's mostly so I don't forget important things.

I come up with a spine for the play: What is the one thing *all* of the characters want *all* of the time? That's the hardest thing to find. I believe my biggest contribution to a play is if I can come up with a spine that unifies the play. That is the bedrock for me. It enables me to meet with designers and begin to think about casting. I can speak with the playwright about where the play goes away from the spine, where it digresses. Unless I can come up with a spine, even a rough one that I refine later, then I'm not ready to do the play.

What kind of work do you do with the playwright before going into rehearsal?

ARVIN BROWN: It takes years to come to this, but you have to believe in your gut that you might *not* have the answers. Don't fake it, don't ask a question that you are very proud of (a question you think will lead the playwright to your preconceived answer), but approach a script in such a way that you are going to the heart of the material, that which is beyond any easy solution. Ask yourself, before you ask the writer, "What really doesn't work for me in this play?" Ask the playwright questions when you haven't a clue what the answer is.

CAROLE ROTHMAN: A lot of times playwrights think they're making a certain point which their play doesn't actually do. If you know where the playwright thinks she's going, you can help get her there. You point out where the focus is off. You question every line. This questioning process also helps you make sure you're on the right track.

JERRY ZAKS: If you accept that you're working toward an ideal which you'll never reach, it makes the journey a lot more fun. You can be a lot freer in your impulses. Either it's there in the text or it's not. I don't believe that you can leave things to the last minute. I try to be as hard as I can on the playwright: "Am I involved?" "Am I confused?" "Do I care?" "Is it clear?" I have to go into rehearsals with as few unanswered questions about the play as possible.

TOM MOORE: I go through every beat of the play, helping the writer shape, structure, and slice away any material that doesn't belong. I serve as a sounding board for the author. I can't write myself, but I'm very useful in helping others rewrite.

GREGORY MOSHER: A playwright chooses a form that makes sense to him—kitchen-sink dramas, slapstick comedies. Who cares what form he chooses or where he sets the drama? Chekhov set his plays in the country, not because of some bullshit idea about "the country," but because he lived in and knew the country. The *intention* of the playwright is all that should matter to the director.

MELVIN BERNHARDT: I like to sit down with the writer and ask about all the things I don't understand or don't immediately connect to, and say, "What did you mean?"

GERALD GUTIERREZ: When I read *Isn't It Romantic* it was funny, witty, and a mess. It was all over the place. I had to ask Wendy Wasserstein what the play was about. A play can't be about everything; it can only be about one or two things.

The weekend before I do a play I like to go away with the playwright, get out of New York. I like to hear the play read by the playwright, an act a day. It's my chance to ask questions line-by-line, just to make sure that no question I have goes unasked. Then, when you and the playwright arrive at rehearsal you are arriving to do the same play.

How do you handle rehearsals?

LLOYD RICHARDS: Rehearsals begin when you think the play is ready. Never go into rehearsal without being certain the spine of the play is there and works. You can fix a lot of things in a rehearsal period, but you can't fix the spine if it's not there. Go back for another reading if you are unsure of what you've got. Another reading is much less costly—both in terms of money and in terms of everyone's sanity—than going into rehearsal too early. Rehearsals are like a toboggan slide: You pass a certain point and you are going all the way; there's no getting off.

CAROLE ROTHMAN: The first day of rehearsal is always a nightmare, yet you've always got to be coherent and excited about the play. It's very nerve-wracking. The playwright is there for the first read-through. Playwrights want to hear what I have to say to the actors, and they might also have something to say. At the first read-through the play shifts from the playwright's to the director's hands. It's no longer how the playwright sees the play but how the director is interpreting the play.

JERRY ZAKS: Having the actors read the play on the first day of rehearsal gives me a sense of what their impulses are going to be, what I have to watch for, and how each actor responds to the slightest bit of performance pressure.

Everyone has the right to express an idea in rehearsals. People have to feel that they have the right to talk and suggest. The danger is anarchy. If someone has a brilliant idea, even if that brilliant idea comes in the middle of forty not-so-brilliant ideas, it's worth listening to. I, as director, have the right to accept or not accept ideas and suggestions.

ARVIN BROWN: The early days of rehearsal are a constant clarification of the playwright's intentions. I'm not saying those intentions might not be flawed, but you must understand what they are.

MARSHALL W. MASON: When I begin rehearsals, we talk about the play, the shared goals, and how we're going to go through the play. I tell the actors the beats; they mark them in their scripts. I require the actors to learn their lines before we work on each beat. When you work beat by beat, the actor is working on a very specific terrain instead of trying to take in the whole world of the play.

CAROLE ROTHMAN: A week or a week and a half of rehearsals is enough time to go through every scene of the play. I have the actors come in with their parts memorized. Since the actors don't have their scripts in their hands, they're on their feet from the first moment. I don't believe in sitting around a table reading a play.

ARVIN BROWN: I get the actors on their feet almost immediately. I feel that that is how their instrument gets operating. What I don't do is sit around a table with the writer having academic or theoretical discussions about what this play is about. I only accept actors' questions about meaning when they are questions coming from lack of emotional understanding. I always encourage actors to use their instincts.

GERALD GUTIERREZ: I spend a lot of time around a table early in rehearsal—so much time that producers used to think I didn't know how to block and would get worried.

Blocking is the easiest thing in the world. You can even block *Three Sisters* in a day if need be. Who cares whether an actor moves to the sofa or the chair, as long as the actor understands his character and is helping the playwright make his point? As long as we are all agreed that *this* is where we begin and *this* is where we have to end up, getting there is each person's job. That's why I spend a lot of time talking and I want everyone to talk. It's very important that everyone be involved.

EMILY MANN: Usually, I will have the actors improvise staging with text in hand and see if they come up with anything better than I have devised before rehearsals began. I then stage the play, incorporating what the actors discovered. I edit and put together a rough staging of the whole thing by the end of the first week.

JERRY ZAKS: I usually come into rehearsal with a first-draft staging. It might not be inspired but it's a beginning, something for the actors to work with. I want to provide a structure that will stimulate the actors to improve on my ideas. That will, in turn, allow me to improve on theirs.

GREGORY MOSHER: The whole idea of rehearsing a play in four weeks is a ridiculous convention; it has nothing to do with the needs of the play. Some plays need three weeks' rehearsal, some need three months. The rehearsal process changes for each play. As a director you're always trying to create an atmosphere where real chances can be taken, where risk will be supported. The process of exploring the human soul is not always easy or even pleasant. Every time you see a good director work you see extraordinary patience.

I don't say very much in rehearsals. As I concentrate on making the text work, there's less need to talk. I don't think directors are the creative font of the production; the text is. I'm not saying directors don't do anything. I'm saying the task of giving a play direction doesn't necessarily involve talking a whole lot. It involves listening a hell of a lot. The standard photograph of a director has him standing with his mouth open and pointing his finger at the actors. A photograph of a director *really* at work would show him sitting forward in his chair, absolutely still, watching, concentrating on the play and what the actors are doing.

MELVIN BERNHARDT: Directing is a self-destructing job: You let go of the production in stages until you're no longer needed. During the first days of rehearsal, I'm sitting at the head of the table as we begin our discussions. Everyone wants to know what I think. We start blocking the play in a rehearsal room somewhere—the set just tape marks and folding chairs—and I'm running on and off the playing area. I'm still a kind of focus for the actors, but they are building a life of their own on that stage. When we move into the theater, I jump up onto the stage and off again as we sort this life out, fine tune the play. Eventually I'm sitting in the theater and the actors are playing the show to me; I've become the audience. During previews, I stand in the back with the audience between me and the actors. The day after opening night, I may as well not exist.

How do you work with the playwright during rehearsals? Do you encourage the playwright to speak with the actors?

EMILY MANN: Once the new play goes into rehearsal, that play—not the ego of the director, writer, or actors—has to come foremost. You have to look at the play as being separate from all of you.

PAT BROWN: Ideally, a playwright can be very helpful in discussing his plays with the actors and with the design staff. I always want and seek this kind of involvement, but tentatively at first, and with caution, to test personalities and their compatibility. Often, the playwright is not the best judge of what he or she has written. What a play "means," what its boundaries are—its circumference, depth, dimension—is very often not apparent to the playwright until all of the key production elements are there.

MELVIN BERNHARDT: I let playwrights decide how often they want to attend rehearsals. The danger is that the playwright is going to expect results too early. I don't want actors to try to *perform* for the playwright.

ARVIN BROWN: I find all writers so result oriented that you have to protect the rehearsal process from them. No matter how much practical experience they have in the theater, playwrights are strangely ill-equipped to deal with the actor's process. A director has an eye that tells him if something an actor is doing is a problem or simply a station on the way.

MARSHALL W. MASON: Part of the difficulty a new playwright has with actors is that the playwright is thinking in terms of the results and, therefore, the actors are pushed to results sooner than they ought to be. If you're doing *Hamlet*, everyone knows where Hamlet is going to end up, so if the actor is mumbling along for the first three weeks nobody says, "Is he really going to play it like that?" You know the actor is going to say "To be or not to be" with complete conviction. With a new play, you don't know what the true result is going to be, which can be very frustrating for the playwright. It's one of the reasons why actors and playwrights seem to have a mutual antagonism from the beginning. The new playwright, especially, is impatient for the actor's process to be finished.

Generally speaking, I encourage playwrights to attend as many rehearsals as they can bear, as long as I can get enough time for the actors to create free from the pressure of a playwright's presence. Actors need time to fuck around with the play, try different things. But for playwrights it's very trying to sit through that. I find it more helpful for playwrights to come the second time we run through something rather than the first. This way they don't have to go through so much of the actor's process.

ARVIN BROWN: I want the writer with me through the staging and all the initial grapplings with the text. I want him to be aware of what I'm doing and of the shape of the production, so that he can tell me about any frightening gaps he sees between our mutual understanding of the play and production and what is becoming the performance. I'm there to put the writer's intentions on the stage; I'm not defensive about the writer speaking up during these early stages.

CAROLE ROTHMAN: When the playwright is in rehearsal all the time I don't think he or she has any objectivity, and, therefore, isn't any use to you at all. You want the playwright to come in as an audience, not as someone so blinded by the process—the little steps the actors have taken—that he or she can't tell that the play and the production are growing.

LLOYD RICHARDS: When actors are trying to put down their books, and the lines aren't there, it can be a frustrating time for the playwright. He can do nothing except sit and agonize. Many valid feelings that the playwright has about the actors' work become invalid under the pressures of the rehearsal period. The actors need their own space to work in and the opportunity to make mistakes and grow.

It is often very valuable for the playwright to withdraw from rehearsals and then come back. The director's whole process is one of going from a position of subjectivity to a position of objectivity: to be involved subjectively with the actors in creation and then to become an objective judge. The difference between progress and achievement is something that the director defines. You have to be objective to define achievement. The playwright can help if he leaves the rehearsals for a time. He can then come back and see it fresh, with objective, not subjective, eyes.

ARVIN BROWN: There does come a time when I invariably ask the writer to take a walk. There has got to be a period of at least a week or so—when the actors are beginning to do their deep emotional work—for the actors to have the freedom to say, "What the fuck does this mean? I don't understand this scene. Why do I have to say this line? I think this is all a piece of shit." All the stuff most actors will not say in front of the writer has a chance to explode. It's better not to let that explosion damage the writer-actor relationship.

GERALD GUTIERREZ: I don't like playwrights to talk to the actors, though they can say hello. The director has got to control the flow of information. There has to be one voice speaking. That voice can incorporate notes from the playwright, notes from the producer, notes from the designers, but it's got to be one person or you've got anarchy.

I once directed a play by a college professor. It was hard for him to keep quiet in rehearsals. One day he told an actress who was having troubles that her character was "a snowflake in the middle of a blizzard." Actors love that because it sounds artistic. But how do you act a snowflake?

What does a snowflake do? What does a snowflake want? What's its objective?

MELVIN BERNHARDT: "I love having you in my play" is the best thing for the playwright to say to the actors. I don't think they can help by getting into specifics. They should say everything they want to say to the director.

LLOYD RICHARDS: In rehearsal I allow the playwright to talk to the actors in selected situations. There are also times when actors ask the playwright questions, but I usually communicate those to the playwright. The playwright is an important resource, and I like to see him as a resource and not as a codirector.

TOM MOORE: When I was younger I never would let any author into rehearsal. When you're younger you're more insecure. Now I like having the author around. I don't let the author communicate directly with the actors, but I have no hesitation in turning to the author at any point and saying, "What do you think?" Sometimes, when a moment in the play isn't clicking, I have to work alone with an actor, so I will send the playwright home. The actor needs the freedom to try things.

If I'm having trouble getting a certain scene, I will let the playwright speak with the actor, but I don't allow any kind of codirecting. I think that confuses the actor. Also, the author seldom talks in terms the actor can understand. Most authors will use literary terms, which the actor will have trouble latching onto.

MARSHALL W. MASON: I encourage the actors to talk to the playwright. Our company of actors is used to creating new works. They are very concerned and eager to have the playwright's contribution. There are certain circumstances in which actors feel the playwright is the natural enemy, and then they can't do their work properly. When the playwright starts being disruptive to the actor's process, then the playwright has got to be barred from rehearsal or has to understand that he or she can't speak. In the beginning I refused to let Lanford [Wilson] ever speak to the actors directly. But now, twenty years later, I encourage Lanford to speak directly to the actors because it saves me a lot of time. I know we're solidly in agreement.

GREGORY MOSHER: I love having Mamet at rehearsals. David and I have an informal understanding that he has final say on the text and I have final say on the staging. I always listen to him. He always has good ideas and I will always try them.

How do you work with the actor in rehearsal?

MARSHALL W. MASON: I found early on that a great deal of directing involves the teaching of acting. You only have a month to rehearse and you spend the first half of it teaching the actors common acting principles, a shared technique and language, and then you have two weeks to rehearse the play.

TOM MOORE: I don't consider myself an acting coach. I consider myself a director. When I have terrific actors capable of doing a number of things, then I serve as a grand editor. Most of my productions bear my stamp to some extent, but they are all shaped by the actors playing the parts. I don't like working with younger actors nearly as much as I do with more experienced actors, because I don't enjoy having to coach them to get them to a certain point.
I trust actors' instincts enormously—if they are in line

with the vision of the author. If a piece of blocking is uncomfortable, I immediately change it. If an actor has something he or she wants to try, we certainly try it. But I am leery of actors saying that something is uncomfortable before they've locked into what the author is doing. You should never please the actor at the expense of the play.

CAROLE ROTHMAN: I allow a tremendous amount of freedom. I know what I want from the beginning and try to shape the performance. But I want the actors to bring their own ideas, their own business, to their roles. The kind of actor I like to work with experiments constantly. The work of such actors inspires me and inspires the other actors.

PAT BROWN: I very much believe in giving actors freedom in developing character. Any play, when it is filtered through an individual actor's personality, becomes transformed by that unique personality to some extent. Consequently, what the actor brings to a role is of the utmost value to me in shaping the play.

LLOYD RICHARDS: I do have something in mind for each role, but I always expect the actor is going to make a major contribution. I give the actor full opportunity to create within my boundaries. If an actor doesn't at some point, in some way, surprise me by his character revelations, I'm disappointed.

At first the playwright knows more about a character than anyone else. In the process of rehearsal, a point comes when the director knows more about every character than the playwright. Then a point is reached at which the actor knows more about his or her individual character than either the playwright or the director.

MELVIN BERNHARDT: Each actor gradually becomes *the* specialist in his or her character.

ARVIN BROWN: If a rehearsal is going properly, the actors are as surprised as the director with what is realized. The director learns every time out. I never end a rehearsal without feeling that I have learned more than I have taught.

DOUGLAS TURNER WARD: Actors drive me out of my mind when they don't capture the *sense* of a line in their readings. A lot of actors think that acting consists of doing something other than what's common sense—they will put the fucking emphasis on the article or the conjunction; they will put the emphasis on a word that will change the whole sense of the line. That is just sloppy.

Actors have an abstract idea that acting is not connected with logic. It's "art." They play around with their lines when I know that the playwright spent months coming up with the right order for the words. There is a certain amount of dramatic writing that lends itself to two or three different stresses, but much dramatic writing has only one reading that makes sense. A director has to know when and how to tell an actor that there is only one way to read a line.

JERRY ZAKS: You have to make sure actors know where something wonderful they did in rehearsal came from so that they can repeat it in performance. It won't be the same every night, but the impulse will be. When you know what all your landmarks are, you can just go. Actors have to be convinced of that.

How do you deal with an evolving script?

MARSHALL W. MASON: One should go into rehearsal with the feeling that, even if not a single change is made on the script, the play is still worth doing. The only kinds of changes that should be made in rehearsal are cuts and little line changes here and there. I don't believe one should be involved in the process of major rewriting in rehearsals; rewrites should happen before rehearsals begin.

MELVIN BERNHARDT: From the time you go into rehearsal to the time you open is a finite time. Everything you can do with the script before rehearsals gives you more work time later.

CAROLE ROTHMAN: I hate to go into rehearsal with a play that is not finished. I think that is unfair to everyone. The script must be in the best shape you think it can possibly be, until you find out it's not.

We did a significant amount of cutting in *Painting Churches*. There were scenes we'd rehearsed for weeks that we cut out. The actors were very flexible, though after the first week of previews they didn't want any more changes. We have to beat our heads against a scene a lot of times before we begin to talk of cutting. You must let the playwright see the scene as well as it can be played for them to realize that it doesn't work.

DOUGLAS TURNER WARD: The first version of *A Soldier's Play* that Charles Fuller gave me was the version we did. By the time it went into rehearsal, the few loose spots had been tightened. In rehearsal it basically didn't change at all. The ending had been overwritten, but we found we had to cut out only the sermonizing. We didn't have to rewrite. We just pared the ending down to its essentials.

EMILY MANN: The director makes sure the text is clean and right and absolutely dead-on. Where the playwright can't cover the flaws you have to try to cover for him or her. If the words don't give a scene the power it should have, and the writer has done everything he can do, and you've done everything you can to inspire the writer, at a certain point, you as director have to say, "The writer can't do it, can I? Can I, with my actors, staging, and design make it work?" You try to make it happen.

PAT BROWN: With a new play, if an actor has a strong feeling about whether a section of dialogue or scene works or does not work, I will certainly trust that instinct, and make attempts to adjust. With a new play, the actor can often be very helpful in refining dialogue and finding implausibilities, or adding a new dimension to a scene.

ARVIN BROWN: When an actor I admire and respect, who has really made a deep attempt to get a moment to work, says to me, "I can't get to it emotionally. I know what the writer means, but I can't get there," then either the actor isn't capable of getting there, or the actor knows better than the writer. A really good actor won't lie. If the scene isn't working I'll say to the writer—and I've said this to major, established writers as often as I've said it to young writers—"Go home for a couple of days and write everything you know about that scene. There is something missing here and I don't want to tell you what it is. Come back with everything you've written and we'll discover the scene together."

TOM MOORE: When an actor is asking for a scene to be rewritten and the playwright is saying that perhaps the actor hasn't quite gotten it, what I do is decide for myself which one is right, and cajole the other into realizing that. Actors always make suggestions that end up being incorporated in the script. If you don't put the author into an outsider position, it is easier for him to accept that sort of contribution. What the director does is serve as moderator and ringmaster. At one point on 'night, Mother, I kept insisting a scene wasn't working because it was too long. I asked

Marsha to shorten it. She solved the problem by *lengthening* it. She understood what I was saying and realized what she needed to do.

MARSHALL W. MASON: No matter how beautifully an actor may do something, if it's a rotten line, it's a rotten line. If the line's not cut, it can certainly ruin a moment. On the other hand, you don't know if the line is rotten since the actor hasn't reached the full, finished performance yet. The director is supposed to understand the playwright's intention, as well as the actor's process, and serve as a bridge between the concept of the playwright and the performance of the actor.

LLOYD RICHARDS: When a scene does not work, there is usually a whole series of reasons why it doesn't. The problem may seem to center around some event or line, but it might not be that at all. It might be that the scene, or a particular section of the scene, has not been set up properly earlier in the play.

GREGORY MOSHER: When you know exactly what the through-line of the play is, you can make cuts and not harm the play.

GERALD GUTIERREZ: After a show opens, I'll sometimes go back and rework something that never quite worked the way I wanted it to. I've done four productions of *Isn't it Romantic* and they're basically the same, but it took the fourth production for me to solve one scene.

What are you looking for when casting a new play?

CAROLE ROTHMAN: I do happen to agree with that standard wisdom that casting is ninety percent of the production.

You get the right cast and your life is much easier. I know actors hate to hear this, but there are certain plays where you can't *act* the character, you have to *be* it.

MELVIN BERNHARDT: I always look for intelligent actors. It's easier to communicate. The brighter the actor, the more he brings. If I can't visualize the actor in the part during an audition, I probably can't get it to work on the stage.

EMILY MANN: You look for the best actor. I often base my plays on real people. The important thing for me is to get that real person out of my mind and cast the essence of that person.

ARVIN BROWN: It's very difficult to get the writer's mind past physical restrictions he may have given himself when visualizing his characters. Physical characteristics are very much tied up in the writer's mind with modes of behavior, modes of character: "My mother was a big woman. She came into a room and dominated it." Well, there are many ways of dominating a room other than by size. There are many big people who come into a room and disappear; there are many tiny people who come in and immediately become the center of attention. Very often you are better off with an actor who understands the need to dominate than someone who is physically prepossessing.

MARSHALL W. MASON: It's important to cast the play—understanding what the playwright's desired results are—perhaps in ways that are not in direct line from start to finish. Quite frequently, the playwright has a vision of the characters so firmly in mind that he really thinks "she's a blonde." The director will, too often, give in and only audition blonde actors. You must be looking for the inner quality of the character and for the actor who has the craft and technique and artistic sensibility to accomplish your goals in a four-week rehearsal period. It's the director's job to be able to spot the potential in an actor that will lead to the result he and the playwright want.

GERALD GUTIERREZ: I fight looking for a "short blonde." You have to fight slamming doors. Casting is so difficult and important. It's all a crapshoot. Sometimes you'll get a wonderful group of actors, but the chemistry of the company is all wrong. Sometimes a nice person is more important to the success of a play than a less nice person with a little more flash. A great actor who screws up the ensemble feeling isn't worth having.

I don't think it's wrong to replace an actor once you're into rehearsals. I don't shy away from it as much as other directors do. If you made a mistake you should fix it, otherwise the play ain't going to work. And a production, especially of a new play, is all about the play working.

GREGORY MOSHER: Once you've cast the actors and okayed the designs, so much of giving the play a direction has been done. I try to serve the play in casting, but I also think, "Do I want to spend the next three months with these people? Are they going to bring something special to the rehearsals? Do they love the play?" That's crucial. The actor's love of the play comes across the footlights. Doing the play merely as a job also communicates itself to the audience. An actor who is perhaps slightly less skilled but who has an astounding love for the work is the one I'll always cast.

ARVIN BROWN: I love to cast in a way that redresses balances. If I get a strong image of a character while reading the play, I like to think about what will produce the deepest realizations of that character. For example, whoever you cast in a tragedy has to have a wonderful sense of humor; and you're dead if you cast a comedy with people who can't feel.

Describe your working relationship with a production's designers.

EMILY MANN: A director can find a play through the designers. I like to get them into the process early. Even as a writer I've often found a play first through a designer.

MARSHALL W. MASON: Sometimes the directors and designers can help playwrights an awful lot by giving them a world of three-dimensional reality far beyond their imagination. When Lanford Wilson brought me *Mound Builders*, he said he had no idea what the play was to be like physically. There were virtually no stage directions. My work with John Lee Beatty created a set that served both the play and the production. The set helped Lanford a great deal when he rewrote the play.

CAROLE ROTHMAN: I like to work with the designers really early. Since *Painting Churches* was about an artist dealing with light, the designers and I looked at a lot of Impressionist paintings. The paintings gave us a feel for the play, a common ground out of which the set, the lighting, and the costumes developed. Directors want to work with tangible things, which is why you go to books, paintings, photographs, and so forth for stimulation.

LLOYD RICHARDS: I feel it is very important for the playwright to be exposed to the design process. The designer is a very imaginative, yet logical and mathematical person. He needs certain information in order to draw lines on the paper. He asks very factual questions that are good for the playwright to hear.

The visual concept for the play is the vision of one person—the director—although many people may make creative contributions.

MELVIN BERNHARDT: In order to work with the designer on the set, you have to decide where you want to play your key scenes, what kind of movement patterns you want, then you can work out the ground plan together.

JERRY ZAKS: *Bette and Boo* had thirty-two scenes, and I knew those scene changes had to be played either in the same rhythm that had been established in the scene or in a tempo that would be a springboard to the next scene. The scene changes could not be random. When I could see all the action of the play taking place on the designer's ground plan, I couldn't wait to get into rehearsals.

TOM MOORE: I usually have some kind of idea about what the design should be. I try at the first meeting not to limit the designer's imagination, but I do give the designer the elements I know have to be there. After I've done a couple of shows with a designer, the process becomes really remarkable, because then we speak the same language.

GREGORY MOSHER: I sort of have to do the ground plan myself. I want to be able to place the actors in relation to each other and to the audience. I tell the designer where each scene has to be played on the stage.

For the first act of *Glengarry Glen Ross*, I knew I wanted the actors to play on the same plane and be very close to the audience. At one point I wanted to do *Glengarry* on a bare stage—just a restaurant booth without any other scenery around it.

Never, never in the design process does it become "What would be interesting?" Or, "What would be theatrical?" It's always "What would be best for this play?"

GERALD GUTIERREZ: If the ground plan is right, the set will work. Everything has to be in the right place. There has to be room for the actors to act. I want to know I can deliver the play on that space as it's defined. There's something boring about everything having to happen downstage center. The set shouldn't stifle the play.

MELVIN BERNHARDT: Beth Henley always thought of *Crimes of the Heart* as more realistic than I did. The first time she saw the set, she wondered why the wallpaper wasn't peeling. The challenge in directing Beth's plays is finding just the right style. We had to achieve a balance so that the old man in a coma was going to be both believable and funny. John Lee Beatty's set created an environment where we could do a lot of funny things without being grotesque.

Do you find reviews helpful or harmful?

GREGORY MOSHER: There are good critics and bad critics. I admire anyone who devotes his or her life to any form of the theater. Obviously critics have a special place in the theater community. Some critics don't think of themselves as members of the theatrical community, but I think they are.

LLOYD RICHARDS: I don't generally read reviews. I don't consider the critic, in most cases, to be a partner in the work. I'm uninterested in what he has to say, unless I respect him as a person, a thinker, a writer—and as a theater person.

There have been a few important critics—those who have a stake in the theater and who make a contribution to the theater through their work—but most of them lived in the past. *Modern* critics are an aspect of marketing, not theater. For the most part, they are selling personality and papers. They live off the theater.

MELVIN BERNHARDT: We don't have anything to learn from reviewers except how long we're going to run. So they are a very important part of my life, damn it.

JERRY ZAKS: I read my reviews. Unfortunately, I believe them—though less and less. If I read twenty positive reviews, it's still not enough. I wish I could appreciate the good reviews I get in the same way I appreciate good reviews when they're for someone else. If someone says anything negative about my work, that's what I'll carry around. I'm just beginning to be less vulnerable. The more I believe in a project, the angrier I get about negative reviews. Everyone is entitled to his or her opinion. But when the expression of that opinion determines if someone comes to see your work, oy, it's rough.

GERALD GUTIERREZ: I read every review written. I ignore every review written. I think critics are ignorant of the process. I don't believe they recognize their position in the chain. I'm not saying critics have to write, direct, or act. They are too quick to praise for all the wrong reasons, and they are very quick to destroy for the wrong reasons. They bring a hit-or-flop mentality to every play they review. As papers fold and we have fewer and fewer critics writing, the problems are exacerbated. Critics will recite you chapter and verse the plays they liked that didn't run, plays they didn't like that ran—which is horseshit. These are the exceptions and not the rule. The play the *New York Times* likes is the one that runs. The play the *Times* doesn't like, doesn't run.

I'm very disturbed when I read the reviews of new writers. The playwright is always the one to take it in the face. Critics inevitably say, "The actor did the best he could with this material." The critics seem to have no interest in developing the new writer.

TOM MOORE: I've never been angry with the critics. Long ago I realized that if you are going to believe the good ones you have to believe the bad ones. Critics do what all of us do when we go to the theater, and that is to judge it from a very personal point of view. Some things affect some people more than others. There are very few critics who really know what happens and why it happens. They simply judge the result. There is not a critic today who can tell the difference between the script and the production. If the director is clever, he can hide many of the play's faults. Critics know directors tell actors where to go, but they don't know how much a director does in terms of shaping a performance. So often critics are geared to seeing what they want to see in a certain director's work. If the show is in New York, and my survival depends on the reviews, I will read the critics right away. When it comes to regional theater, I never read the reviews until four weeks after the show has opened, because then all the reviews, good and bad, seem irrelevant.

GREGORY MOSHER: I don't think anyone but another director can tell what's directing and what's not. Often, even directors can't tell. You literally have no way of telling if a bit of business was invented by an actor, a director, or a playwright.

MARSHALL W. MASON: I think it's very important that actors don't read the critics until after the production is over. We have a rule here at Circle Rep that no one is to discuss critics. We try to split our openings over several days so that one night isn't all critics. We have a very small theater, and if fifty seats out of one hundred fifty are filled with critics it's death. We also try to keep who is coming when a secret. People who want to know can find out, but they are under an obligation not to spread that information.

We have tried to persuade actors that it's better not to read the critics because they have to go on and perform no matter what the critics say, favorable or unfavorable. It certainly makes the moment a critic may have spoken about a very self-conscious moment, and acting must be free from self-consciousness. The publicity department saves all the reviews, and at the end of the run we give all our actors a packet.

As a director, I respect and listen to the point of view of certain critics. The questions some critics raise can be good questions, and a playwright can use those almost as a blueprint for rewriting. Not that you rewrite to a critic's specifications, but critics can point out areas that are unrealized for a first-time viewer of the play.

The theater has become so expensive that no one wants to attend without "knowing" something is going to be "good." I think the critics have to act as consumer reporters because that is what their readers expect of them. When Frank Rich or John Simon says, "Go see it," it's the *Good Housekeeping* Seal of Approval. What the public wants is guidance on how to spend its money.

GREGORY MOSHER: I think *we* vest too much power in critics. We say they don't matter and then we quote them in our ads.

What would be your advice to a director just starting out?

MELVIN BERNHARDT: There's no sensible reason why anybody in the world would want to direct plays for a living. If you want to direct, you don't need any advice from me. Be happy in the work itself. You can't go into theater for fame and fortune.

GREGORY MOSHER: Early in your career, no one will ever ask you to come and direct a play. Get five friends together and direct a play.

GERALD GUTIERREZ: I think you learn more from assisting and watching people direct than from going to a classroom.

JERRY ZAKS: The most important thing is work, work, work. Learn your craft. Get the stars out of your eyes. The only reason to direct a play is to bring something to life on the stage because of the response you had to reading it. Any other reason is not going to sustain you.

TOM MOORE: Work begets work. It doesn't do any good to theorize productions. Get out and do workshops. You have to latch yourself onto young writers with whom you share a common sensibility. Almost every director I know has formed an alliance with a writer. That is how you learn.

ARVIN BROWN: Keep meeting writers. Seek them out, read their plays. Find writers who are as hungry as you are and befriend them. Once you've found something that speaks to you, then seek out the ways in which the play might be done. Don't wait for opportunities to come to you. They won't. Don't be too critical of the auspices under which you work. Work! If you like a play, just do it.

CAROLE ROTHMAN: You have to get a playwright to hire you first. Most theaters choose plays and not directors. They pick the play first, and the playwright generally brings along his or her director. Get playwrights you want to work with to see your work.

JERRY ZAKS: Your directing style will define itself as you help a play come to life. Don't think about your style. It's a big mistake.

GREGORY MOSHER: You get older. You learn. You try not to make the same mistakes over again. It's no different from being a cab driver.

What do you consider the ideal training for a director?

GERALD GUTIERREZ: Acting training breaks down inhibitions and liberates your talents. I think it's important for directors to act every couple of years. One tends to be very isolated in one's own discipline, and that's bad for a collaborative art form.

JERRY ZAKS: I knew many "rules" of directing by virtue of my years of acting. It's very helpful to have been an actor. I wouldn't know what to tell someone who's never acted and wants to direct. You have to know where actors are coming from, why they do what they do.

ARVIN BROWN: I've never done anything in the theater but direct. I acted only when I had to pass a course at Yale. I was petrified about this when I started to direct because it was generally thought that one needed an acting background to go into directing. I realized that I was going to have to learn a vocabulary other than personal illustration. This has served me in very good stead. Because I can't illustrate for an actor what I want, I must find another way to make him realize what the moment needs.

MARSHALL W. MASON: I'm a true classicist at heart and firmly believe it's very important for anyone in the theater to have a real, working knowledge of the classics.

CAROLE ROTHMAN: Working on the masters helps you to learn what the structure of a good play is. A directing career in regional theater is almost totally based on doing the classics.

PAT BROWN: Young directors will shortchange themselves if they do not work on the great plays of the past. It is impossible to give full expression and full dimension to a new play without some knowledge of the plays which came before it. Whether a young director wants to believe it or not, all new plays have profound connections with the work of the past. For a director to deepen her work with new plays, she must travel all roads backwards, as well as forwards.

EMILY MANN: If you don't deal with the classics, you'll settle into mediocrity and bland naturalism that will smother you as an artist. Contemporary, naturalistic plays, if you cast well enough and have a good enough designer, tend to make the director obsolete. You will constantly surprise yourself as an artist by coming into contact with the great minds and spirits behind the classics.

GERALD GUTIERREZ: I realize every time I do a new play that classical training liberates you to do anything you want to do. You have to begin with the classics. If you can do them, you can do anything. Playwrights who have grown up on movies and television—more loosely constructed forms—often need a director with a sense of classical construction and form to help them shape their work to succeed on the stage.

What is the philosophy underlying your directing? What makes for good directing?

GERALD GUTIERREZ: To be unnoticed. To stand behind the play, not in front of it.

CAROLE ROTHMAN: To serve the play in the most creative way you know.

MELVIN BERNHARDT: Good directing, for the kinds of plays I tend to like, is not noticeable. Good directing clearly conveys the words on the page, and the play's intellectual and emotional experience to an audience.

MARSHALL W. MASON: The director must serve the play. Therefore, the director's ego must not interfere with the work. It's very important for the director to be able to articulate his vision of the play so that the playwright knows the director and he are trying to accomplish the same goal. Often, far too much is left unsaid at the beginning of a collaboration.

JERRY ZAKS: The greatest responsibility a director has is to bring a play to life: Insist that the choices the actors make serve the life of the play, and not their own egos or their own sense of what is funny; then, if the play has life, it will take care of itself.

TOM MOORE: I don't believe directing is an art. It is a skill. Your purpose as a director is to take what the author wrote and find an ultimate expression for it. The words are the principal factor in the production. The play must become personal.

ARVIN BROWN: If there is an art to directing, then that art brings the director who is willing more and more in touch with himself. When your craft is there, you can afford to be as open and spontaneous as you pretended to be when you were less sure.

LLOYD RICHARDS: The director is the objective person between the audience and the play.

DOUGLAS TURNER WARD: I deal only with what's essential. The essentials of the play will always hit the audience the hardest.

GREGORY MOSHER: Writing a play is an act of expression. You have to make every effort as a director to ensure that the integrity of that playwright's expression is preserved. The play is going to have fingerprints on it by the time it faces the public, even though it's not the director's job to actively put fingerprints on the play. It's his job to present the play as purely as possible.

The play must come off the printed page, through the director's imagination, to the audience. Invariably, when something goes wrong with a play it's because the director just hasn't made the play clear. Not that he didn't "fix" the play, or make the play "work," but he didn't make the play *clear*. Millions of things can go wrong, but they all fall to the director. The playwright has already done his job—writing the play.

MARSHALL W. MASON: The director's job is to fulfill the playwright's vision through the actors, movement, set, costumes, lighting, pace—all the elements of the production. Everything should support the vision of the playwright. I don't mean the play has to be faithfully reproduced in terms of a single vision. The playwright and director working together have two points of view, and that gives the work depth; it's simple physics.

JERRY ZAKS: If you are *truly* answering the questions, "Is this right? Is this believable? Does this serve the play?"— *then* you're directing.

ACTORS
AND ACTRESSES

American actors today have become true collaborators in the development of new plays. They have a commitment to the success of the play as a piece of theater, a work of art, rather than merely as a vehicle or a stepping-stone to film or television. Having worked extensively in readings and workshop productions of new plays, today's actors understand the craft of putting together a play and balance their acting talents with a knowledge of directing, producing, and playwriting.

Actors are intelligent readers of plays and depend as much on their minds as on their instincts when fashioning a character. They are constantly questioning and speaking their minds at readings and in rehearsals. Through the creation of character, actors enable the creation of the play.

The fifteen actors and actresses in this chapter speak their minds on a variety of areas: training, workshops, rehearsing, working with the playwright, director, designers, and other actors. They give advice and offer opinion.

Tanya Berezin is a cofounder of the Circle Repertory Company in New York. She has created roles in Lanford Wilson's *Serenading Louie, Angels Fall,* and *The Great Nebula in Orion.* She received an Obie Award for her performance in Wilson's *The Mound Builders.*

Hume Cronyn is a playwright and director as well as a stage and screen actor. He co-wrote and acted in *Foxfire,* which also starred his wife, Jessica Tandy. His other stage credits include *The Gin Game,* and Marsha Norman's *Traveler in the Dark.* His extensive film work includes *The Seventh Cross* and *Cocoon.* In 1974 he was elected to the Theatre Hall of Fame for his outstanding contributions to American theater.

Mia Dillon received a Tony nomination, Clarence Derwent and Los Angeles Dramalog awards for her performance in *Crimes of the Heart.* She has also appeared on Broadway in *Da, Hay Fever, The Corn Is Green* with Cicely Tyson, and *Once a Catholic,* for which she received a Drama Desk nomination.

Elizabeth Franz was nominated for a Tony Award for her performance in *Brighton Beach Memoirs.* She also acted in Liviu Ciulei's *Hamlet* at the Arena Stage, Andrei Serban's *The Cherry Orchard,* and created the title role in Christopher Durang's *Sister Mary Ignatius Explains It All for You.* She has performed at the Berkshire Theatre Festival, Baltimore's Center Stage, Yale Repertory Theatre, and the Mark Taper Forum.

Barnard Hughes won Tony, Drama Desk, and Outer Critics Circle awards for his performance in *Da.* He has performed on Broadway in *Angels Fall, The Iceman Cometh, The End of the World,* and *The Good Doctor.* His extensive Shakespearean credits include a Tony-nominated performance in *Much Ado About*

Nothing. His film and television work includes *Midnight Cowboy*, *Where's Papa?*, *The Hospital*, and *Doc.*

Tom Hulce played the title role in *The Rise and Rise of Daniel Rocket* at Playwrights Horizons and in its subsequent public television telecast. His other roles include Alan Strang in *Equus* on Broadway and in Los Angeles, Ned Weeks in *The Normal Heart* at the Long Wharf Theatre in New Haven, Connecticut, and Romeo at the Milwaukee Repertory. His films include *Amadeus*, *Echo Park*, and *Animal House.*

Linda Hunt won an Academy Award for her performance in *The Year of Living Dangerously* and an Obie for her work in the acting ensemble of Caryl Churchill's *Top Girls*. Hunt has acted in *Mother Courage*, *A Metamorphosis in Miniature*, *Elizabeth Dead*, *The Tennis Game*, and the films *Popeye*, *Dune*, and *The Bostonians.*

Željko Ivanek originated roles in Athol Fugard's *Master Harold . . . and the Boys*, Woody Allen's *Floating Lightbulb*, and Neil Simon's *Brighton Beach Memoirs*, for which he was nominated for a Tony Award. He performed in the American casts of Caryl Churchill's *Cloud Nine* and David Hare's *Map of the World*. His films include *Tex* and *Mass Appeal.*

Robert Joy is Canadian and a former Rhodes Scholar. He has performed extensively Off-Broadway at such theaters as the Public, Playwrights Horizons, and the Ensemble Studio, as well as at such regional theaters as the American Repertory Theatre in Cambridge, the La Jolla Playhouse, and Long Wharf. He has created roles in A. R. Gurney's *What I Did Last Summer*, John Guare's *Lydie Breeze*, and Donald Margulies's *Found a Peanut*. Joy has appeared in the films *Atlantic City*, *Ragtime*, and *Desperately Seeking Susan.*

Swoosie Kurtz received Obie and Drama Desk awards for her performance of Rita in *Uncommon Women and Others*. She received Tony awards for her work in *Fifth of July*, *Tartuffe*, and *The House of Blue Leaves*. Her other credits include *A History of American Film, The Effect of Gamma Rays on Man-in-the-Moon Marigolds*, and *Children*. She co-starred with Tony Randall in the television series *Love, Sidney*.

Valerie Mahaffey created the role of Emily Dickinson in Peter Parnell's *Romance Language*. She also created roles in James Lapine's *Twelve Dreams*, Elan Garonzik's *Scenes and Revelations*, and Joanna Glass's *Play Memory*. She won an Obie Award as a member of the acting ensemble for Caryl Churchill's *Top Girls* at Joseph Papp's Public Theater. She has appeared at the Mark Taper Forum, the Milwaukee Repertory, and Long Wharf.

Donald Moffat starred in *Painting Churches*, *Play Memory*, *Terra Nova*, and *The Iceman Cometh* in New York. Moffat studied at the Royal Academy of Dramatic Art and has been a member of the Old Vic. He has performed in such American theaters as the McCarter in Princeton, Cincinnati's Playhouse-in-the-Park, and the Great Lakes Shakespeare Festival. He received a Tony nomination for *The Wild Duck*.

D. W. Moffett created roles in Larry Kramer's *The Normal Heart* and John Pielmeier's *The Boys of Winter*. He co-starred in the NBC television movie *An Early Frost*. He was a founding member of the Remains Theater in Chicago.

Pamela Reed has appeared in *Fen*, *Aunt Dan and Lemon*, *The Sorrows of Stephen*, *Standing on My Knees*, *Getting Out*, and *The Curse of the Starving Class*. Her films include *Melvin and Howard*, *The Right Stuff*, *Eyewitness*, and *The Best of Times*.

Frances Sternhagen has won Tony Awards for her performances in *The Good Doctor* and *Equus*. She received an Obie Award and the Clarence Derwent Award for *The Sign in Sidney Brustein's Window*.

What is your background?

SWOOSIE KURTZ: Mine is a classic story: It was a dark and stormy day at Hollywood High. . . . The drama teacher there lit the fire for me, and he's the reason I'm an actress today. He taught me about stage energy—that heightened sense of reality.

I went to the University of Southern California and gave it up after two years because I couldn't stand not doing theater all day long. I got accepted at the London Academy of Music and Dramatic Art. I came back from England and didn't know anybody in New York, but I went to auditions and ended up getting a lot of offers. Some were pretty low on the totem pole—scrubbing the stage and sewing costumes. Some were legit acting offers—not leads, but things like spending an entire season in Cincinnati doing whatever came up. "As cast" they call it.

I went from one regional theater to another for three or four years. I liked being an itinerant actor. My father was in the Air Force. I went to seventeen different schools, so I was used to being itinerant.

D. W. MOFFETT: I have a B.A. in International Relations from Stanford University. I started taking acting lessons at night while working as a commercial banker in Chicago. The St. Nicholas Theater, which David Mamet founded, had a non-Equity ensemble called the New Works Theater, which did only new plays. I quit the bank to join this ensemble.

I started a company with seven other actors called Remains Theater. At that time Chicago theater had a real wide swath of people in their mid-twenties who all sort of said to themselves, "Well, hell, I'm not going to wait around for someone to give me a job. Why don't we do it ourselves?" That's what we did. We rented a storefront. My father lent us two thousand bucks and we built a theater.

ROBERT JOY: I grew up in Newfoundland, where community theater is very strong. Later, I went to England for a short while on a Rhodes Scholarship. While I was in England, a bunch of my friends set up a comedy group. We'd get together five or six weeks before opening night and create the show. We wrote, directed, choreographed, produced—everything. That was, in a way, the best kind of training I could have had.

We weren't highly disciplined by any means. A week before we were to open everyone would panic, and we'd work incessantly for that week. Adrenaline productions is what they were.

The best thing about that kind of training was that I had to make very fast choices, instinctual choices, and stick with them. Our motto was, "Do it with a bold face." In other words, choose what you're going to do and do it with absolute conviction, and something will happen. Things did happen. We did six shows in three years, and we were quite a success.

ŽELJKO IVANEK: I wanted to be an actor from the beginning. I chose a college specifically for that; I went to Yale.

The training was primarily Stanislavsky, post-Stanislavsky, neo-Uta Hagen. Once you've learned that basic actor's language you're almost halfway there no matter with whom you work.

Most of the acting work was scene work—picking a scene, working on it outside of class, bringing it into class, having it critiqued, and maybe working on it some more in class. That was the pattern. What an actor comes out of Yale with is knowing how to pick up a script and start work, knowing what to ask yourself. Basic actor's questions about relationships and circumstances start coming naturally when you begin to read something: "Who are these people?" "Why are these people here?" "What do they want?" "What do I want from the other person?" "What do I want from this situation?"

Toward the end of my time at Yale I began to feel that as much as I had confidence in my work—I knew how to approach the text if someone handed me a scene—I didn't feel I had any real technical background. I didn't feel *trained*. Intellectually and emotionally I could start wheels turning, but I didn't feel justified arriving in New York calling myself an actor.

I went to the London Academy of Music and Dramatic Art for two years to get the technical training I felt I needed. There is something very cold and English sounding about the term "technical work," but all it means is a lot of physical work: stage fighting, movement, singing. All of this physical work is strictly about opening up, getting rid of your bad habits, not allowing your limitations to get in the way of your potential. Being open, vulnerable, and accepting.

BARNARD HUGHES: My early training was in Shakespeare, with a teacher who remembered every reading he'd ever heard from the great stars. We had to parrot those readings, stress for stress. The rhythms were pounded into us. Not the best way to be introduced to acting! After that I was in a stock company which played forty weeks a year.

I remember one rehearsal. I was making an exit. I pulled out a white handkerchief and I waved it as I went off stage. The director said, "What's that for?" I said, "Well, I thought . . ." He replied, "You're not paid to think. Say the lines. Say them fast. Let's hear them. That's all. You start thinking and your head is going to swell up like a balloon and bust."

I stayed with that company five or six years, but I never asked anyone anything again. If I had a problem in motivation or anything I would never subject myself to the embarrassment of asking. I think it was, in a sense, the best thing that could ever have happened to me, as I was thrown on my own resources and imagination. That's when I first began to really *think* about acting. I had been going through the motions before that.

MIA DILLON: I was acting purely by instinct until my first year in New York, when I did *Da* on Broadway. I did *Da* for a year and a half, and being onstage with quality, talented actors was like having a one-and-a-half-year scene study class.

You learn by doing as opposed to studying, reading, or hearing about acting. You learn so much more when the technique becomes a part of you and your being, instead of merely intellectual conceits.

ELIZABETH FRANZ: While I was at the American Academy of Dramatic Art in New York I was told I wouldn't work until I was Mildred Dunnock's age. I didn't know who she was but I understood what they meant. I remember this little voice asking, "Do you mind if I try?"

VALERIE MAHAFFEY: Somehow, before I came to New York I got myself together and I wasn't scared. I knew I wanted to be as prepared as I could be. I cornered this girl I knew—she was a dancer who had come back from New York to visit Austin—and I made her tell me everything I wanted to know about New York. She told me where to get my pictures taken, gave me a subway map, told me I had to have a telephone service, something I had never even heard of.

TOM HULCE: I came to New York from the North Carolina School of the Arts to be in a play I liked very much, *Total Eclipse,* but the producers didn't know that, so they neglected to hire me. About six weeks later I worked my way into an audition for *Equus* and was hired.

What do you look for when choosing a new play?

ROBERT JOY: It's not mystical. Sometimes I read a script and think, "I'm not connected to this character." I know then I couldn't play that character with conviction.

TOM HULCE: I want to do a role when I feel a connection with the writing. It's a chemical thing, the same way as when you're attracted to another person. I don't know why it happens sometimes and why it doesn't happen other times. Somehow, it's a kind of music I hear or don't hear.

I read a lot of things I think are very good, but I don't feel I would be the best instrument for them.

SWOOSIE KURTZ: Something speaks to me from the script on first reading. Ninety-nine times out of a hundred it doesn't happen. It's so easy to eliminate those plays you don't want to do.

PAMELA REED: So few really good plays come along that it's easier to say what doesn't attract me. I'm infuriated when characters don't learn anything about themselves or the world around them. We go to the theater to learn things about life, society, ethics, religion, politics.

MIA DILLON: What I want to find in a new play is a character that challenges me to learn something new about myself, take me beyond where I currently am. It's hard to read a play without mainly looking at the character you might be playing. If that character is interesting, you tend to think the play is interesting. Unfortunately, the audience doesn't always agree.

ŽELJKO IVANEK: I don't read a script and think, "What an interesting character." Being impressed that a character is offbeat or peculiar doesn't interest me. What I usually come away with after reading a play is an emotional sense of what it's about, what its issues are. What I get hooked into is relationships—what happens between the people in the play.

I look for recognition. A lot of times when I read a script I don't recognize the people; I don't recognize the situation; I don't recognize the behavior. I just don't understand what these people are like, and therefore I don't have any interest. On no level does the script spark anything I recognize as human.

DONALD MOFFAT: I felt both *Painting Churches* and *Play Memory* were absorbing. They were "page-turners," as they say in Hollywood. I read *Painting Churches* three times through on the same day.

The interesting thing to me is showing a person's life in transition, the changes. That's always something I look for—what is the progress? Certainly a character who has his life changed, or who chooses to change, is the most interesting. This is what an actor does: illuminate the human condition in some way. "I see" is the ideal reaction from an audience. There has to be something in the part that will provoke that reaction.

TANYA BEREZIN: When I was a young actress, if the role was wonderful, that was all that mattered. I've done enough of those to know you're not communicating anything if the *play* doesn't work, if the audience doesn't experience the *play*. I'm more willing, truly willing, now to play smaller parts than I was when I was younger. When I was younger it was about showing off. Now it really is about communicating.

SWOOSIE KURTZ: The play has to be good. I used to have tunnel vision: I just looked at my part to see if I could stand out. As you get older you learn to look at the whole picture. If the play isn't good no one is going to pay any attention. If the play isn't any good, it's not going to have a prayer.

ELIZABETH FRANZ: It's much easier when you like the whole play, but there's no reason why if half a play works you shouldn't do it. I love working on a play to try to help the playwright get the whole play to work. Working on one play can help a playwright on his next one.

PAMELA REED: You always look at a script in terms of its overall success. You've got to take into account the thrust of the whole play, but if you're looking for the perfect play you might as well start selling shoes.

Plays are not meant to live in books. Plays are meant to live on stages. There are some plays that read very well. There are also plays that don't read well on the page, but, boy, do they come to life on the stage.

FRANCES STERNHAGEN: If I want to keep turning the page, then I'm grabbed. If I find after reading the first act that I simply don't care what happens to the people, I know I'm not going to want to do that play. And the language should be interesting, provocative, fun-to-say.

LINDA HUNT: I love plays where there is actually style in the language. I like plays that have a sense of language that is exact and exacting, almost pristine in its simplicity. A play's language should have an inevitable musicality that leads to the play's emotional and intellectual center.

SWOOSIE KURTZ: If I'm interested in doing a play I'll sometimes ask to do an informal reading of it with other actors. The way the words feel as they come out of my mouth will tell me if I should do this play. Reading it out loud to myself wouldn't be the same. If the words don't come out of my mouth right, I know no matter how important the people are I'd be working with, or anything else, I shouldn't do the play; somebody else should.

HUME CRONYN: I choose plays by sitting down and reading. I read as an audience member. The second, third, and fourth times I read as a critic, but the first time is just how this play speaks to me. Hardly ever do I consider whether this will be a good "vehicle" for either me or my wife [Jessica Tandy]. I optioned several Beckett plays not because we could play in them, but because I was swept away by the scope of his concept. It's the way the playwright thinks, the imagery, the metaphor, his or her sense of theater, that makes me want to do a play. I've been known to make some terrible choices. I can show you the scars.

DONALD MOFFAT: Robert Morley said when he chooses a play he looks at the name of the character and then thumbs through the script to see the size of the part. And if he has the last line in two of the three acts, he takes the part. It's a facetious answer, but there is a grain of truth to it. At this point in my life I look to see if the part is significant enough to warrant looking at it further.

BARNARD HUGHES: The size of the part is involved in the decision, absolutely. I don't want to come to the theater and sit up in my dressing room all evening, while people onstage are doing wonderful things. You want to be involved. At my age, if you are going to give your time to a production, you want to be very much involved.

VALERIE MAHAFFEY: Sometimes you take roles because you need the job, though it's better when you actually like the script.

Do you find a difference between acting in new plays and acting in revivals or classics?

ŽELJKO IVANEK: I didn't leave drama school thinking "I want to do new plays," but after doing four of them, I'm caught up in it. You don't have a burden of accumulated interpretation—on a revival your thinking can't be as clean as on a new play—and you've got the playwright there. If things aren't working, things can change. If you are hitting a wall, and hitting a wall, and hitting a wall, finally someone will move the wall.

D. W. MOFFETT: I certainly enjoy the freedom of being the first one to do a part, because if you have a sensitive playwright, he will trust your instincts and the text will evolve to reflect your input.

With revivals I don't feel constrained by what was done

before. I don't think I've ever done a play where I had an idea of what had been done with the role before.

ELIZABETH FRANZ: I can't help but be affected by the people who've done the roles before. If you were to give me the role of Alma in *Summer and Smoke*, it would take me time to get away from what Geraldine Page did in the original production. It would be hard to get her performance out of my mind. When you go into a revival you must find your information about the character from the playwright's words and not from what's been done before by anyone else, or from what any critic has said about how the role should be played.

TANYA BEREZIN: Maybe it's because I've done so many new plays, but when I do a classic, I don't decide to do something "different." I don't think about my interpretation. I approach it the same way as I do a new play—"What is this character about?" "What does she want?" "Where is she going?" Interpretation comes from my decisions on those questions. I don't need to be different from somebody else, I just need to find something I think is true. It's exactly how I also approach a role in a new play.

LINDA HUNT: What you never know in advance with a new play is if it will work. That's why I do new plays: You have to act it in order to find if it works or not. You know *Mother Courage* works. You don't know if you can pull it off, but you know the play can work and has worked.

TOM HULCE: The one thing you don't have when working on a revival is the opportunity to think so creatively that it might demand a rewrite. Some of the most exciting times I've spent are the times we've taken an absolutely fresh look at a play people *think* they know. Usually they don't really know what's there, they just know the myth surrounding the play. I love to approach plays without preconceptions. It can be as much of an adventure as working on a new play. It's a matter of discovering for yourself the path you know has been laid, the road you know has been completed, as if it had never been traveled before.

MIA DILLON: A new play is a blank canvas. You can go anywhere, try anything. If the playwright is willing to work with you, you can add part of yourself to the character.

ROBERT JOY: There's an excitement around a new play not present in a revival. What's exciting about working on a new play is to see the writer go away and come back with new material, changes that make the play better.

PAMELA REED: A play's a play. The main difference doing a revival is that you know there aren't going to be any rewrites. In revivals there are always places where you'd love some rewrites. You approach both a new play and a revival with the same amount of integrity and hard work.

ELIZABETH FRANZ: When bold concepts are used a revival is new again. Just a revival for revival's sake is not as exciting as a new play.

ROBERT JOY: If someone offers you a role in *Long Day's Journey into Night* you know it is a good part. History tells you so. If it had been a brand new play you might be tempted not to do it. Because you know it's been done and it's a "great" play, you're willing to go with the challenge. I always like the idea that a play is new, and that I can *create* the character. If something is difficult and has no track record, you might be a little faster in saying no. If it is a "classic" and difficult, you make the extra effort to see the connection. Actors should give new plays the benefit of the doubt more.

TANYA BEREZIN: In a sense a new play is easier than a revival. I read it and try to understand what it is. I try not to have preconceptions. Making choices is really much easier when you're simply working on the given circumstances of the play and not with the given circumstances of the play's *history*. You become defensive, even if subconsciously, when working on revivals. You're fighting memories of Colleen Dewhurst or Julie Harris.

MIA DILLON: If you're doing a well-known play, chances are people have already seen productions of it. Audiences do come in influenced by former productions.

In one Philip Barry play I played the "Katharine Hepburn" part. How do you get away from that? You try to go in a different direction, but you'll always find someone who is disappointed you're not Katharine Hepburn.

PAMELA REED: When I did *Standing on My Knees* I kept telling the director I didn't want to do a copy of his earlier production. I hadn't seen that production, but I knew I was a very different woman from the original actress and wouldn't be making some of the same choices.

I remember a huge row about these bulky sweaters the first actress had worn, which the director wanted me also to wear. The first actress was quite tall and I am very petite and can't wear clothes like that. The director ultimately realized he was trying to impose on me what worked before and that it wasn't working now.

SWOOSIE KURTZ: A new play attracts me more than a revival because nobody has any preconceived notions about it. No visual images come to mind. I never wanted to play Juliet or Lady What's-her-face or any of those. Everyone's seen them a million times. Even during my school auditions, my classical piece was from *Puntilla* by Brecht, a virtually unknown play. I was thrilled I confused the people auditioning me—you can't hit a moving target!

I'm much more fascinated by new plays. Anything can happen. When you sit down at the first rehearsal to read it, that's not what you're going to have on opening night.

Do you like participating in informal sit-down readings of plays-in-progress?

SWOOSIE KURTZ: I love readings. I'm asked to do them a lot, and I do them whenever I can. I feel totally at ease in them, because the pressure is not on the actor, but on the playwright.

The main thing is not to make something work that doesn't. I'm really good at doing that, so I have to be careful. It's a tendency all actors have. So often, we're in the position of having to save our asses by making something that isn't quite there into something "interesting." It's the survival instinct. In a reading you have to let the playwright know how bad or good the play is. If there are sections that are dead, you have to just let them lie there. You can't try to pump them up, or finesse them.

PAMELA REED: There's no way the writer can know what to rewrite if you try to be cute and "correct" everything. First of all, you can't correct anything: You're an actor, not a writer.

BARNARD HUGHES: I feel a responsibility to work with new plays. If I can go and read a play-in-progress, I get involved as much as I can. To let the author hear what the play

sounds like out loud is important. I have the feeling readings are more valuable to the playwright than to me, but
it is one of my responsibilities to the theater to be involved.
I'm always so caring about a playwright who has to turn his
play over to a bunch of strangers.

ROBERT JOY: I've seen producers make decisions about new
plays on the basis of sit-down readings. I've seen good plays
founder because the reading goes badly. It's a terrible responsibility. I try to do my best possible work.

With an informal sit-down reading—having read the
play once on my own—I try to be as clear as possible for
the writer. I try to do the most natural thing, without
forcing, and not make the interpretation bizarre. I try to
convey the impression the role had on me at my first reading. I don't want to call attention to my performance. That's
not what a reading is about. It's about the playwright seeing
if his words work, or the structure works, or the character
motivations work.

TOM HULCE: I try to be simple and coherent in sit-down
readings. Chances are neither a playwright nor a director,
if there is one, is interested in your questions. Otherwise
they would have held rehearsals. The best thing to do is
to show up and be simple and honest, let everyone hear
the play for what it is.

It's dangerous to make big acting choices about a play
you haven't worked on, because they can obscure what the
reading is for—to hear what is written. A sit-down reading
is just like your first reading of a play to yourself—you try
not to come to any conclusion, but just to give it a hearing.

PAMELA REED: I don't do a lot of preparation for readings
because then I start performing. The purpose of doing a
reading of a play is to let the writer hear his play. That is

the *only* reason. Even if there is an audience, a reading is still to let the writer hear his play.

I prefer to get together with the other actors, read through the play once, and then do it. If it's a very informal reading in the playwright's home, I'll read the play a couple of times before going there.

MIA DILLON: I don't read the play too many times before a sit-down reading or I begin to have lots of questions which will never get addressed, and that ultimately hurts my performance. In a sit-down reading you should just go in, seat-of-your-pants, and let your emotions take over. That way, you don't have time to think out your performance carefully.

TANYA BEREZIN: I've done some of my best work in unrehearsed, around-the-table readings. While simply listening to the other actors, feeling the rhythm of the play, wonderful things have opened up for me. I think it's actually better for the play to be read fairly cold. Then you're more involved with its forward movement.

ELIZABETH FRANZ: My role in a reading is just to speak the character, to play the character with enough passion to fulfill the needs of the play.

VALERIE MAHAFFEY: Since I'm the sort of actress who has barely read the script twice through before going into rehearsals, I'm doubly that way before doing readings. But it works for me. I will usually ask how to pronounce certain words, or how full out the playwright wants the reading to be. Is it very relaxed or should I be chewing on the end of the table?

I get emotionally involved, otherwise the playwright might as well just have people who can read well. Sometimes you have to ignore the people you're reading with because you think they're awful, or you just don't click in with them at all. Other times you get very excited about a reading because all of a sudden the actors connect with the script and a real performance just comes out of nowhere.

SWOOSIE KURTZ: I think around-the-table readings are sometimes disasters because the playwright doesn't get the actors he or she needs. Sometimes the actors don't come up with the goods. If someone is wildly wrong for the part, it is a disservice to the play and the playwright.

DONALD MOFFAT: I try, as an actor, to bring an energy to my reading, some semblance of what a performance might be like. There is a tendency in first readings to sit around a table with no energy and mumble. That's of very little benefit to anyone.

It's important to make a strong choice about the character, even if it's wrong. At least it's something for the author to recognize—"That's not the way to play that."

FRANCES STERNHAGEN: I really think in a sit-down reading you have to have a sense of the character. You have to have read the play and have decided that you can play it. It's important that you like the lines, relate closely to the character—you don't have enough time to let things happen slowly.

Do you enjoy working on staged readings? Do you think they help in developing new plays?

PAMELA REED: Staged readings are often not "readings." You're between a rock and a hard place.

TANYA BEREZIN: Staged readings are awful for the actor. You've asked questions that you haven't really answered. You've answered them intellectually, off the top of your head, but you've not emotionally realized those answers. Also the director is giving you ideas for the rhythm and movement of the play, the peaks and the valleys. The performance is all external. I am more nervous before a staged reading than I am under any other circumstances.

FRANCES STERNHAGEN: There you are wandering around with a book in your hands. It's like the second day of rehearsal. You can't give as much of the inner part of the character because having the book in your hand is awkward. You just don't feel the flow.

ELIZABETH FRANZ: An actor's process is so vulnerable. When an actor starts working a voice starts coming, a body starts coming, a vision of who the character is starts happening. When you can only go so far with the character, as in rehearsals for a staged reading, and can't complete your process, you get a very strange, distorted character.

LINDA HUNT: I think there is little to be learned from readings. I think there is a great deal to learn from a workshop where rewriting takes place during the actual process of rehearsals, and then another workshop follows. That's exciting for the actors, director, and playwright.

DONALD MOFFAT: I try not to get involved in staged readings. Such a lot of effort for so little result. I feel the actors can do more spending that extra rehearsal time on the script, so the actor is really free from it, rather than learning blocking. Seeing the actors move may help the director figure out some staging problems, but if the director really does his homework he should be able to figure out the same answers by himself.

TOM HULCE: Some staged readings almost require an approximation of what you'd do if you had the time to rehearse fully. The best approach is to work as fast, but as honestly, as you can, as far as you get before the reading. It has been very useful to do staged readings with three weeks of rehearsal. Leave out the technical elements—sets, lighting, costumes—but give what is essentially a performance of a play everyone is agreed isn't quite ready for full production.

SWOOSIE KURTZ: I think staged readings can be useful. The playwright and the director come away with a very good idea of what that play could be like in a full production. A play should have gone through several drafts and two to three around-the-table readings before it gets a staged reading.

In a staged reading you are not just moving, you are *performing*. Sometimes they will tell you that you don't have to do a performance—bullshit. They'll say "Nobody expects a performance," but they *all* expect a performance. You don't have to give a tear-your-eyeballs-out performance, but the commitment must be there.

ROBERT JOY: In a staged reading you have an opportunity to examine, reinterpret, and contribute to the play by digging as deeply as you can and giving the writer new ideas or, at least, showing the writer the weaknesses in the play. Sometimes in a sit-down reading you try to make things work, you try to gloss over any flaws. In a staged reading you really can't hide the flaws. You have to dig into the role, commit yourself to choices, and develop emotional lines so the writer can see what's strong and what's weak in the play, and can really identify flaws and difficulties.

I did a staged reading of Donald Margulies's *Found a Peanut* with two rehearsals. It went quite well, though it showed up the flaws. It showed up where similar things happened in two or three scenes—one confrontation was a lot like another confrontation, even though the scenes involved different characters. The script was rewritten on the basis of that reading and became much denser, more compact; it worked better.

After a reading how much input will you give to the playwright?

SWOOSIE KURTZ: I don't have that much confidence in how good I am in judging a reading. If I'm asked I will say what I didn't understand or what seemed to go off on a tangent. A new play seems like such a precious thing; you have to protect the playwright.

I have to sit on my prejudices. For instance, I always think things are too long. I am rah-rah for cutting. I'm the sort who probably would have suggested cutting the "Attention must be paid" speech if I'd been involved in the original reading of *Death of a Salesman*.

BARNARD HUGHES: If I talk about the play I might talk about it from the wrong point of view. I tend to talk too personally of how it affected me as an actor.

VALERIE MAHAFFEY: If asked I will just focus on my character and the scenes she is in. I feel presumptuous telling the playwright what works and what doesn't.

TOM HULCE: There's something dangerous about too many cooks at that early a point in the process.

I also feel the experience of working on a play makes me so involved that I'm not clear enough about it to respond right away.

PAMELA REED: Usually a writer will invite comments. The responsibility you have to him is to be specific. You talk about your character: what made sense and what didn't.

MIA DILLON: The playwright will sometimes ask you questions, but I'm not going to volunteer what's wrong with his play unless he wants my opinion. When asked, I usually focus on my character, how the play works from her point of view.

Do you find an audience helpful at a reading? Should there be a discussion with the audience afterwards?

ELIZABETH FRANZ: A reading can become too sedentary and conversational without an audience. After all, a play has to have a performance energy to it.

MIA DILLON: No actor wants to go out and be bad in front of an audience. Even in a reading you run the risk of abandoning the play and just saving your skin. You use a lot of tricks and perform a better play than is on paper. That's a disservice to the playwright. No play is finished without an audience in attendance.

DONALD MOFFAT: After the reading the playwright really shouldn't want to hear too many opinions. A first reading is a very traumatic experience—whether the reading works or not. He should protect himself from overload. If he has any sense he doesn't invite too much input.

D. W. MOFFETT: It's helpful for a playwright to find out what impression his play has made on an audience. At the same time, he has to take any and all comments with a grain of salt. It's always annoying when someone talks about a certain actor's or actress's performance, instead of the character itself or the play. It's a special responsibility for the audience at a reading to try to see the play through the performance.

TANYA BEREZIN: At Circle Rep we invite our subscribers to the staged readings. It may or may not be all that helpful, but when 150 people don't know what was going on in a scene, the playwright learns something.

How do you prepare for a role before rehearsals start?

PAMELA REED: If you approach every character in the same way you'll probably end up playing them all in the same way.

DONALD MOFFAT: Other actors look at me askance when I say I don't do any reading outside of the script. If it isn't in the script, it's only going to be a hindrance. Some years ago I did a wonderful play called *Terra Nova*, by Ted Tally, about Scott's expedition to the Antarctic. I started to read outside the play, but dropped that almost instantly because I realized the author had already done all the exploration, had already filtered the raw material, and given us his point of view. My job was to flesh out what Ted Tally felt about all this. Dragging stuff in that isn't in the script confuses the issue and can only get you in a fight with the author's intent.

VALERIE MAHAFFEY: I don't do a whole damn lot before rehearsals begin. If the play is something I'm excited about, I assume something is going to strike me in rehearsals, and it usually does. I try to go in very open.

BARNARD HUGHES: I came to *Da* prepared in lots of ways I don't with most plays. I am Irish, very Irish, in my personality, and it just ran off the spoon. The Irish background—my parents were both born in Ireland—made me aware of these people. My character wasn't anything like my father's, but I took a piece here, a piece there, and finally got it all together.

SWOOSIE KURTZ: If the part is close to me, I don't do any research before rehearsals begin. I just keep reading the play, just let the whole thing wash over me. Somebody once said, "Let the play work on you before you work on the play."

I write down what the other characters say about me, what of that is true and what isn't; what I say about them and what is and isn't true; how I act with one person as opposed to another person.

ELIZABETH FRANZ: I read the play as many times as I can. I also sleep on it; I literally put it under my pillow.

LINDA HUNT: You must work with the text before rehearsals in a way that leads you to great discoveries without making decisions that will interfere with the rehearsal process. You have to explore, but not discover, not go "Aha!" I think a state of not knowing is very important; you must come to rehearsals like a baby.

I'm someone who's never gone into rehearsal knowing lines. It's a very important luxury to learn the lines along with the movement, the motivations, and everything else.

That moment in rehearsal when you find you actually *know* a scene is when the entire rehearsal process begins to come together for you.

MIA DILLON: I like to read the script until I'm familiar with it and have all my questions ready. But I don't want to begin trying to answer those questions until I have the other actors, the director, and the playwright around me.

I can't stand memorizing scripts before rehearsals. If I memorize, I spend the first week trying to remember my lines instead of exploring the character and the situation.

ROBERT JOY: I read the play once, cover-to-cover, then I leave it alone until the first rehearsal. The important thing is to read the play as a play and not as a vehicle or as an acting problem. I try to be its audience. If the writing is at all effective, there is a very clear image of my character.

ŽELJKO IVANEK: Relationships are the first thing I see and the first thing I try to figure out. That's why I have a lot of trouble working on my own. At best I can reread and reread and reread. When I try to force myself to sit down and consciously make decisions, I get very restless and can't do it for more than ten minutes at a time. There is no payoff until you are in a rehearsal studio opposite somebody. I feel much more strength having somebody to play off than I do having made a set of decisions about what a character is like away from the rehearsal situation. The real work on a script is testing out your thinking in rehearsal, testing out possibilities, isolating things.

SWOOSIE KURTZ: I usually create a role from the outside in. Such things as shoes, types of walks, accents, really tell me about the character.

D. W. MOFFETT: I work on the center first and then find the outside stuff. Usually there is something internal that clicks and then I start to find out how the character holds a pen or touches something.

DONALD MOFFAT: Externals are important to me. Central to my creating a character is observation. It's dangerous, because it can lead to prejudice and instant categorization. It's a matter of objectively looking at people and guessing what they do, who they are, what their backgrounds are. A great deal of what we know about people is what we see. You can tell an awful lot about someone from his speech and voice. You can tell where he has been and where he's going.

FRANCES STERNHAGEN: I am the kind of person who tends to work from the outside in. I like to think of the way a person looks, and how I'm going to fit into her walk and mannerisms. Then I start building the character's inner self within that framework.

ŽELJKO IVANEK: With *Brighton Beach Memoirs,* I went out to Brighton Beach and walked around. I looked at old magazines, listened to that period's music, and things like that, but once I'd done that I literally never looked back on it. If it sinks in, it will help. If it doesn't sink in, looking at old Lucky Strike ads four weeks into rehearsal won't help me make something happen.

A lot is subconscious. I feel silly when I try to articulate things. If I sat down and tried to write out "Who am I and what do I want?" I would feel as though I were in kindergarten. I'm not denigrating that, but there is something false about making it so physical and so blatant. If you are not reacting to something in the first place, you can do all that work—it's work anyone can do—and it still doesn't make you a good actor.

ELIZABETH FRANZ: I always write a sort of novel about my characters: where they came from, what they were like as children, what their families were like. The "novel" on a new play is far larger than that for a revival.

BARNARD HUGHES: Working on a character is like spilling a bunch of beads on the floor, and working to get them all on a string. The author gives you the guidelines. An actor fails if he doesn't do what the playwright requests.

I've done hundreds and hundreds of plays. I can pick up a script and read it like a musician reads music. You can see how it builds, the mathematics of the thing.

What is your rehearsal process?

ŽELJKO IVANEK: I'm very bad just sitting down and trying to intellectualize, because it feels so cold. If you don't have some emotional understanding of the play, nothing else can follow.

SWOOSIE KURTZ: I don't like to sit around a table for too long. I'm a physical actor. I like to be standing. You can only go so far sitting around a table. Being on your feet, working with props and the other actors, teaches you about the play.

TOM HULCE: Every path taken from the first reading through *closing* night, whether finally used or not, is enriching, deepening, layering. The more choices I discover, the more fully I can commit myself to one—as opposed to many—choices, making it hard to choose one. I cover all the possibilities so I have enough information to make what for me will be the best choice.

ELIZABETH FRANZ: When you start to learn the lines, you think the role's never going to work. You're all feet. You're all hands. You start to put on a funny voice, a funny walk. Anything to make the character work. Then you realize all the actors are having the same trouble, so you drop that stuff and get back to basics. There is no way to hurry the process.

When you're memorized you can begin to play off the other actors. Suddenly, what another actor says makes sense to you. You find out why you have to say your line. Suddenly you have a real voice and you are answering honestly as the character.

TANYA BEREZIN: When we start tearing everything apart in rehearsal, the hardest thing for me to do is to put it all back together. What I have finally learned is to go back and ask, "Why did I want to do this play?" It's funny, but usually that will help me put everything back together. Once I've discovered in rehearsal what the playwright wants, what the director wants, what each moment requires, I finally ask, "Where am *I* in all this?" and then I can pull it all together.

VALERIE MAHAFFEY: When I worked on James Lapine's *Twelve Dreams*, Tom Hulce and I improvised certain scenes because James wasn't sure what he wanted. It made Tom and me crazy, but we trusted him. At one point James asked me what my character could possibly see in Tom's character—this ridiculously shy student. I said, "I don't know. Room for improvement?" He liked that and put it in the script!

TOM HULCE: With *Twelve Dreams*, because it was episodic and an ensemble kind of event, it was an effort on our part to realize what Lapine had written. The script was a kind of blueprint, made more specific by his direction and by his willingness to commit himself to his intention. He kept us spinning, so we arrived at more ideas, choices, and directions than we otherwise would have. Our work was realizing the most variations on any given moment. He didn't want us to settle for what we would arrive at easily.

You never felt anyone was pulling away and saying, "I don't want to work this way," or "I want to know what's going to happen." It was an intensely free kind of approach.

TANYA BEREZIN: Improvisations on a scene, particularly on a new play, don't help me. Usually, when you're rehearsing you don't know the character well enough to come up with something that is true to her given circumstances. You're going to come up with something that is coming out of your impulses of the moment, which are half involved with the given circumstances of the play and half involved with who you fought with last night and what you had for breakfast this morning.

What helps me most of all is running lines. Not for memory, but for embedding them into my consciousness. Questioning the words and letting the words sink in seems to be the thing that most helps get me centered on the scene and on the doing of it.

I also find it really helpful to list facts. What do I know about this character? All of her personality is captured behind those answers.

MIA DILLON: The first thing you do as an actor is discover what your character's function in the play is. You find out where the playwright wants the character to go. Anything

I don't understand or that doesn't work for me, I will ask the director or playwright about, because they might be able to tell me a way it will work or what it means. If they can supply those answers, I'm being more faithful to the playwright's play than if I make up the answers.

You can't find the truth of what *you* think the character is; you have to find the truth of the character by understanding what the playwright wants. Once you find that truth you can question the playwright about those things that don't work for you.

Are rehearsals for a new play different from rehearsals for a revival or a classic?

LINDA HUNT: The difference between rehearsing a new play and rehearsing a revival? When I did *Mother Courage,* everyone asked me how I was going to do the famous silent scream. On a new play no one knows what the "famous" moments will be.

How do you feel you contribute to the final draft of the play?

DONALD MOFFAT: Authors very, very seldom dash things off overnight, and with any great text—one that has withstood the test of time—the answer to any question an actor might ask lies in the text. In a great play, there's not a question I can ask as an actor that isn't answered right there in the text. My method is always to give the script a try.

Especially in new plays, you find things that don't work right away. In early rehearsals, it seems to me, the energy should be spent on trying to make the play work.

TANYA BEREZIN: The trick to rehearsing a new play is to assume the playwright is as right as Shakespeare was. Assume the play is written correctly when a moment isn't working. Don't run to the playwright to change things, but work to find a solution. The director and the playwright will see what isn't coming together. Then maybe later, if there are still kinks, and you question those kinks, you might say, "What do you think?" I think it's very, very dangerous to question the writing of a particular scene because it's not happening for you at the moment.

The answers are in the play. If you look at the given circumstances of the play, then you should be able to figure out what the character wants. You ask questions that clue you in to the specificity, the humanity of that character. If you can figure out *what* she wants, the *why* will follow.

ROBERT JOY: To make a play work, you become a writer if you have to. To respect all the compartments in the theater superstructure is to cut yourself off from really participating in a new play. To do your best work as an actor, you've got to think and sometimes act like a director, a producer, and a writer. You always have to be sensitive about how much input the playwright can take, but I find that, by and large, directors and writers welcome suggestions from actors.

TOM HULCE: It's tricky to know when to treat a new piece of writing as if it were *not* in progress, to just deliver what's there, or to stamp your feet and say, "There's something missing here," or, "It's not clear here," or, "What if . . . ?"

D. W. MOFFETT: We went through five different endings on one play I was doing before we opened. The playwright and director would come up to my dressing room and say, "What did you think?" I'd tell them what I liked and didn't like, and sometimes those suggestions were taken. That's what I love about new plays—I get to have that much input.

TANYA BEREZIN: I always assume it's me if something doesn't work, but there are times when a play's just not good enough. There's not much you can do about that. You can make suggestions. You can't say, "Make it better." You should ask questions. If the playwright or director can explain it and make it clear to you, terrific. Sometimes, by asking a simple question you make the playwright change something, but it is changed from his vision, not from yours. That's collaboration.

MIA DILLON: I've known John Pielmeier since I was seventeen. He wrote *Agnes of God* with me in mind. I feel my stamp is on Agnes, although many other actresses have gone on to play the role. In the creation of Agnes, through many conversations and work on scenes with John, I infused the role with my own spirit.

How do you deal with rewrites during rehearsals?

TOM HULCE: I love to be surprised. I love to have my lines changed. I like to feel that something truly collaborative is happening.

When a script is changed in rehearsal, I look at what's new and I'll have an opinion whether it's a solution to the problem or not. But my job at first is simply to let the writer and director see it, to be an instrument and deliver the material as best as I can. The best thing I can do is show them what it is.

TANYA BEREZIN: It's not my place to judge a new scene. You think of how it fits into the movement of the play, not what you lost or gained.

HUME CRONYN: Sometimes, even with work, you not only don't improve the piece, but can actually dig the hole deeper. I place very little faith in rewrites. You can't take something the playwright has conceived, if he's done the job professionally, tear it apart in rehearsals, and start all over again. You end up with a patchwork quilt, and it ain't very pretty.

It's quite a different thing to take a play out somewhere and say, "This is work-in-progress. We're going to read it for people, get an audience's reaction, do more work, give some staged readings, then put it on a bare stage." You progress that way. That developing process is necessary.

As soon as you get into rehearsals, you're going to find places where you can improve the play, where you were wrong, where suddenly the play takes on a life of its own and completely distorts your original concept. You're going to make both happy and miserable discoveries.

BARNARD HUGHES: I think the plays that aren't sufficiently explored by the playwright before they get to the actors are the hard ones. With a good play, everything you want to find out about a character is said right there in the text. You don't have to go looking for sense memories, or faking, or anything to give you a bridge to get to the next piece of the play you can understand. Everything is laid out totally and completely. You can find out everything you need to know about the part from the text.

TANYA BEREZIN: I speak up when there is too much in the script. I say, "I don't need this." Usually, the playwright, in trying to make something clear, has put in too many steps. If you are investigating the play, or even a scene, moment by moment by moment, you'll find there are moments in the progression that are really unnecessary. If a moment is unnecessary, rather than just in your way, you ask to get rid of it. The main way to help the playwright is just to act the part—investigating, acting, and questioning the character.

DONALD MOFFAT: At the beginning of the second act of *Painting Churches*, my character originally quoted "The Wasteland." We had that right up until previews. Then, Tina Howe got a letter from the Eliot estate saying we'd not be allowed to use it. Overnight, I was presented with a new poem. It took me some time to learn the poem and fill it out. It's always a shock to be thrown something on such short notice—especially the night before the critics come.

MIA DILLON: If I can see that the changes are helping and making the play better, I'm always in favor. If the play is being changed because no one knows exactly what's wrong, then I'm frustrated.

LINDA HUNT: I have become more philosophical over the years, more open to trying things. I have learned to speak my mind in the most constructive way I can, to trust myself more, to keep my own counsel.

TOM HULCE: Occasionally, new material comes in that you didn't want in the first place. Sometimes people's instinct is to fix what works because they don't know what to do with what doesn't. They'll try to improve what is already working just fine.

When the script changes, it's difficult to try to forget the earlier version. Even though the material is no longer in the play, it could be useful. The old version can often be used to fill in a blank in a performance.

What's really difficult is when something is changed or removed that was a vital step in the race you were running. It's as if they take out part of the track and you have to make this great hurdle in the middle of the race.

D. W. MOFFETT: What I've had to learn as an actor is that if the director and the writer say, "This is no longer necessary," I have to find that moment's source elsewhere in the play. You take the spirit of that moment—the critical essence for the character—and disseminate it somewhere else.

ELIZABETH FRANZ: When scenes are moved from place to place, it's jarring. I do the new lines over and over so that, by rote, I learn where the new bridges have been placed.

PAMELA REED: It's fun and challenging to deal with rewrites. Transitions will be different, and that can drive you crazy, but it keeps you on your toes. You just jump in and do it. You have to remember that everyone wants it to work.

How do you feel about reworking the play or the production during previews?

SWOOSIE KURTZ: I'm a great believer in everything changing in front of an audience. In previews you make glorious discoveries with the audience. It's all so scary, wonderful, and surprising. The audience teaches you so much about the play, but it doesn't mean that you can sit back in rehearsals, do no work, and wait until previews.

DONALD MOFFAT: Ideally, textual changes can wait until previews. An audience teaches you more about what you're doing than any amount of rehearsal. They don't necessarily provide an answer; you still have to find that. You constantly make little adjustments.

FRANCES STERNHAGEN: *On Golden Pond* was running three and a half hours long going into previews. This was the director's decision, and it was a good one. We tried it before an audience. It was marvelous to discover for ourselves what did and didn't work, and what had to come out.

D. W. MOFFETT: That first week and a half of previews usually brings pretty intensive rewrites—almost as much rewriting as during the entire rehearsal process, because everyone now knows where the critical issues lie. After the first five or six previews, man, you know what does and doesn't work.

It's amazing how much script surgery can get done in a week and a half. The company spends four weeks of rehearsal saying we might have to change this and that, and the previews say "Change this. Don't change that."

If the play is working, the audience's instincts are amazingly consistent. You must trust their instincts as you do those of an actor, designer, or director. You must recognize the audience's artistic contribution.

VALERIE MAHAFFEY: If the script is constantly changing in previews, you have to remember the director's notes, what's different in the writing, what the preview audiences are responding or not responding to—it's too much. You cannot act if you have notes in your head. That new section of the script comes and you're not free just to be there with the other person onstage, talking to them. Instead, you are thinking, "Now this doesn't work in the old way. I was told to do . . . what?" It's just horrible. You've got a fifty-fifty chance of actually doing it the new way.

What kind of input does the playwright give you during rehearsals?

D. W. MOFFETT: It's incredibly important that the writer be available at rehearsals. If you don't trust the writer, you're in trouble—you start to mistrust your text, and then you mistrust yourself. Working on a new play, you have to have the discipline to try to make problem areas work, but, ultimately, you have the escape valve of saying, "I don't think this text works. Can we change it?"

Some playwrights can get overly sensitive about their stuff, particularly in the early phases of rehearsal. I will paraphrase the script just to find an emotion. I will repeat lines just to find an intention, a basis, a ground. I don't like to see a playwright wince. Some playwrights understand an actor's need, in the beginning, to use the text as molding clay. They know we're going to return to the words as written. Other playwrights wonder, "Is he never going to say my text the right way?" If the playwright can't be laid back early in rehearsals, then I'd say, "Get out."

Having the playwright around in the later rehearsals is really critical, because you get down to identifying those components of the script that may or may not work.

SWOOSIE KURTZ: There usually is a time when the director tells the playwright not to come to rehearsals for ten days or two weeks. It's more valuable to have the playwright return after that with fresh eyes. If he sees every little bit of rehearsal, he'll be so close that he'll lose any distance.

Sometimes, having the playwright there is like having your parents watch you on a date. You think of your work in rehearsal from his point of view. You don't feel free to say, "Why isn't this working?" You may not mean the play; it's just a problem *you* are having. But the playwright's ears don't know the difference.

LINDA HUNT: There is a time of great allegiance to the writer, and a time of great allegiance to the director, and a time for the play to become the actors'. Rehearsals are wonderful when those times are intuited by the company.

MIA DILLON: I've worked with playwrights who have specific ideas about the play but are open to suggestions about character interpretation. I've also worked with playwrights who "knew" every line reading in the play, and exactly how they wanted everything played. That's maddening, because the playwright is not allowing for what an actor can bring to a role and a production.

If the playwright is at rehearsal only to make sure no one damages his baby, then his presence is detrimental. Actors have to experiment. A playwright who allows you to experiment can wind up with a much better play than one who hangs on tight and won't let go.

BARNARD HUGHES: The playwright is always the final authority. I think the playwright's idea—arrived at after maybe years in front of the typewriter—is a hell of a lot more valid than an off-the-top-of-my-head opinion. I think whatever a playwright writes, no matter what stage of development it is in, should be given a pretty fair shake before you start questioning it.

VALERIE MAHAFFEY: I will try to make what's in the script work, beyond all reason. This probably gets me into trouble. I'm frustrated when I'm working on a part and feel changes should be made; but I don't fight.

TOM HULCE: I had trouble in the second half of *Daniel Rocket*. I had to work too hard for it to play. That made me think there was something not quite right. I was able to be very specific with Peter about what *might* happen, and it was really thrilling to see pages from him that were exactly what I was longing for. It was great. It felt like an absolute collaboration.

VALERIE MAHAFFEY: It's bad when playwrights are too much in love with what is on the written page and think everything we're doing in rehearsal is wonderful. Work doesn't get done because they're so pleased. That particular personality shouldn't be in rehearsals. We may be sensing flaws in the play or our performances, but everything is hunky-dory with the playwright, so what do you do?

TANYA BEREZIN: Nobody ever sits down and says, "What do we want this play to do?" "What is the effect?" "What is this playwright's vision?"

It's dangerous not to include the playwright. How can a playwright know what's wrong if he can't see the scene in rehearsal? It's rather arrogant for directors or producers to banish playwrights. I find most playwrights are much more critical of their work than anyone else is, because they have the clearest idea of what they are trying to say. They can see in rehearsal, watching a scene unfold, whether the play is happening or not.

ELIZABETH FRANZ: In rehearsals for *Brighton Beach Memoirs*, some of the actors were having problems because of the presence of Neil Simon. He has a very strong personality. We had to ask him to leave. We didn't know where we were in the play and needed some time alone. We were being trapped into performing it in the way we *thought* he wanted it performed.

There is a time when all playwrights should go away. That should be up to the director. I've found directors who have been actors, such as Gene Saks and Jerry Zaks, to be more sensitive to that. They're more familiar with the process.

VALERIE MAHAFFEY: Every director-playwright team operates differently. In the last week of rehearsals for one play I did, some things were not being done—the director was a very bright person but didn't know how to talk to actors—so the playwright stepped in. He came to us privately and told us what he wanted and what he thought the director was trying to tell us.

I'll be damned to hell for this, but if the director and the playwright have the same idea and the director is just not getting it across to the actor, then the playwright should step in if *he* can explain matters. Ideally, though, he should have the director's permission.

D. W. MOFFETT: I do not want to have access to a playwright because I want some ally with whom to fight the director. I want access to the playwright as a collaborator, not as a co-conspirator.

LINDA HUNT: In the beginning I didn't know how to talk to playwrights. I was audacious in the extreme. I remember cornering one playwright and saying, "If you were going to tell me just one thing about my character, what would it be?" I thought this would be like hearing the word of God. The playwright's response, "I don't know," struck me dumb.

I had another playwright say to me, "What would you think if I told you that the way you were playing this scene was bad, ill-conceived, awful, and that you should do something else?"

I had to learn how to be a true collaborator.

TOM HULCE: I was working on a David Rabe play, *The Orphan.* Rabe talked about what he felt I had done that was so right, and the way he talked had absolutely nothing to do with what I was doing. It really made me see how my performance as perceived by someone, even the playwright, is a subjective kind of thing. That experience has encouraged me not to talk to the writer. The fastest solution to a problem, generally, is to go through the director.

PAMELA REED: I like having the playwright in rehearsals. Sometimes, just by hearing the playwright talk or even laugh you can learn things about his play. A writer's behavior is so idiosyncratic that it breathes as one with the work that she or he does.

ŽELJKO IVANEK: Working on *Master Harold* was different because the playwright, Athol Fugard, was directing. He was not only the playwright, but the play was about his life. I was up there playing him. No other director could have given me the information he gave, or guided me as he did. He gave me confidence, because if he felt I was on the right track, I was on the right track. It was also harder because, playing him, I felt obligations I wouldn't have in other situations.

At one moment in the play, my character has a phone conversation with his father, a man he loves, but who is an alcoholic and a liar. Not much happens in the phone call— there's no event in the lines themselves—but the cumulative effect of the play's action until then, along with the phone call, is devastating, and my character ends up lashing out at the two servants—one of whom is a father figure.

My character winds up taking out all the pain he feels about his father on this servant, eventually spitting in his face.

Somewhere around the second or third week of rehearsal, Athol wanted to look at that scene. He told me to do anything I wanted to do, he didn't care, he'd deal with the consequences. I finally realized that the action had to have something to do with that bottle of whiskey my character brings home for his father.

We did the phone call. As my character hangs up the phone, he lashes out at the servants, and starts packing his things and the bottle. I looked at the whiskey, paused, took the bottle, hit it on the table, and it shattered. I was almost hyperventilating and could barely say the lines. It was as real as anything I've done on the stage.

One of the things I'm proudest of is that the moment of breaking the bottle is now in the play, written into the script of *Master Harold*. It used to be that my character would take the bottle home, and now he breaks it. I'm thrilled no end about that. People for ever and ever will be playing a moment I had something to do with creating.

Describe your working relationship with the director.

HUME CRONYN: Ideally, the director works hand-in-glove with the writer, but the writer should talk to the director and let the director talk to the actors. If the writer talks with the actors, the director must know what is going on and give his permission. You're inviting chaos if you don't funnel everything through the director.

Once in a while, you come to such a situation as when I was doing Edward Albee's *A Delicate Balance*. I was having a problem with a scene. It wasn't that I didn't trust the scene, I didn't know how to do it. Alan Schneider, the director, kept talking and talking to me about it. It didn't reach me, somehow. I asked Alan if I could talk to Edward directly about the scene. I spent a couple of hours in a dressing room with Edward talking about this particular scene, and the problem was solved just like that.

Alan was a very shrewd and conscientious director, but, somehow, there was a failure of communication between us. People talk different languages. In the theater, you realize very quickly that language is a bum medium of communication. That situation in *Delicate Balance* was not a reflection on anybody involved. It doesn't represent a failure for the director, the playwright, or the actor.

PAMELA REED: I don't think playwrights should be forced into a "hands-off" policy by the director. You have to have respect for the lines of communication, so that everyone knows what's going on. Otherwise, you make muddled choices.

TOM HULCE: I prefer to send everything through the director, because his skill is to know how to talk to the actors and to the writer—it's not always the same language. Because I tend not to be articulate in rehearsal, it's much better for me to talk to the director and let him interpret for the writer.

SWOOSIE KURTZ: I always think it's best to say things to the director and let him decide how to pass it along to the playwright. Also, the director might disagree with you wildly, so that's another reason not to bypass the director. Usually, I will defer to the director's judgment, unless I feel really strongly about something.

D. W. MOFFETT: Some actors freak out if a director gives them a result—"Be sad," "Be happy." I cannot work with a director who is unable to help me understand what the character's motivations are.

I recently worked with someone who operated only in results. I asked him what I was doing in the scene. He said, "Don, you're metaphorically naked." "How do I play that?" "I don't know, that's your problem." That kind of director you don't want to work with.

HUME CRONYN: Some actors won't tolerate a line reading, or the director demonstrating something. I love both. The director can carry on for a week in academic, polysyllabic words, when what he wanted me to do was go *faster!* I like being given specific directions. It's my job to cover that direction, to hide the seams so that the audience doesn't see it.

LINDA HUNT: You have to become good at interpreting and translating comments from directors—and from playwrights—who might not know the best way to speak to an actor. You have to feel the freedom to hear what's being said and then turn it into something you can use.

TOM HULCE: I directed a play at Playwrights Horizons. I was astounded to find out that the actors saw, read, and heard something that was planets away from where I was. This is one of the reasons that I'm in awe of directors who can bring a diverse bunch of actors to a *single* view of a play.

D. W. MOFFETT: Partly because I've directed before, I don't bitch when a director wants to change something. I know it can always be changed back.

VALERIE MAHAFFEY: Some directors will work you hard, but in the wrong way, such that they take away any magic you bring. Then I'll say to the director, "Please leave me alone right now. I know what you're saying. You have to leave me alone right now or I won't be able to get it." Some directors know how to make you work hard without taking away that inexpressible thing an actor can bring to a play.

How closely do you work with a production's designers?

DONALD MOFFAT: The practicalities of the theater are such that you don't get much involved with the designers. Good designers understand what the right kind of sweater or prop can do for you. The elements you deal with, the tables and the chairs, evolve through rehearsal to reinforce and reveal your character. You become very attached to *your* table and *your* chair.

ELIZABETH FRANZ: If a design has been chosen and okayed by the playwright and the director, we must try it. If you are familiar enough with your character when you see sketches and diagrams, you can make comments. My costume for *Brighton Beach Memoirs* was to be made of linen, not cotton. I wouldn't have felt right wearing a linen dress because Kate Jerome, my character, couldn't afford linen. But the designers told me linen would stand up better than cotton, and that it would be made to look and feel like cotton. Hearing that made it okay.

In *Brighton Beach*, the kitchen was behind a scrim, so the audience could see movement but not the actual kitchen. Still, the designers gave me a stove and a sink. They allowed me to go propping with the stage manager for canisters and bowls. They gave me beans to snap every night. It was wonderful; it made my performance all the more real. I always went onstage before the show and made the beds in the bedrooms. The boys never made the beds right.

TANYA BEREZIN: I'm short. Sometimes I'm slim. Sometimes I'm not slim. I always start by telling the costume designer how difficult it is to dress me. I tell her what I think is physically good and bad about me. Then we talk about the character. With good designers, you talk the way you would to another actor or a director about the character and her world.

Some designers have in mind what they think the character should wear, without wanting any feedback from you. Sometimes it's okay. Sometimes it's not.

I am fighting with every ounce of technique in every moment of performance to combat my self-consciousness. If the clothing is not comfortable on me, and that makes me feel the audience wants me off the stage, I can't act.

VALERIE MAHAFFEY: I neglect the designers. There will come a time in the last dress rehearsal—the last time you're allowed to go out into the house to see what has been created—when you see the magic of the sets and costumes. I get so busy in my little world, I don't have time to get to know the designers. That's sad.

PAMELA REED: I never played with dolls when I was little, but seeing the set models makes me wish I had.

It's odd if you come in and the costumes are all done. I love to talk to the designers and share ideas about what is right for the character and what will best show that character on your body.

TOM HULCE: It's a very odd thing that actors are the last people to know what anything is going to look like, yet they're the ones who have to inhabit that world. I'm a maniac about clothing. I'm not easy, only because it's very difficult for me to be articulate. I've tried the patience of a number of costume designers.

My discussions with designers are usually based on the character—my vision versus theirs. Their concerns are not specific to *my* character. Their concerns are toward *all* the characters. I don't care what the costume looks like next to somebody else's. I don't care how it goes in the scheme of things. That's the designer's problem. I can't be concerned with that, though I can be aware of it.

D. W. MOFFETT: I am probably one of the easiest actors for a designer to work with. I don't bitch. If that's the set they want, I'll play on it. You want me in shadow? I'll play there. I think the design is the province of the director.

How do you deal with reviews? Are they harmful or helpful?

D. W. MOFFETT: I've finally understood why most actors don't read reviews. Acting is just you and your belief in what you're doing.

You can be so-and-so's darling, but it's not going to get you a job. That's for damn sure. The people who are casting movies in Hollywood are not counting up how many Frank Rich points D. W. Moffett has.

My agent calls me up ecstatic when a critic likes me. But it doesn't get me a job. I'm beginning to realize that reviews only make people come see the play, or not. If critics love the play and think I should get off the stage for the rest of my life—fine. If the *play* gets a rave, then people will come and see it. If I'm proud of my work in the play, what else can I do?

ELIZABETH FRANZ: I miss critics talking about the ensemble. The whole company's effort cannot be denied.

TOM HULCE: If I feel something isn't working, I'm interested in seeing what the critics write. If there seems to be a kind of consensus on where I'm going wrong, then that can be useful information.

Sometimes critics don't see what you are doing as a choice but as the *only* thing you can do. This is especially true when critics only know *part* of your career and not your entire range of roles. It makes me mad when they don't look at what I do as a choice but as if I were a victim of limitations.

PAMELA REED: American critics don't discuss the body of work of an artist. They don't critique within a context. They seem to say either "fabulous" or "I hated it." I don't rush out and buy the reviews. You'll always have friends and enemies who'll leave them at your door.

I believe Teddy Roosevelt's remark, "I'm much happier being in the arena than being a person outside commenting." Criticism is an odd life. A critic is a strange thing to be.

SWOOSIE KURTZ: When all is said and done, criticism is only *opinion*. By definition, different people have different *opinions*. I'm not saying they're not pretty much right about things. If I read three reviews and all say something is boring, I won't go. Yet, I've seen so many brilliant performances unrecognized. When it's in print, people believe it.

I don't read my reviews now until several weeks into the run. If you read them on opening night, or the next morning, it's your whole world. A couple of weeks later, it's old news.

TANYA BEREZIN: I was fortunate when I was relatively young. I did *Battle of Angels*, and I got a "love letter" review from Walter Kerr about that performance. I, of course, felt wonderful. Some of it was true and some of it wasn't true. I thought about that, and it made me realize it was one man's opinion. Some of the things he saw were things I was working on, and other things only he could see. I'm glad he saw them, but they were not anything I did. For me, reviews now are about whether the play is going to run or not, whether the audience is going to come.

VALERIE MAHAFFEY: Usually, critics are very good to me. I appreciate that. You love to be singled out, but it doesn't count for much unless the whole play works.

MIA DILLON: I see whether I can use negative criticism. I have in the past—though not too frequently—been able to incorporate solutions to some of the negative comments into my performance.

ROBERT JOY: I've always had an open mind about criticism. I find that actors overreact and fail to see what a general reader will see. The little reservations critics have about actors just wash over general readers. General readers see only the overall tone of the review—is it positive or negative? You soon realize there is no sense in worrying about reviews.

I've got nothing against critics. I think they're doing a very difficult job and the hardest thing for them is to retain a freshness of approach, as if they went to one play a month instead of one play a night.

Critics can't always tell what is the production and what is the script. I've gone to plays and been very distracted by their bad production. It's tragic when a new play is panned because of a bad production. So many productions settle down after they open, especially those that need a calm, relaxed atmosphere to succeed. Given the tension of previews and opening night, sometimes that calm is lost and the play suffers.

PAMELA REED: When I did John Olive's *Standing on My Knees* at Manhattan Theatre Club, the critics trashed the play. They gave me raves. Where do they think my performance came from? The Carnegie Deli? The man wrote a great role, and the play had some flaws.

No critic ever has the right to say a person should not pursue a career of his or her choice. When critics get into that arena, they are playing God.

DONALD MOFFAT: When I meet critics—which is not very often—I'm always surprised at how little they know about the processes that are involved. They certainly know very little about acting.

MIA DILLON: Sometimes, what you have to take the blame for in print was a directorial choice. Very few critics can separate the acting from the directing from the writing. I'm not sure I can tell who contributes what to a production, even knowing or having worked with the actor, director, or playwright.

SWOOSIE KURTZ: I don't think critics often know the difference between good acting and bad acting. They fall for obviousness. They're not attuned to subtleties. I don't think critics know the process of selection behind a specific acting choice. If they don't like the character, they don't like you.

What would be your advice to an actor just starting out?

SWOOSIE KURTZ: Become a veterinarian. I hate to be cynical, but I wouldn't advise anyone to go into this acting business.

MIA DILLON: Be independently wealthy. If you would be happy acting in the smallest theater in the smallest town for no pay, then you belong in the theater. If you are acting for any other reason, you should think twice.

TOM HULCE: Me giving advice is like the blind leading the blind. Let the flash of the business take care of itself. Make your investment where you feel there's the most to learn.

Nina's speech in the fourth act of *The Sea Gull* is the best advice I've heard: "It's not the fame or the glory or what you've always dreamed of, but the ability to endure, to bear your cross."

ROBERT JOY: Actors have to come to a play with creative energy, instead of a defensive energy about proving themselves worthy.

ELIZABETH FRANZ: Watch. Watch life and watch actors you respect. Stop being selfish and self-observant and observe others.

When I'm out of my own way I can hear the voice of the character. I had the opportunity once to play three different roles in repertory. That was wonderful for catching my personal mannerisms. Each character has specific mannerisms. It's better to stand and say the words with no movement than with false mannerisms.

LINDA HUNT: The greatest acting is simple.

HUME CRONYN: As a very young actor, I was offered a play about which there was an enormous amount of buzz saying that it was going to be a big hit. The director was George S. Kaufman. The leading role came to me. I remember sitting and reading that play and not liking it. I read it again and again. I still didn't like it. I thought, what did I know? The play opened. It was a failure.

Don't go if you don't believe in it. It's always dangerous to go against your instincts. If you don't have a passionate appetite to be involved, don't do the part. Instinct can be fallible, but you've got to listen.

TANYA BEREZIN: Young actors should develop their curiosity. You've got to assume the playwright was after something and use your curiosity to find it out. If you stand back from the play, try to find out what's wrong and have a superior attitude toward it, you never can reach its essential truth.

VALERIE MAHAFFEY: It's best if you are in a school where you have a chance to do a lot of plays. After some actors leave school and give this acting business a shot, they get discouraged, leave and go on to something else, which is not a bad thing. If you're not meant to do this, fine. People get winnowed out, and those who are left are very special. Hold on to that specialness. That's what the critics and the directors want. They want people who know who they are and what is special about themselves. They don't want the people who look and act like everybody else.

DONALD MOFFAT: Success in the theater requires luck, it really does. Luck is an arrow flying through the air, and if you are in the right place at the right time, you get hit by the arrow. The idea is to walk down the middle of the road, where the arrows are flying the thickest.

You have to be unable to live if you don't act. If this isn't there, you really should think twice about acting. This being a given and, also, given that you have sufficient talent to be employable (but almost anybody fits that category), you must simply pursue a career as best you can.

D. W. MOFFETT: Go where the work is. Don't sit on your ass hoping to make it. Why are you acting? Are you acting because you want to act, or because you want to be a star? Once you figure that question out—and you had better figure out that you're acting because you love telling stories—then go and tell stories somewhere. Don't sit around bitching about the fact that you're waiting on tables instead of telling stories. There are wonderful theaters everywhere.

I am damned grateful I spent my twenties in Chicago and that I did not come to New York until I was thirty. I know I'm a better theater artist as a result. I have more experience. I have more to offer.

ROBERT JOY: Try to read as many new plays as you can. When you find one you like, express your interest. If no one else is organizing a reading, you organize one. If you find a play you have some feeling for, the best thing in the world is to take it in your own hands and get a reading together. This is where the theater's division of labor should be more flexible. If actors are going to try to get involved in new plays, they have to take on part of the producer's role.

BARNARD HUGHES: I've always felt that being in the theater was a pretty sensible thing to do. It's as secure as anything else.

What makes for good acting? Good theater?

PAMELA REED: You had better not be lying.

ELIZABETH FRANZ: Great theater is a group of actors spurred by the same purpose: playing the play. It is infectious. It takes your breath away.

MIA DILLON: When you're a professional and know all the tricks that go into making the illusion of theater, it's hard to get caught up in a performance. An exciting evening in the theater is when someone makes me suspend my disbelief, draws me completely into that world on the stage.

HUME CRONYN: Let the audience tear up the seats and hurl them at the stage and want to kill the actors. If the audience is reached and their reaction is to be furious, how wonderful, how healthy! That's what theater is about.

BARNARD HUGHES: Acting isn't making things comfortable for yourself. You've got to get that out of your head as soon as you can. There's nothing comfortable about being on the stage. You're not supposed to be out there feeling cozy.

HUME CRONYN: Very little in the theater is genuinely spontaneous. It's hard to keep that illusion after three or four hundred performances, but you bloody well better do it. That's the real discipline in acting.

LINDA HUNT: Great acting is in the degree to which an actor is able to be in the present, vulnerable, swayed and influenced by whatever thoughts and stimuli are moving among the actors on the stage. I'm excited by the degree to which an actor is able to respond simultaneously to all that. Out-of-this-world acting is a remembered moment being created in the present: it's crazy.

SWOOSIE KURTZ: The most exciting kind of acting, to me, is when the actor is almost unrecognizable in the part. Call it character acting if you want, but I think it goes beyond that. The reason I wanted to become an actor was to get away from my boring old self, not have to be me. To be someone else and to have a whole other set of problems, and a whole other point of view, is like being given a set of wings. It's such freedom.

D. W. MOFFETT: Every*one* in the theater should do every-*thing* in the theater. It is a real gift to have cleaned johns, written checks, acted, taken tickets, placed ads, called critics, prepared press packets. You don't get so defensive about your turf. I'm not into *my* turf, *my* moment.

Great theater takes place in a spirit of "I want the play to work." Look at it this way: Your character ain't going to work if the play don't work.

TOM HULCE: I've worked with a lot of nice people, and boy, am I not interested in nice. I want to work with people who are opinionated, who have a real vision. You might have big or little disagreements, but you know there is a vision at work. I will take that any day, no matter how difficult or neurotic or complicated the people I'm working with are.

I would prefer to be bad, more than I would prefer to be safe. If you're working with people who have a clear vision, then you feel free to take the biggest risks. You know that if you fall they'll catch you; if you go off track, they'll put you back on.

ROBERT JOY: I think being out of work affects people's acting. I think a lot of the tension you see on the stage in New York comes from people who are frustrated about their careers. There is an aura of desperation. If you've been out of work for a while, each audition gets successively worse, less carefree and easy. For an actor, ease on the stage—to be able to approach material without showing effort, to be relaxed, though not facile—is a very important quality.

DONALD MOFFAT: I wish there were an everyday requirement in our lives for the theater. A thirst, a hunger for the theater. I wish the theater were deeper in our consciousness.

DESIGNERS

A successful play creates an imaginary world, a world molded out of the playwright's vision, a world into which the audience is drawn and through which journeys. Production values—sets, lighting, costumes, and sound—can heighten or undermine the audience's understanding and acceptance of that world. A farce may not come across as the athletic romp the playwright intended if it's played on a cramped set, under dim and somber lighting. The designers create the physical reality of an imagined universe for the actors to inhabit and the audience to view.

The designers involved in a production of a new play usually work more closely with the director than with the playwright. Even if they never talk with the designers, playwrights do, however, have their say: in the stage directions, the dialogue itself, the atmosphere the conversations create, the ambience set up by the various relationships and conflicts.

In this chapter, five set designers, two costume designers, and two lighting designers, all active in designing new plays in New York and regional theaters, talk about their backgrounds and mentors, reading a new play for design ideas, creating design metaphors, working with an evolving script, designing within a limited budget, and their philosophies of design.

Jeffery Bauer has designed scenery for numerous plays for the Victory Gardens Theater in Chicago, among them *Butler County* by Dean Corrin, *Levitation* by Timothy Mason, and the premiere of Jeffrey Sweet's *The Value of Names*. Bauer has also designed for Chicago's Wisdom Bridge Theater, the Hubbard Street Dance Company, and the Northlight Repertory Theater Company in Evanston, Illinois. He is a resident designer for The Body Politic Theatre, and on the faculty of the Theater School at DePaul University.

John Lee Beatty has designed sets for Beth Henley's *Crimes of the Heart* and *The Miss Firecracker Contest;* Lanford Wilson's *Talley's Folly, Fifth of July,* and *Talley and Sons;* David Mamet's *A Life in the Theatre* and *The Water Engine.* He is a recipient of the Tony, Obie, Drama Desk, Maharam, and Outer Critics Circle awards.

Allen Lee Hughes is the lighting designer of *K2, To Gillian on Her 37th Birthday, Bent, Sophisticated Ladies,* and *A Soldier's Play.* He has designed at such regional theaters as the Folger Theatre in Washington, D.C., the Arena Stage, and also at Joseph Papp's Public Theater. Hughes has received Maharam and Outer Critics Circle awards.

Marjorie Kellogg designed scenery for *Da, American Buffalo, Steaming,* and *The Best Little Whorehouse in Texas* for Broadway. She has designed such productions as *Total Eclipse* and *Extremities* for Circle in the Square and the Roundabout Theatre. She has also written two science fiction novels.

Ming Cho Lee is the chairman of the Department of Design at the Yale School of Drama. He designed sets for productions of *K2*, *The Cuban Swimmer*, *The Shadow Box*, *Two Gentlemen of Verona*, *For Colored Girls . . .* , and *Much Ado About Nothing*. For ten years he was the principal designer for the New York Shakespeare Festival. He has also designed at the Guthrie Theater, the Stratford Shakespeare Festival in Canada, the Metropolitan Opera, other opera companies in New York, Chicago, and Houston, the Joffrey Ballet, the American Ballet Theatre, and the dance company of Martha Graham.

William Ivey Long has designed costumes for *Nine*, *Sister Mary Ignatius Explains It All for You*, *Mass Appeal*, *The 1940's Radio Hour*, *Passione*, *True West*, *Twelve Dreams*, *The Marriage of Bette and Boo*, and *The Tap Dance Kid*. Long has designed for Playwrights Horizons, the Public Theater, and the Yale Rep, and has won Tony, Drama Desk, and Maharam awards.

Dennis Parichy created the lighting design for *Crimes of the Heart*, for which he received a Tony nomination, a Maharam Award, and a Drama Desk Award. Other productions include *The Best Little Whorehouse in Texas*, *As Is*, *The Sorrows of Stephen*, and *Knock, Knock*. He has worked in such regional theaters as the Guthrie Theater in Minneapolis, The Mark Taper Forum in Los Angeles, and the Pittsburgh Public Theater.

Loren Sherman designed sets for the premiere productions of Christopher Durang's *Baby With the Bathwater* and *The Marriage of Bette and Boo*, as well as Mark O'Donnell's *That's It, Folks*, Albert Innaurato's *Coming of Age in Soho*, Peter Parnell's *Romance Language*, and A. R. Gurney, Jr.'s *The Dining Room*. His regional credits include the Williamstown Festival, the Actors Theater of Louisville, the Seattle Repertory Theater, and the Kennedy Center.

Patricia Zipprodt has received eight Tony nominations for her costume designs, winning the award for *Fiddler on the Roof*,

Cabaret, and the Broadway revival of *Sweet Charity.* Her other designs include *Sunday in the Park with George, Brighton Beach Memoirs, Chicago,* and *Pippin.* She has designed costumes for the American Ballet Theatre and for the Metropolitan Opera. Zipprodt has also received two Maharam Awards and three Drama Desk Awards.

How did you become a designer?

MING CHO LEE: My introduction to theater was as a teen-ager in Shanghai during the Japanese Occupation between 1942 and 1946. American films were, of course, not available. Without American films—none of us wanted to see Japanese films—there was a renaissance of theater, opera, ballet, and symphonic activities. I was introduced to modern plays—essentially Western theater spoken in Chinese and adapted to a Chinese situation.

Later, when I came to Los Angeles, I enrolled at Occidental College as an art major. I found my early love for theater had never really left me, so I became a speech major in my junior year. I went to work as an apprentice to Jo Mielziner in 1954. I'm one of those few designers who didn't go to Yale, though I did end up teaching there.

PATRICIA ZIPPRODT: I remember, even in kindergarten, I loved my drawing classes the best. One day my mother told me I didn't have to go to school because I had a bit of a cold. I insisted on going because that was the day we had drawing class. I ran all the way.

As I went on, I knew by instinct I was going to be a professional artist rather than a hobbyist. I passionately wanted training in the visual arts. I had no notion of what this training might be; I knew it must nourish and put to full use the connection that existed between my hands, eyes, and inner vision.

Like a lot of people, I made my way to New York in search of what to do with myself. Living on the cheap in an unheated tenement flat, I painted in my free hours, supporting myself with odd jobs—ushering at Carnegie Hall and the like. One evening I saw a Balanchine ballet called "La Valse," which Madam Karinska had costumed. In the costumes I saw so many colors at the service of this extraordinary piece of dance that something clicked in my head. At that moment, costume design seemed to become the trunk I was born in.

MARJORIE KELLOGG: So often the reason for going into a field starts out as one thing and ends up another. When I first worked in theater in high school, design was something not many theater people could do. Those who could draw were automatically shuffled into design. In the beginning, for me, design just seemed a way to be in theater, use my talent for drawing, and have a physical object happen as a result of my efforts, Now I find that design is a perfect expression of my desire to re-create place, to feed my nostalgia for place.

I apprenticed under Ming Cho Lee. An apprentice learns on the job. You build models, draft shows, do historical research, hold the designer's hand during technical rehearsals, give notes to the crew. It's a very good way to learn the practical parts of the business, as well as watch the design process in action, as opposed to the theoretical, academic approach of graduate school.

JEFFERY BAUER: I began as an actor at Jacksonville University and, eventually, because all actors were obliged, got involved with tech work. I always found it frustrating to be onstage and not be able to see how things looked.

The acting experience I had—even before college I had had quite a lot of acting experience in professional theater—was probably one of the most valuable things to me as a designer. It gave me a more complete understanding of the entire theater process. It definitely influenced the way I design, what I take into account when I begin designing a show.

DENNIS PARICHY: A lot of what I do and how I do it comes out of the experience of having done almost three hundred shows—failing sometimes, succeeding sometimes, working in all different kinds of theaters, encountering all the challenges and problems involved in creating for the theater.

JOHN LEE BEATTY: The strongest part of the Yale preparation was that they thought you'd become a designer and not a teacher.

WILLIAM IVEY LONG: I am a second-generation theater person. My father was tech director and my mother did costumes at the University of North Carolina at Chapel Hill. I used to be put to sleep in the scrap bins underneath the cutting tables. It was wonderful to feel that theater is normal life, that this is how everyone lives.

What designers have influenced your work?

PATRICIA ZIPPRODT: My mentors have, oddly enough, been mostly scenic designers, rather than costume designers. My first mentor was Boris Aronson, who took me under his wing, reviewed my work, wrote my recommendation to the union, and kept good track of me. I always say that Boris was my Yale, because he taught me so much as we worked together on shows: the relative values of color, how many whites there actually are, just what makes a simple garment a theatrical garment.

MING CHO LEE: As an apprentice to Jo Mielziner, I started out by filing away old drawings. I drafted ground plans, did elevations, built models. When Jo was designing *Cat on a Hot Tin Roof,* he allowed me to draft the bar for him. I worked with his assistant on the bus-and-truck tour of *Can-Can,* and that led to design work on my own in regional theaters.

JOHN LEE BEATTY: Because I grew up in Southern California, I saw a lot of road company productions of Broadway musicals. I was very much influenced by Oliver Smith. He was the big, commercial, musical comedy designer in vogue at the time.

DENNIS PARICHY: Critical to my training was an acting teacher at Northwestern, Alvina Krause. She was primarily an acting teacher, but also directed a number of shows. The experience of encountering her approach to the theater— the importance of the text, knowing what the play is about, and understanding and being responsive to that—formed the way I design.

Part of the reason Marshall Mason and I work so well together is that he also was a student of Miss Krause. We share that background and see theater in very similar ways. There is probably far less verbal communication between Marshall and me than is necessary in some other director-designer collaborations, because we share basic assumptions about the process of putting together a production.

JEFFERY BAUER: It's hard to pinpoint one role model when there is such a vast body of design material. When you look at a photo, or go to the theater and see another person's work, the possibility exists that some kind of influence, subconscious or otherwise, is going to occur. It's hard for me to identify any direct influences as far as my own work goes, because I don't particularly try to emulate other designers.

I think everybody develops his or her own style.

Is designing a new play different from designing a revival or a classic?

WILLIAM IVEY LONG: I mostly do new plays, I've done very few revivals. You can't help but be influenced when you design a revival. On a new play you're working with two live people, a live playwright and a live director—as opposed to a dead playwright and a bored director.

MARJORIE KELLOGG: The difference between designing new plays and designing most revivals is having the playwright around. Designers, when asked about the playwright-designer collaboration, say, "Oh, it's so wonderful working with playwrights." The playwrights say, "We never see the designer. The director keeps us away from the designer." Designers *think* they work with the playwright because they deal intimately with the script. They really don't see the playwright that often, which is too too bad. I sense the presence of the playwright, but the playwright isn't really around that much.

JOHN LEE BEATTY: It's always different. You're not just approaching a new script but approaching a new script with a certain director and a certain author. Designing a play by Neil Simon, directed by Gordon Davidson and produced by Emanuel Azenberg, is different from designing a new play by Lanford Wilson, directed by Marshall Mason and produced at the Circle Repertory. The first time you do a play, you can't divorce the identity of the play from the identity of the people involved.

MING CHO LEE: I think designing new plays and designing revivals are equally exciting. If I have nothing new to say about *Death of a Salesman,* then I probably shouldn't do it. If I can come up with a totally new look, a revival is as exciting as doing a new play.

Though a revival carries a lot of baggage, one must approach designing it as if the revival were a new play. Designing a new play is sometimes more difficult than designing a revival because you don't have other designers' mistakes to look at. It's harder to "hear" a new play than something you have heard before.

LOREN SHERMAN: You have to have a point of view toward whatever you design. That's even more important on new plays, where a point of view hasn't been established.

DENNIS PARICHY: There is a subtle difference between designing a new play and designing a revival. With a traditional play, a Shakespeare, you can't avoid remembering productions you've seen before; they've influenced your vision of the play. To get deeper into some classics before I form specific design ideas, I consult critics and books on the author and the play—all as a place from which to take off. This might give me new ideas of what the play is about and how to approach it, how to imagine it for myself.

Your response to a new play inevitably comes out of your personal experience. The characters in most new plays are more immediately contemporary than those in classics. I can identify with a person or several persons, their lives and what their problems or conflicts are. I can find some element that relates personally to me.

WILLIAM IVEY LONG: There is a tendency when designing classics to conjure up so many famous productions in your mind that you are forced either to echo previous designs, creating a kind of pastiche, or consciously go for a completely different look.

JEFFERY BAUER: Other than the fact that there is no precedent, the major thing about doing new plays is that they are always changing. It is exciting to work on a play while it is in a rough stage. As the play goes into rehearsal, or even as the scenery is being built, you have to deal with changes in the script. You may have planned on doing a scene change during intermission, but then the intermission is moved to another spot in the script. You depend on your ingenuity.

MARJORIE KELLOGG: I find that new plays are more exciting to do than most revivals I'm offered. I'm not interested in doing any more Clifford Odets. I've done three productions of *Death of a Salesman*. There comes a point when it's more interesting and challenging to do new plays.

LOREN SHERMAN: It didn't occur to me until about a year and a half after school that I was working on new plays a lot. That's not something I intended, but it evolved and now feels very natural. It has become more than a preference.

How do you keep your work fresh, free from the influence of other designers or previous productions?

PATRICIA ZIPPRODT: I will not look at photographs of previous productions. Your inner vision is like a chalkboard—once it becomes streaked, you can never erase it clean.

JOHN LEE BEATTY: The major joy in designing new plays is not having to copy the ground plan out of the back of Samuel French. It's ironic to know that somewhere out there someone is being forced to copy my ground plan out of the back of Samuel French. Nothing says that the ground plan or design for the original production is necessarily right.

Copying the original is no sin, but I don't think it is a terribly rewarding thing to have to do. Realistic plays like *Fifth of July* or *Crimes of the Heart*, or *A Life in the Theatre* are not going to be improved by making the action take place somewhere that wasn't intended.

It's harder not to copy with musicals: Try doing *Chorus Line* without copying. How the hell are you going to do that? You're stuck. Those mirrors are the set for the show; there's no way around it. How can Dolly not wear a red dress? How can she not come down a set of stairs? The design is now inseparable from the material.

DENNIS PARICHY: Copying can often be blamed on those Samuel French scripts, in which all of the staging and the ground plan of the original set is included. You must throw all of that out and imagine the play anew.

Delve into the play to the point where you know it on a personal level: how you respond to the characters in the play's situations, what you think of them. The only way to make a design really your own is to get so immersed in the world of the script that you reimagine it.

LOREN SHERMAN: When I do a play that's been done before, I'm not afraid to look at the original ground plans. You have to have some respect for the fact that the original design was developed in collaboration with the playwright. For instance, I worked directly with Chris Durang on the set for *The Marriage of Bette and Boo;* every subsequent production of the play will need the input of an imaginary Chris. If the designer is really trying to be true to the playwright's intentions, then he or she has to realize that some of those intentions are embodied in the ground plan the playwright approved.

I wouldn't advise anyone to try and copy the original scene design, but they should have respect for the ideas behind the original design. As an actor and director interpret the words in the script, the designer can interpret the ground plan in the script.

MARJORIE KELLOGG: Each design is your vision. You react to the script as you read it. Read the play over and over and you'll start to see the play your own way. There are times when your solutions may look like those of some other designer you've worked with, but it's not the same set, merely the same approach.

JEFFERY BAUER: There are certain painting techniques all designers use over and over again in different combinations. Sometimes you may use the same combination but come up with a totally new effect. Yet there are only a certain number of ways a designer can hang a door. A designer shouldn't waste time trying to make the basics of set design and construction unique.

How do you read a new play for design ideas?

DENNIS PARICHY: The design process for a new play begins with an intensive study of the text. How intensive depends on how complex a particular play is—how clear it is or is not on the surface. In order to feel familiar with the world of the play, with the playwright's intent, I need three to five readings. I need to understand the action of the play and the through-line that ties the whole thing together.

MARJORIE KELLOGG: I read to see if I like the play, regardless of the design possibilities. If the play says something that wants to be said, I will do it. If the play works and is offensive, I will not do it. If the play says something worth saying, but maybe doesn't quite work yet, I will still be glad to do it.

MING CHO LEE: One, you read the play. My first reading is very much *not* as a designer. I tend to read the play strictly as an audience member, so that I can get the total impact. My reaction is like the audience's—not strictly from the head, or analytical, but much more emotional. Some plays really grab me, and out of that first reading comes an urge, a need, to design the play. With a play I have to keep putting down, have a terrible time finishing, I tend to feel I may not be the right person to do it.

At some point in reading the play, there is a flash, an idea that perhaps the production can look a certain way. Again, it is clearly a visceral kind of reaction, an excitement. Then it is time to talk to the director or, if it is a new play, the playwright.

WILLIAM IVEY LONG: When you read the script you look for the story: Who grows? Who changes? Who goes from here to here? You look for technical things: Is there blood? Does the dress have to tear away and reveal five pygmies? Does she give birth onstage? Is there a child who grows into a man? Is there water thrown? You get your artistic and humanistic approach at the same time you're breaking down the technical aspects of the design.

LOREN SHERMAN: Deciding to do a certain play has to do with finding something in the play that speaks to me. *The*

Marriage of Bette and Boo has so many things I consider to be true about relationships. It excited me.

The best designs always come from images that flash in your head as you're first reading the play. I've learned to follow my impulses. I don't like to burden myself right away with "How am I going to do this?" I like to go into a first design meeting with a director and playwright and just talk about the images that came into my head while reading the script. I may not yet know how to turn those images into actual set designs. But I find that liberating, not scary; it keeps my work open to the collaborative process.

How do you start the process of translating the playwright's works into physical reality?

MING CHO LEE: I teach my students that there is an *ideal* process to the designing of a play, yet I realize everyone's design process is necessarily different.

DENNIS PARICHY: A play is a journey. You start out from a certain place and you end up somewhere else. I try to identify where the people in the play start—what is their situation, their relationship to each other, what are their main concerns. If I understand that, I understand the central action of the play.

I make copious notes, writing down anything that occurs to me along the way. I usually do a script analysis similiar to what a director might do. I break the script down into beats, name the nature of each beat, and mark down the essential action of each beat. Particularly with complex or confusing plays, I need to sort out the play's structure, so that I understand what is going on. Once I grasp what is going on, I feel ready to deal with the director and the playwright.

JOHN LEE BEATTY: I read the play the first time through and actually don't think about scenery very much. I look at the play as a literary piece. Usually, I keep my thoughts to myself, talk to the director, and whatever pours out at that point is what happens. I try to analyze the problems and virtues of the play at the same time: What could be misleading? What could be a pitfall? How important are various small actions in terms of the entire action of the play? What kind of movement does the play require? A basic question you have to ask of every new play is: "Is it a comedy or not?"

ALLEN LEE HUGHES: I like to think there is one design that is right for a play. You start with all the possibilities in the world and work to come up with the *one* right answer. I cannot put pencil to paper until I know that answer. Putting a light plot together has very little to do with design. That's technique, not *design*. Finding the correct answer is *design*.

MING CHO LEE: I have a series of questions, some major choices, to get me started. Is it *really* a realistic play? I think everyone has to face that question. Is it a domestic play? Is it a play of huge issues? How do the people behave? Where is it? When is it? Who is in it? What happens to them? Designers have to deal with those things.

PATRICIA ZIPPRODT: First comes a really careful study of the script. Simultaneously, or immediately thereafter, you get together with the director. I'm a firm believer that the theater is a collaborative business run by a dictator, the director. The director holds the natural seat of authority. I like to think designers physicalize the concepts, the interior images the director has conjured up in his head. Designers often have to mind-read the director, because it is very hard to talk about visual things: There is no direct translation of the visual into the verbal. Designers and directors often talk *through* the medium of painting, sculpture, architecture, or music.

The smallest thing can illuminate the whole approach. For example, the first task in working with Bob Fosse on *Pippin* (we were put together by the producers and didn't know each other on a one-to-one basis) was setting up a mode of communication. I asked Bob over coffee how he saw the show. He thought for a while, and said it should be "magical" and "anachronistic." I thought that was great, but when I got home I realized I didn't quite know what he meant. I called him up and asked him what he meant by "anachronistic." He thought for a moment, and then replied, "Jesus Christ in tennis shoes." That image gave me the show! Also, if your focus goes dim in the design process, especially on massive projects, you can pull out those key pictures or phrases and trust them to pull your work back into focus.

LOREN SHERMAN: With new scripts there are no rules. The creation is really intuitive.

JEFFERY BAUER: I will read a script and just let an image—fuzzy or specific—form. It's not necessarily a set. Sometimes it's a certain way I see light shining or, more often, the essence of a mood. I take that image and see how it fits the technical design requirements of the play. I usually don't deal with specifics or technical problems before I can establish that mood.

MARJORIE KELLOGG: When a play interests me, the first question I ask is "Can I design the set?" Is the set possible within the physical limitations of whatever theater it's going into and the budget?

Sometimes you get a project where everyone is asking

for the moon and it's suicide to take on the assignment. You're crazy to even consider it unless there is something really great about the play. If the production has to be absolutely realistic and you only have twenty cents, it's better to just go away because everyone is going to be mad at you at the end. There's no point.

If you think you can give the play a good set, then you start thinking about how to visualize it. I don't think about *scenery*. I think about what images I saw when I was reading the play. Those images can be a place, a particular painting, a color, an arrangement of light and shadow. When I sit down to design, those initial images are going to be my truest reactions to the play and, therefore, the most interesting to try to put onstage.

MING CHO LEE: Quite often, when a rough sketch feels right, I may take the chance of quickly making a one-eighth-inch to a one-foot scale model. However, the problem with making models early is that you sometimes begin to commit to a specific design. Ideally speaking, I like to be able to draw as many different kinds of sketches and explore as many different approaches as possible, and then meet with the director again.

I feel that after the initial meeting with a director you shouldn't meet again unless you have something to show. The first meeting is words and talk. If the second meeting ends up to be more talk and words, then something is wrong, because the second meeting must really be related to something visually concrete you've created—a series of sketches or a rough model.

JOHN LEE BEATTY: In *Crimes of the Heart* the set description didn't make sense. It asked for a bed in the kitchen, stairs that came *down* into the kitchen, and a door from the kitchen into the grandfather's bedroom. These were all things you don't normally get in a kitchen. I heard myself saying that it didn't make sense and then I got it: It didn't make sense on *purpose*. The fact that the set didn't make sense made perfect sense in terms of our style of production for this play.

LOREN SHERMAN: One of the images that came into my head when I read *The Marriage of Bette and Boo* was leafing through a family's photograph album. In a sense, the movement of the sliding panels I designed captured the effect of a camera's shutter, a series of snapshots from the lives of the two families in the play.

I also imagined that Chris Durang, as the narrator, had a mind like an apartment complex with all these rooms. We'd open a door, visit that scene, and then go to another one, but that first scene was still going on all the time. I wanted to get on the stage the impression of an infinite number of rooms. I wanted a set where the act of closing one scene would be the act of opening the next scene—a set that urged the play forward.

Romance Language is about moving toward the West and the open frontier. My design image for *Romance Language* was of a conveyor belt: a scene would be brought to you, then it would pass, and you'd be pulled deeper and deeper toward the West, each scene coming down the conveyor belt being more open, more spacious than the last. I thought it conveyed a sense of American ingenuity.

PATRICIA ZIPPRODT: I do a lot of research. I like to do my own research if I have the time, because I can think, mull over ideas, while researching. As you are thumbing through books, your subconscious is active, reacting to the pictures you see, to the words you read. You are looking for things you can use.

MING CHO LEE: I do research. It tends to be generalized research—research that has a kind of emotional value, that somehow gives a sense of the place, the weather, the altitude, the sounds you might hear in the place. I'm beginning to feel that if you can't *hear* the play, you really can't *see* the play.

WILLIAM IVEY LONG: I'm a fanatic about hair and shoes. People look first at the face and then the feet. The irony for a costume designer is that this omits the body in between. Hats were invented so you can find the face under them. The bigger the theater, the more you have to focus on the faces. You don't create designs that sabotage the audience's ability to find the person.

ALLEN LEE HUGHES: I'll make a wish list—write down anything I want, or think the show needs. I give my imagination rein, even if the show is to be in the smallest theater with only ten-foot ceilings. Then I'll cut that list according to priorities and possibilities.

Do you ever depend on a visual metaphor or a production "concept" when creating a design?

WILLIAM IVEY LONG: When I was younger and more pompous, I consciously started from a concept or a metaphor. Now I've learned that you start from what the play is telling you. I don't consciously say, "This is my metaphor, this is my conceit." It should evolve organically.

MING CHO LEE: I have no idea if I use metaphor. I've always found that when the design is good, you see the metaphor. I don't know how to design one consciously.

LOREN SHERMAN: Metaphoric images make the design better, even if they exist only in my mind. I don't think the audience has to say "Aha!" to benefit from those metaphors. Set design can subliminally reinforce what the play is trying to say.

A good design should really embody a metaphor that resonates with the playwright's metaphors. It should strengthen the playwright's vision. A playwright expresses what he feels through his words. A designer expresses what he feels through visuals.

DENNIS PARICHY: If I find a problem in making my response to the play clear, I will develop a metaphor for clarification. If I can't translate the metaphors into concrete design terms, they're no good, no matter how clever or appropriate.

Sometimes a play's metaphors help me create a design. In the beginning of *Talley's Folly*, the character of Matt says, "This is a waltz and a valentine." That line translated into the most romantic lighting I've ever done. I had to create a world so fully that everyone saw it as a romantic ideal we all would like to experience.

With a show like *As Is* I never had any metaphor, but I had a very strong aesthetic response to the script on first reading. I knew it was a presentational play—straight out to the audience, not to be complicated by complex lighting. The lighting had to be integrated with the text, support the text, not try to do too much or too little. It had to communicate the play without any fancy visual elements to impress anyone—those things that are fun for designers but have nothing to do with the text.

MARJORIE KELLOGG: Concepts are mostly used to bring new life to classics. Why do that to a new play? Let it exist in its natural state first before you start overlaying it with bloody ideas. When you're doing Shakespeare you can play around. He's survived the test of time and been done in numerous ways. When you're doing a new play, there is something egotistical about taking an offbeat track because you don't really know what the play is unless you've done it. Why overlay it with something that comes from the outside before you know what's on the inside?

What is the designer's role in rehearsal?

JOHN LEE BEATTY: We had some problems with the set for *Fifth of July* because we weren't prepared for the play's reception as a comedy. On paper—a woman who's had all those operations, can't conceive, can't do anything, is burned out totally—the subject doesn't look especially amusing. Onstage, the character, with Swoosie Kurtz playing her, became vital, a life force instead of a negative experience.

Faced with a stronger comedy than we'd thought, we painted all the gray shingles of the house yellow; from dessicated bones it became buttercup yellow with white trim. As you get closer to the play through the production process, you see those things.

LOREN SHERMAN: I like to go to the first rehearsal and talk to the actors about the design. I don't attend rehearsals religiously. I do like to see a run-through every once in a while to see how the project is coming along, but I rely on the stage manager for my latest information.

JOHN LEE BEATTY: I really don't like to see a lot of rehearsals. As a designer you are always waiting for someone, and so you have time to poke your head into the rehearsal room, pick up what's going on, get the tone of the rehearsal. I see bits and pieces. I may see a scene. I like the freedom of staying on the outskirts of the show, of hovering around rehearsals.

My work doesn't require me to see a full run-through before we move into the theater, but I like to see one a few days before we move, so that if there are any last minute changes I know about them. Then, in the shop, I can make those little adjustments that make all the difference.

How do all the changes a new play goes through during the rehearsal period affect you?

PATRICIA ZIPPRODT: Change is the name of the game. "If the song doesn't work, change the dress" is the sort of thing you hear constantly. The more accurate you are in guessing what will and won't work, the better off you are. The subsequent adjusting, tuning, fixing, affects everybody. Until the show is "frozen"—that can be five minutes before the opening-night curtain goes up—you know your work is not done.

MARJORIE KELLOGG: Minor design changes happen all the time; they're a pain in the ass. Some people will wax romantic about keeping things fluid. To tell the truth, designers work in concrete things. They have time pressures, material pressures, budget pressures. It's better to do the design work up front. Wood, Styrofoam, paint, and canvas can't be changed as easily as the written word. You can't put those in a word processor and play around with them. They are expensive.

If you have a basic living room set you can rewrite the script from now until opening night. If you're going to need a dining room suddenly, it can be devasting. You can be as inventive a designer as possible and the dining room will still look cobbled on.

MING CHO LEE: I'm not good at changing scenery; it just boggles my mind. It is up to me to realize the play, to create the visual counterpart of the playwright's word, to create the world for this play. I tend to be very bad at dealing with a production built on quicksand. I've never been a designer who can come up with solutions to problems right on the spot. I feel I have no time to discover how to make a connection between the asked-for change and my overall design approach.

JOHN LEE BEATTY: A lot of new plays I've done have only been partially written—especially Lanford's plays. The first play of Lanford's I did was *Mound Builders*. He hadn't even finished the first act when we started, let alone the second. We were going on a bare description of what *might* happen in the second act. The problem, of course, was that I could only go by the part of the play I had read and Lanford's description of what he thought the rest of the play was going to be. We later found certain aspects of the play weren't as important as they appeared to be when described.

You don't get upset by changes. You expect them. It's more upsetting not to be involved in the decisions. If you just get orders phoned in to you that something doesn't work, it's frustrating. You do what you can, but a certain point comes where, in terms of time and money, you can't do much about changes.

Scenery is very important to a play, but the script is the most important thing. Even the most visually gifted directors and playwrights really haven't made their script revelations by the time you've done almost all of your design work. The designers are usually the first to do hands-on work on a production; directors, playwrights, and actors sort of ease into the production at a later point. In a sense, they have to catch up to you and your design.

LOREN SHERMAN: Most set designs for new plays allow a certain flexibility. You don't want the set to cause the director or playwright not to be able to make the changes they want. The fun of a new play is that it grows more in those few weeks of rehearsal than it will ever again.

DENNIS PARICHY: A lighting designer has to approach a new play with a very flexible attitude. Changes are usually not major adjustments of style or tone, but minor corrections, attempts to make some part of the play or production clearer or more effective. For instance, the director might restage a scene, or a scene will move from the beginning of the first act to the middle of the first act. You just have to be ready to cope with those changes.

Small changes can affect an entire series of lighting cues. Usually, changes happen at the last moment in tech rehearsals, or in previews. You can only say, "Okay," then rearrange the lighting cues and do a quick fix. You think about the change overnight, and the next day you make it work in an effective, lasting way.

ALLEN LEE HUGHES: These days, with computer boards, it's easier for the lighting designer to stay on top of script changes. I will sit in rehearsal and watch what is going on. If the director is reblocking, I want to be there. The best thing is to be around and be interested.

A lighting plot has a certain amount of built-in flexibility. A plot should be specific enough that it is designed for that particular show, but general enough so that you can deal with changes. You have to deal with moving a morning scene to nighttime without rehanging all the instruments.

JEFFERY BAUER: Everyone who works on a new play knows it is going to change. Every project you work on goes through a certain amount of evolution, but, of course, new plays change to a greater degree.

A designer has to rely on the stage manager to find out what has been changed during rehearsals. You can't always be there, but you should be in daily communication whether directly or via your telephone answering machine.

I worked on a show recently where we decided we'd have the act break in a certain place. The show was designed so that a major scene change could be made during intermission. About two weeks into rehearsal, the director said he was thinking about moving the intermission. It was shocking. The director had not tracked that proposed change through the entire show. In the end it stayed as is. If the director or playwright had insisted, we would have had to do it. Ego aside, I can't say "no" to the director or the playwright. All I can do is let them know how the change is going to affect the production. But ultimately it's their decision.

JOHN LEE BEATTY: With some shows you end up designing a set that I call "one size fits all." You get a basic scheme, that you hope will fit all the scenes they're going to add and subtract. You leave a few blanks around the edges to fill in later.

WILLIAM IVEY LONG: Usually, you're not allowed to go over budget when changes are made, so you've got to salvage whatever costumes you can. You have to work on your feet. If you work with any director who is at all alive, the play always changes. In fact, you want it to.

DENNIS PARICHY: We did four separate productions of *Angels Fall*. Each time the script was significantly changed. It was Lanford's process of discovering what he was writing about and making it clearer to everyone else. *Angels Fall* seemed weak and confused when I first read it. Each production was part of the process of making the play the best possible.

After that many productions you get the feeling you've designed the play fully. When you have limitations of time or money, you often feel you have missed some little details here or there, that you have missed the tone in a particular scene, or that the production is slightly off somewhere. Usually, shows are limited runs and you don't have the time to fuss with them. You don't often get the chance, as we did on *Angels Fall,* to work on a project over a period of years.

Does your design process change when you have to work within a limited budget?

WILLIAM IVEY LONG: I always work with a limited budget. A million dollars can be a limited budget. I know no one will believe that or give me any sympathy whatsoever.

When you don't have the money to build costumes, you start collecting costumes from other productions, other theater companies, actors' closets, your closet. I had to wear a corduroy blazer to the opening night of *Nine,* my biggest show, because all my evening clothes were being used as costumes for another show.

When you have a tight budget, you really have to work closely with the director because you can't make mistakes. You can't just go in and throw out Act Two.

Even if you only have ten cents, you should do a design that is magical and really sums up the play, and then it's amazing how you can find things to make that design work. You shouldn't start with the negative approach of "I don't

have any money." Forget the money. Pretend—within reason—you've got the world. Design what is in your heart
of hearts.

LOREN SHERMAN: I usually put the budget figure in the
back of my head and don't think about it directly. You
can't worry about what each piece of scenery is going to
cost as you're designing it. You'd drive yourself crazy. Producers sometimes don't want to tell you the budget before you design, thinking it's going to limit you somehow,
but it's useful to know if the budget is $500, $5,000, or
$50,000.

Once the set is designed, it's tricky to have to cut it
down to fit the budget. If you have to cut it down too much,
you no longer even have your design. The design dissolves.
Sometimes you are better off designing more cheaply from
the start. Sometimes, with a great design, you can convince
the producers to find you more money.

When the budget is $500, you have to come up with a
$500 idea. It doesn't do any good to come up with a $50,000
idea. But just as there is a "best" $50,000 design, there is
a "best" $500 design for any particular play.

MARJORIE KELLOGG: All budgets are limited. The first thing
I say to the director when we have a severely limited design
budget is, "Look. You're not going to get everything." A
little bit of everything is not as good as a lot of a particular
design element. You can spread your resources so thin they
are almost invisible, and people wonder where the visual
impact is. Whatever leaps to mind as the most important
thing to make the play happen is where to put your money.
You have to figure out what the play's essence is and get
the most for the money you have, rather than shoot for the
moon.

MING CHO LEE: There are impossibly limited budgets. Sometimes a limited budget brings an increase in imagination. If you are given enough time, the distilling, the process of elimination, can give you something very strong with rich, sharp imagery. There are other times when the demands are so big and the budget so small that all your energy goes toward how-the-hell-to-put-it-on, and quality be damned.

It all depends on expectations. For example, if *K2* is done in a small room, I would not mind putting up a platform and calling it a mountain. It would be just as exciting. However, if you are in a normal theater—forty feet wide and twenty feet high—it will never work to put up a platform and call it a mountain. Each situation brings with it certain expectations, and those expectations must be fulfilled, or the audience will be disappointed.

JOHN LEE BEATTY: Imagination is a very idealistic word for the best way to design on a tight budget. The money matters, of course—it's very hard to do an entire set of mirrors if you can't buy the mirrors. That is a big problem, but you can arrive at the same idea with a different attitude.

Where you really get into trouble is in a large theater with a small budget, or the opposite: where the money does not match the situation. There is a sliding scale of perception on the part of the audience and the critics. I did a musical at Goodspeed Opera House and it got perhaps the best reviews I've ever received. The scenery was moved to Broadway pretty much intact, and there I got my worst reviews. What was really slick and glamorous in one setting looked small, tacky, and cheap on Broadway. The same scenery had moved out of its realm. Money is not a problem; appropriateness is.

ALLEN LEE HUGHES: I'm not going to do the same kind of lighting design for a production as I would for a workshop. The workshop might be done with clip-on white lights, but on Broadway it won't be clip-on lights and they won't be white. Because that's not what is appropriate.

You figure out what you absolutely need, or want, and then pare that down to what you absolutely have to have. Then do it. Part of the idea of theater is to have fun, but if you really care about the production and what it looks like, it is silly to do a show to which you don't think you can contribute your best. I remember almost doing *Hair* early in my career for a director who had fifty dollars and ten lighting instruments. *Hair* on ten instruments didn't interest me at all. Maybe someone else could have done it, and done it well. I would not change the way I design. A lot of bad lighting gets blamed on not having enough instruments. My job is to do lighting; it is someone else's job to get the money so that I can do my job properly.

DENNIS PARICHY: Usually, inherent in any play is a set of contrasts—dark scenes and light scenes, blue scenes and yellow scenes. The most important contrasts must be identified. On *Angels Fall*, whatever else I did, the *important* lighting task was that it appear to be hot outside the church and relatively cool inside. Nothing else mattered, as long as the audience understood that this place was a sanctuary, that people could come here for a moment and take a rest in their crisis-ridden lives, find out where they were coming from and where they were going. A simple contrast was set up, which helped make the dramatic situation plausible, concrete, and palpable. You must find that major contrast, or some other central lighting quality that is important, then decide how to light the actors most effectively within whatever budget you have.

Usually, at the climax, or the resolution or end of most

plays, there has to be something that is visually more stunning, more effective, than anything else in the show, or else the show doesn't have a final impact. The end of *Talley's Folly*, when Matt and Sally get into the boat and have their first kiss, should be an apotheosis of romantic, moonlit moments. In a sense, you have to design from that moment backwards. If you have limited numbers of instruments, you use what you have to make that climax work, and then you use the remaining instruments to do the rest of the show. The rest of the show doesn't have to be as vivid. I've learned you can't light every dramatic moment of the play with a special accent. If you give each important moment the same visual weight, none of them will mean anything. If you accent everything, nothing is accented.

PATRICIA ZIPPRODT: I never like to know what the budget is until I'm through my design work. I have people who must be covered up with costumes. I need to solve the design problems first and the fiscal problems later. If I have to think about how much money I've got for shoes, that will be in my way while I'm drawing a heel. I want to be as creative as possible, then readjust and redesign when I get bad news about the size of the budget. When you have to make compromises you always go back to the script for guidance.

JEFFERY BAUER: I try not to think about budgets until I have formulated a vision, a concept of the show. I don't want the thought of money to influence my initial vision. There is always a creative solution to communicate what you want with one hundred dollars, as well as one hundred thousand dollars. Almost every show has limited funds, and the budget size doesn't have to influence the design. It's nice to have a lot of money, but you can probably achieve the same effect, communicate the same mood, or establish the same historical period, with any given amount of money. It's like a car. A $5,000 car will take you to the same place as a $25,000 car.

After you have your initial ideas, you get involved in shifting, changing, "making do." This brings you to an essence of design. You distill your ideas down to a couple of simple, elegant design elements that can be as expressive as if you had filled the entire stage with elaborate scenery.

What's your working relationship with the director?

MING CHO LEE: Everything has to be filtered through the director. That doesn't mean that at some point, especially if I'm working on a new play, I won't talk with the playwright. If the director is keeping the playwright from entering into the process, I get a little bit nervous, because I wonder if a problem exists that eventually is going to infect the whole project. I prefer the director to express his personal excitement, how he feels about the play, to bring some kind of immediacy to the work, as if it is happening right here, or is happening to people you know. Sometimes, of course, they have to talk about theme, and theme is important, but talking about it is notetaking time. Eventually you have to get to the actual design for this production.

MARJORIE KELLOGG: Some directors I've worked with made the design process so painless it was astonishing. The two of us seem to share a kind of shorthand or sensibility. You can trust a director like that with rough sketches because the two of you are in tune; he can read your rough sketches the way you read them.

The design images are reached in concert with the director, over the telephone at first, then over coffee. Then over ground plans or in the theater itself, if you're fortunate enough to be able to sit in the theater for a while and dream. If you're lucky, the design just appears in your head. Then it's just a matter of working out the physical details.

There are also times when you and the director don't have this shorthand, or the director is not very visual. He may not be articulate enough, or he's not done his homework. Whatever the problem, he is unable to tell you what he really wants. You work your way through a number of ideas, and through his responses to these ideas you'll understand what it is he wants.

LOREN SHERMAN: I will talk to the director several times before I start to show him any designs. If we both think my ideas are a good approach to the script, then I become pretty wedded to what was agreed upon. I liked my design for *Baby With the Bathwater,* but both Jerry Zaks and Chris Durang were worried about it. I was going to rethink the whole thing, but after staring at the design for a couple of days I realized it was good. We did it and, at the end, they also thought it was a good design.

JEFFERY BAUER: A play I worked on a couple of years ago took place in a combination gas station/grocery store in the middle of farm country. The initial mood or feeling I had from the play was of a panorama, a strong horizon-line, and I saw light coming through cracks in wood. In that instance, the director liked the images and we were able to carry the design through.

The outgrowth of all these discussions is a preliminary ground plan. You really can't do anything without this. It might not be the same one you finish with, but it gives you something to play with. A lot will be dictated by the script. If the script says you have to have a door, then where do you put it?

DENNIS PARICHY: The most important thing to find out from the director is whether we are talking about the same play. We must understand the play in similar ways, or I at least have to know what the director feels so that I can adjust my own thinking. There are occasions when I think a director might be wrong about the play's meaning, but if I'm going to take the assignment, my job is to design the production the director has in mind, and not the production I might have in mind.

Sometimes I will have a conference with the director in which we don't even talk about lighting, except in the vaguest terms. I find that the most satisfying productions, the shows that just flow, are those in which the director and I talk about the play—what the characters are like, the relationships, the playwright's world—and out of that discussion comes a very clear idea of what I need to do. A specific set design, with a particular look, will say many things to me about the lighting.

MARJORIE KELLOGG: I will not work without a model of the set, because most directors only know how to work with models. Very few know how to read ground plans or a sketch. They look at a sketch and see what they want to see. That's very dangerous. With a model there is no possibility of confusion or misinterpretation. The model tells you, for instance, how big the set is, what the access is, where the actors can stand and where they can't.

If I have time I make a rough model out of white stock. I can then give the director scissors to play with—let him cut the model up, try things. If you spend little time putting together this model you have no commitment to it and don't mind slashing it. Of course, you still have a commitment to the ideas represented in the model.

Once you've got something everyone is happy with, you do a more finished, detailed model. The detailed model is the document you show the actors. It makes everyone relax about the set. It becomes a known quantity. Some directors need the model to be able to work the show out, but most, once the final design is agreed upon, keep the design in their heads. In most cases, the model vanishes from rehearsal pretty early on.

LOREN SHERMAN: I work mostly with models. I do rough sketches mainly for myself. I have no problem chopping apart a model with the director. At no point in the process should you feel the model is such a precious thing that you're afraid to experiment with it.

One of the reasons I don't like to rely on sketches is that a designer can make sketches that can be read in so many different ways that they don't really communicate anything in particular. I don't think anyone has problems reading models.

MING CHO LEE: Nowadays, when I make models I tend to include the first several rows of audience, and some sense of the proscenium arch, so you are looking at the set in the context of an audience instead of merely looking at it as a set. I feel that, unless you have those seats, you are really fooling yourself about the relationship of the set to the audience.

JEFFERY BAUER: A gray area exists as to what the designer and the director each bring to the design of the production. Sometimes it is totally up to the designer because the director doesn't wish or require input. A good bit has to come from the director, because he pulls the whole thing together.

What about working with the playwright on a new play?

MARJORIE KELLOGG: Playwrights tend to be very polite to designers. I've never heard one say, "You really made a mess of my play." I never know if I'm realizing the playwright's vision.

In the initial stage directions you are given a précis of the playwright's vision of how the play should look onstage. Sometimes it's a line saying, "Afternoon. On the street." Others, like Shaw, go into unbelievably detailed descriptions.

What I want to hear from the playwright is not where the door should be, but what effect the room should create on the audience's mind, and what the playwright *felt*, not *saw*, about that environment. What I'm good at is visualizing things. What the playwright is good at is expressing things in words.

I always want to know what the playwright had in mind. I always ask if the playwright is available. I always offer my phone number to the playwright so we can talk. Surprisingly, they don't often call. Most designers hunger to talk to the playwright. Knowing the playwright, understanding his personality, his point of view, can give you another insight into the play. It's another help to make sure you've got it right. It would be great to have the playwright at all the production meetings.

DENNIS PARICHY: Oftentimes the playwright is not directly involved with the lighting designer. Playwrights generally say very little to me. The set design seems to be the primary focus of the playwright. I often don't get involved in the process until at least the major outlines of the set design have been hashed out.

MING CHO LEE: After reading Marsha Norman's *Traveler in the Dark,* I realized it was kind of abstract, but at the same time not abstract. What is not written in the play is written in the scenery—one of the hardest things to design. I told the playwright I didn't know where the play was set. She said it was deliberately obscure. I told her I didn't know the season of the year. She said she always liked writing plays where someone puts on a sweater. Fine. That was all that I needed to start.

ALLEN LEE HUGHES: People are sometimes amazed that designers read the plays and are intelligent human beings.

JOHN LEE BEATTY: Sometimes I won't see a run-through of a show until it's on the set. Because I've not seen any rehearsals and I'm not daunted by the problems of the actors, or of rewriting, I'm seeing it with rather fresh eyes. I can be useful to the director even if I have only a few comments. This is the last time fresh eyes will see the show before previews.

JEFFERY BAUER: Having the playwright around is really valuable because you can answer questions for each other. If you can't find the answers, you make the necessary changes. When the playwright isn't able to be around I send him copies of renderings and ground plans, and we talk over the phone so that he is still included in the production.

MARJORIE KELLOGG: The playwright is so vulnerable. The producer feels he's bought the playwright. The director feels he's the playwright's father. The actors feel they are the playwright personified. What's left except to go across the street and drink? When a playwright is stubborn and willful, the process gets more interactive; the playwright has to be part of the team.

What about working with the actors?

PATRICIA ZIPPRODT: The actors come to my studio and I photograph them—front, profile, back. Thus I have both their images and their body measurements in my head while I'm designing. I design by accommodating and using their body types.

When I was designing *Accidental Death of an Anarchist,* I went to Patti LuPone's house. I tried her in skirts of different lengths, hats, berets, big jackets, small jackets—until we blocked out her best proportions. I wanted to get her into a very Italian, avant-garde look. I got hold of all the Italian fashion magazines I could, borrowed an element from this designer and an element from that one, and made this wonderful "mongrel" of an outfit that looked absolutely right on Patti.

WILLIAM IVEY LONG: Meeting the actors can throw all your plans into the trash can.

DENNIS PARICHY: I get a lot out of rehearsals, hearing the director discuss the play with the actors. I attend as many rehearsals as I can fit in, which gives me an insight into the inner workings of the characters. The way the actors are going to approach a scene, and the specific details they are adding, give me insight into the play, and thus my design.

JOHN LEE BEATTY: We all knew the floor of the set for *Fifth of July* was going to be old boards with cracks between them. Swoosie Kurtz's high heels went between all the cracks, and she couldn't walk across stage without her shoes being pulled off. This was a serious problem, but Swoosie insisted she wear her heels; they were important for the part.

If people have problems walking on cracks onstage, they'd probably have the same problem in real life. It seemed to me that in real life people would put carpets on the floors. I dragged in all these cruddy old carpets and started whacking them down on the floor. It dressed up the set a lot, and added another element, another facet to this family's house and to them.

JEFFERY BAUER: Unlike a costume designer, I don't get to work with the actors as much as I'd like. With a new play, you are much more involved because you go to many more rehearsals. I enjoy a certain amount of actor participation. After all, it is their environment, and their character has to be part of it. Actors usually are concerned about what sort of dressing or props will be on the set, but not about such things as doors. However, once I had to redesign a doorway for a six foot six actor. Other theater companies, in fact, have borrowed that doorway when they have used the same actor!

LOREN SHERMAN: A scene designer doesn't have to be as concerned with actors' egos as a costume designer does.

JOHN LEE BEATTY: I would never take a note from an actor and then go do something without asking the director. The director has the overall vision of where the production is going.

Describe your working relationship with the other designers on a production.

PATRICIA ZIPPRODT: Designers usually work closely, showing each other work. I place characters within the set designer's context or world. I set the characters' colors against scenic colors, their shapes against scenic shapes, their textures against scenic textures, so it becomes a unit of work. That's the ideal: an integrated whole.

DENNIS PARICHY: Lighting should support what the sets, costumes, and actors are doing.

JOHN LEE BEATTY: I like to meet with the director alone first. The set designer usually comes first in the production situation. From then on I like to get all the designers together with the director and the playwright. Often, the costume designer or the lighting designer will have an idea you don't. An important dress may often be involved in creating the color scheme of the entire show.

When all three designers get together, a lot of shorthand communication goes on. More often than not you have a source of inspiration, such as Monet, the pre-Raphaelites, Caravaggio, a page ripped out of a magazine, an advertisement, a piece of stained glass. You pass whatever it is around and talk about it, how it relates to the production design. That's basically how we develop a common approach.

LOREN SHERMAN: Perhaps this is scene designer chauvinism, but ideas for the set itself should come first. The set design locks in the overall approach and the other designers work within those boundaries. But it's nice to include the other designers early on.

If I design a set such that certain lighting positions can't be used, I, as much as the lighting designer, have lost those lighting positions. It's not one designer against another. We're all working on the same play.

ALLEN LEE HUGHES: Some set designers don't want the lighting designer around, which is probably due to a certain insecurity. I feel the lighting designer should be part of every production meeting right from the start. Even if I don't say a thing at a meeting, I can take in a lot of information that is going to help me. Sometimes a director may say that he sees the play as such-and-such, then not say so again or forget he said it. So if I'm brought in later in the process, I may miss information that is crucial to my designs.

JEFFERY BAUER: The production has to have a coherent design style. I'm tired of seeing productions where the actors are doing one thing, and the staging is doing another, and the design elements are somewhere else. I like to discuss with the director and the other designers how specific ideas are going to work together and be consistent with the chosen production style.

The more you decide together in early production meetings, the easier it is going to be later. In initial meetings, everyone's input is valuable. At later meetings— sometimes just with one of the other designers, or only the director—I discuss specific problems. The process varies with how willing your colleagues are to compromise.

WILLIAM IVEY LONG: In some of the productions I work on, we designers all work at the same time. But on most productions the set is already done when they call the costume designer in. The ideal thing is to have the designers sit and banter ideas around about the production. Design starts with "Hey, come look at this."

What advice do you have for designers ready to enter the profession?

MARJORIE KELLOGG: Young designers become involved in new plays instantly. They often begin their careers designing workshops and showcase productions, most of which involve new plays.

LOREN SHERMAN: Get to know directors and playwrights who are at the same point in their career as you are in yours. Work with them. Grow with them.

WILLIAM IVEY LONG: Designers are often misled in their training to feel that they are decorators, that only their nimble stitching fingers, not their minds, are important. A lot of designers don't want to dig in and become a part of the show. If you are interested in being part of a team, then it's worth making a fool of yourself, getting your hands dirty, doing five times the number of sketches just to realize an idea.

If you want to see the great designers at work, they're in New York. Young designers should study other design-ers. I am a pupil always. I'm a great fan of a dozen designers. I go to see all their shows, talk with them, study their sketches. There is always stuff to learn.

You have to start with the play, the written word, and then the director's dream. Designers are there to serve the play, to interpret it, and to give the playwright's words and ideas a physical reality.

DENNIS PARICHY: What a lighting designer sets down on paper when sitting at his drafting table is only the beginning of the design. The design is what you end up with when the show opens. You have to come into the theater with your lighting plot knowing you're going to change it, adapt it. It may take five days to figure out what to do to make just one moment work right. You fiddle.

When the play is evolving significantly throughout the rehearsal period, you may end up with a lighting plot rad-ically different from what you started out with. Your design slowly evolves into what has to be done for this particular show. That evolution is what is really exciting.

JEFFERY BAUER: First, there are certain skills, a craft, involved in designing that have to be learned. Whether they are learned in school or learned by doing is a matter of choice or circumstance. Second, being a designer is work. It is years of hard work. If you don't enjoy being a designer, don't do it. I'm convinced that when design stops being fun, I'll stop.

JOHN LEE BEATTY: It really helps to write down what you think about the *play*. After you've done that, see if it is reflected in the *design*. It's very hard, of course, when you aren't used to working on new plays. You feel very much at sea, yet you must realize that everyone else is out in that boat with you, too. If you trust the author and the director, and they trust you, some beautiful things can happen.

PATRICIA ZIPPRODT: Advice is hard to give because good advice is specific to the person receiving it. Every time I would ask one of my mentors for advice, the answer I'd get would be, "It doesn't matter what you do, *just keep working*." I would rail against that and have fits, but it is what *I* tell people now who are starting out. You solve more and more problems the more you work. You develop your style. You build work relationships that can serve well in the years ahead.

MARJORIE KELLOGG: When anyone asks me if they should go to graduate school I say yes, because designers today can't afford to have as many unskilled assistants around as they used to. Ming Cho Lee took me on virtually unskilled. There were two or three assistants in his studio then and

I learned from them as well. I picked things up, absorbed like crazy.

MING CHO LEE: The Master of Fine Arts program in design is deadly, too narrow. It is all about how-to and doesn't touch base with everything that feeds the theater, feeds the work. The range of essential humanistic knowledge for a designer makes mere knowledge of theater too remote and unreal and nostalgic. Suddenly the point of reference becomes so narrow, which I've found very frightening.

ALLEN LEE HUGHES: Advice? Just tell the story through your design. Make it accessible to the audience.

What is your design philosophy?

MARJORIE KELLOGG: Good design is design that's responsive to the play. I have seen some pretty designs that didn't serve the play, so what good are they?

DENNIS PARICHY: When I was young I thought I had to know everything at the beginning. I've learned that the process for the designer is as ongoing and evolutionary as it is for the actor and the director. You start with a rough sketch and end with a finished painting. It doesn't matter what you begin with, but what you finish with.

JOHN LEE BEATTY: The production is going to be best when it is itself, and unique. A world is created which is that play alone. When you approach a new play you don't want it to look like any other play. You don't want it to look like *Little Foxes* if it isn't *Little Foxes*. You have to reflect the script.

One problem is that a designer is only as good as the

script. There are plays I've followed right off the cliff. You can't design a play that isn't there.

ALLEN LEE HUGHES: People often don't realize the effect lighting has on a production. I've seen shows killed by bad lighting. Because theater is so integrated, if one element is off the whole production disintegrates.

Lighting, along with scenery, should tell you where you are. If you put something arbitrary on the stage, the audience looks at it and thinks, "Why is that happening?" While asking that question they've missed dialogue, they're not paying attention, and the production goes down the tubes. The script doesn't have a chance.

JEFFERY BAUER: The essence of theater is communication. Design is a form of communication. The audience hasn't met you, but they know who you are through what you put on the stage. We channel our entire personality and experience through what we design. The design has got to be true to the play or else it is art work instead of theater. When all the elements of theater come together, it's unbeatable.

MARJORIE KELLOGG: It is part of your responsibility as a designer to help the audience understand the play. You owe that to Shakespeare as much as to Lanford Wilson. Perhaps you can play around more with Shakespeare, but if you muddle Shakespeare you're being just as naughty as if you muddle Lanford.

You are a communicator as a designer; you're not just making pretty pictures. Your primary responsibility is to put the audience in the right frame of mind to absorb the play. By designing a lousy ground plan you can make the play impossible to happen.

WILLIAM IVEY LONG: We are not here for ourselves. I'm afraid that much design training supports this erroneous belief. We're not here to put a pretty dress on the stage. That pretty dress had better tell who that woman is; support her actions, supply a subtext. So few people understand this.

I've had producers ask me what show I've always wanted to do, or what style I've always wanted to design. I just look at them and think that they can't be real. That's the dumbest approach I've ever heard. You tell me what the play wants to say and I'll give you the best design I can.

MING CHO LEE: There is not a single play that does not touch somehow on culture, on values and human relationships. Theater has to speak to us. Theater design is not just turning out work, but absorbing the play and expressing it through your design.

THEATER COMPANIES
AND PRODUCERS

No matter how wonderful a playwright's play, no matter how inspired a director's interpretation of that play, it will not reach an audience without a theater company or a producer who is willing to finance a production.

Today's producers balance their love of the theater with an accountant's understanding of profit-and-loss statements. The economic pressures within professional theater have forced producers to test new plays through readings and workshops, instead of through the old-fashioned out-of-town tryout. The same pressures have encouraged regional theater companies to no longer wait for Broadway to supply next season's scripts. They have begun commissioning new plays, funding residencies for playwrights, developing new plays through workshops.

During the first half of the century, powerful producers found a play, called in a director, rounded up actors, dictated rewrites, and put on a *show*. Today's producers and theater company artistic directors are advised by literary managers and dramaturgs, specialists in theater history, literature, and criticism. The emphasis in contemporary theater has changed from the *show* to the *play*. Many of the major regional and developmental theaters in the country are run by artistic directors who were affected by the rise of the not-for-profit, Off-Broadway, and Off Off-Broadway workshop theaters of the late sixties. These men and women have been influenced by modern methods and attitudes, yet they retain their artistic ideals.

In this chapter, three major Broadway producers and representatives from six developmental theaters discuss their criteria for choosing plays, their feelings toward readings and workshops, and why they are committed to new plays.

Andre Bishop is the artistic director of Playwrights Horizons in New York. Playwrights Horizons has presented the work of over 200 playwrights, producing such plays as *Kennedy's Children, Vanities, Gemini, Coming Attractions, Say Goodnight, Gracie, Romance Language, March of the Falsettos, Sister Mary Ignatius Explains It All for You, The Dining Room, Geniuses, Isn't It Romantic,* and *Sunday in the Park with George.*

Thomas G. Dunn and Lynn Holst are the director and literary manager, respectively, of New Dramatists, a forty-five playwright workshop organization. New Dramatists has served over 500 playwrights by allowing them to work with actors and directors without the pressure of a production deadline. Among the current member-playwrights are Steve Carter, Gus Edwards, Amlin Gray, Jack Heifner, Emily Mann, John Olive, Eric Overmyer, John Pielmeier, Jeffrey Sweet, and August Wilson.

Peter Hay and David Parrish are the president and executive director, respectively, of First Stage, a workshop in Los Angeles for developing new plays. Among the playwrights and directors who have worked with the company are Terrence McNally, Paul Jarrico, Charles Nolte, John Patrick Shanley, Tom Alderman, Thomas G. Dunn, John Olive, Mark O'Donnell, Rene Auber-jonois, Paul D'Andrea, and Gail Wronsky.

Bill Hemmig is the literary manager for the Circle Repertory Company. Among its world premieres are *The Hot l Baltimore, When You Comin' Back, Red Ryder?, The Sea Horse, Knock, Knock, Fifth of July, Angels Fall,* and the Pulitzer Prize-winning *Talley's Folly.* Circle Rep has been honored with over one hundred awards including the Tony, Pulitzer, Obie, Drama Desk, Outer Critics' Circle, and Villager awards.

Bernard B. Jacobs and Gerald Schoenfeld are the president and chairman, respectively, of the Shubert Organization. The Shubert Organization operates seventeen theaters in New York, Chicago, Boston, Philadelphia, Los Angeles, and Washington, D.C. They have produced such plays as *The Gin Game, Master Harold . . . and the boys, Little Shop of Horrors, Children of a Lesser God, The Real Thing, Amadeus, Good, Ain't Misbehavin',* and *Whoopi Goldberg.*

Gail Merrifield is the director of new play development for the New York Shakespeare Festival/Public Theater. Under the leadership of Joseph Papp, the Festival has presented over 300 plays and musicals. Among their productions are *No Place to Be Somebody, Sticks and Bones, Short Eyes, For Colored Girls Who Have Considered Suicide When the Rainbow is Enuf, That Championship Season, Streamers, The Pirates of Penzance,* and *A Chorus Line.*

Lloyd Richards is the artistic director of the Eugene O'Neill National Playwrights Conference. The Conference has presented new plays by over 225 playwrights. During the Conference, the playwright is joined by a director, dramaturg, and actors in re-hearsing and rewriting the play. Each play is given two staged readings before public audiences, and after the performance all Conference participants discuss the presentation.

Frederick M. Zollo has produced the Pulitzer Prize-winning *'night, Mother*, and *Ma Rainey's Black Bottom, Hurlyburly, The Basic Training of Pablo Hummel, On Golden Pond*, and *Paul Robeson* on Broadway. Off-Broadway he has produced *Key Exchange* and *Funhouse*. In London, Zollo has produced *Breaking the Silence, Camille*, and *Glengarry Glen Ross*.

Why do a new play?

DAVID PARRISH: Ask Shakespeare, Molière, Shaw, Ibsen, Chekhov. Or, since none of them are around to answer, try Samuel Beckett, Eugene Ionesco, Harold Pinter, or Edward Albee, each of whom wrote new plays that someone believed in and that changed the face of contemporary drama. We remember the Elizabethan age for the *new* plays it produced; we study the drama of ancient Greece to see what was new *then*. New plays have always been the order of the day; revivals, rare. In five hundred years, no one will care about our productions of Shakespeare. Instead, they will look to see what our new plays were.

BERNARD B. JACOBS: Nothing else in the theater has the impact of a good new play. Good plays come along only rarely. Even if you go back to Shakespeare and count the plays that have had a significant impact, you're not going to find very many. When people say the theater is dead or dying, they mean that a really good play hasn't come around lately.

PETER HAY: Theater is not just an interpretative art, and original plays tend to push performers, designers, and directors to their creative limits. Lawrence Olivier called his favorite part that of Archie Rice, which he created in Osborne's *The Entertainer*. Not even the experience of playing the greatest classic roles can compete with the godlike feeling an actor has for a part he helped create.

BILL HEMMIG: If a theater has the remotest interest in serving playwrights, it has to do new plays. A theater that does just revivals is serving only its directors, actors, and designers.

Circle Rep was founded with the full cooperation of the playwright, director, and actor. Our resident playwrights don't write in isolation. They have a professional theater with all its resources behind them, and its entire staff ready to support them at any stage of the writing process in which the writer feels he or she needs help: from germinal idea, through first draft, all the way to a fully-mounted production.

And Circle Rep offers something that very few professional American theaters offer—a chance for the playwright to write for an ensemble of actors, to create roles for specific actors, which, as Lanford Wilson would probably be the first to tell you, makes the play richer as well as giving the actors a stronger sense of being partners with the playwright in creating the characters.

How do you and your organizations go about finding new plays and new playwrights?

GAIL MERRIFIELD: You find new playwrights in a great variety of ways. The Public gets at least three thousand scripts a year. We read every one. The longer you stay in the theater, the more likely it becomes that you'll find plays through friends. It's a good sign when a director brings in a new play. I like those close director-playwright relationships.

FREDERICK M. ZOLLO: I look at everything that comes to my office. I'll read the beginning, middle, and end of a script. I'd much rather read it by myself than go hear a reading by actors. I'd rather make up the voices and sets myself.

GERALD SCHOENFELD: The Shubert Organization can't see every play being done in New York and at the regional theaters. If we hear a worthwhile play is being produced somewhere, we'll go and look. Our network is large enough that we don't miss significant works. We also read hundreds of scripts that are submitted to us.

BERNARD B. JACOBS: We read about five or six hundred scripts a year. We look to see if a script both has the potential to be a Broadway success and says the sort of thing we think should be said on the stage. After seeing and reading a thousand or so plays a year, we come up with very few we really want to produce—our standards are very tough.

LYNN HOLST: When you're reading hundreds of scripts, you generally know what's good and what's not. You don't really miss much. I rarely don't finish a script, but I understand those people who think they can tell if a script is good or not in the first ten pages.

THOMAS G. DUNN: New Dramatists has two "slush" readers who read all the plays that come in. If both readers say no to a script, it goes back to the playwright. If they're split, a third person will read the play. Before we decide to invite the playwright to join New Dramatists, a total of seven readers read the two plays we ask the playwright to submit, and all seven readers have to be positive about his or her work.

DAVID PARRISH: At First Stage we don't so much look for new plays as look for new writers who we feel have potential. We have found writers through word-of-mouth, through relationships we have developed at such places as the O'Neill National Playwrights Festival and the Sundance Institute, and through production work at regional theaters.

Since First Stage does only readings and not full productions of plays, we are concerned entirely with the quality of the play and its potential. We don't have to consider budgets, audience appeal, or the casting difficulties inherent in a play. Our audiences have heard historical plays with casts of over thirty, minority plays from Hispanic and Asian writers, and plays in very sophisticated nonrealistic styles.

What attracts you to a new play?

FREDERICK M. ZOLLO: In all the plays I produce I look for a statement, a political, social, or emotional statement, that appeals to me. I speak through the playwright's voice. In *The Basic Training of Pavlo Hummel*, David Rabe's condemnation of the Vietnam War was a statement I wanted to make. I'm always excited by plays that are fearless: *'night, Mother, Hurlyburly, Ma Rainey's Black Bottom.*

My second criterion for choosing a new play is: Does the play have a unique language? The measure of a great playwright is his or her ability to create a unique vocabulary, a distinct voice. If you are an astute playgoer, you'll know the voice of David Rabe when you hear it. You'll know Lanford Wilson. You'll know David Mamet.

GAIL MERRIFIELD: The playwright's impulse has to be truthful and passionate. I never look for a particular kind of play or something on a particular subject. I'm constantly surprised by what people choose to write about.

ANDRE BISHOP: I try not to analyze the play as I read it. I work on instinct. I don't apply any critical functions to my reading of a play except those that are on automatic pilot. Of course I'm biased by certain things: who the author is, whether I've heard anything about the play, the title of the play, even the way the script is typed. All these things clue me into whether this is a play I want to do and, more important, whether this is a writer to whom I want to commit someone who will be able to take advantage of what Playwrights Horizons can offer.

BILL HEMMIG: Every theater has its own artistic vision, which usually boils down to the artistic director's personal vision for the theater. In order to give Circle Rep's artistic director, Marshall Mason, as broad a range of plays to choose from, I try not to put blinders on myself as to what is a Circle Rep play. I try not to look for any particular style, but simply look for the best plays I can find. The literary department channels our selections into Circle Rep's sit-down reading series, which is the first time Marshall gets to hear a play. From the reading, Marshall decides whether something is right for our company.

Circle Rep has a reputation for doing realistic plays. The play doesn't necessarily have to be realistic, but it must be peopled with three-dimensional, fully faceted human beings. We like characters that we can identify with and have an interest in as people.

BERNARD B. JACOBS: The quality of the writing attracts me. Also, the play must be a theatrical event, with confrontations an audience can relate to and characters an audience can sympathize with, characters who have an appeal. When

I'm considering a play, I also have to take into account who I can get to direct it, and what actors are available.

ANDRE BISHOP: When I read a play I read it more as an actor than as a critic. I immediately translate the play into something that exists in performance and not just on the page.

I'm attracted to idiosyncratic comedies. I believe comedy is a very difficult and honest way of writing. I'm upset when people dismiss comedy writing as fluff. The kinds of comedies we do at Playwrights tend to be rambunctious, iconoclastic, satiric, dark, socially relevant comedies. Someone once said that the writers at Playwrights were a bunch of "worldly wisecrackers."

GAIL MERRIFIELD: There is a certain kind of vitality in a good play regardless of the subject matter. I can sense it in a script I don't understand or even like, but when I can feel that surge of vitality I'll read the play again and again.

Reading a script is very difficult. I often read scripts out loud. What functions best in a play often is not evident on the page. I try to imagine the script performed in the very best production it can be given. I look for possibilities in the script, rather than for a finished product; something suggested but perhaps not developed. You try to make the playwright aware of what he or she has got.

If I already know the writer's work, of course I will read that personal knowledge into the script. James Lapine sent us a rough draft of a script. If it had said "Written by James Smith" on the cover I would not have known what to make of the play. Knowing Jim Lapine, however, I knew there was something there. That play turned into a magical work, *Twelve Dreams*.

ANDRE BISHOP: I decided to do James Lapine's *Table Settings* after reading ten pages of notes and dialogue. It was a very strong ten pages, theatrical and evocative of so many emotions.

LYNN HOLST: If you are reading a play and have a lot of "buts"—"I like this act, *but* . . ." or "This is an interesting character, *but* . . ."—the play probably won't be chosen.

You look for a play that is true to itself, that doesn't pander. You look for a voice that is honest, rings true. The writer must have a commitment to his or her play.

BILL HEMMIG: A play's theatricality is the first thing that excites me. One of my major criteria for judging the quality of the script is, "Does this have to be a play?" A play has to belong on the stage and can't be a film or television script. Plays can't just imitate real life.

GERALD SCHOENFELD: You can tell in the first few pages whether the person can write. If you decide the person can write, then you consider the dimensions of the project— how complicated is the script, what shape is it in, is there a particular director interested, a particular actor?

LLOYD RICHARDS: An artistic director gets very involved in production when considering plays. I'm concerned with the size of the cast, how the play will fit into my season, and whether I have the money to create the play's technical requirements.

BERNARD B. JACOBS: Budget is never a consideration when choosing a play. If you want to do a play, you spend what you have to spend in order to give that play the best possible production.

GAIL MERRIFIELD: Some plays are acting vehicles. If you could get a certain performer to be in it, you'd do the play; without the performer you might not do it. There's nothing wrong with doing a play for a specific actor. That's a glorious reason. The choice of a play doesn't always ride on the script.

Does the possible audience appeal of a new play come into consideration?

BERNARD B. JACOBS: Once you've decided you want to do a particular play, you have to determine what its audience is and how to go about attracting that audience. Every play has an audience. Some plays appeal to the young, some to the old, some to minorities. *For Colored Girls . . . ,* which you would think would have a big black audience, didn't develop a black audience until well into the run of the play. Sometimes, what you think will be the audience for a play turns out not to be. Different audiences perceive a play in different ways. If a play speaks to a minority issue, it does not mean the majority is not going to want to acquaint itself with that issue.

GAIL MERRIFIELD: When you read some plays you may think they will appeal only to a narrow audience, but you never know; you're always surprised. You'd think *For Colored Girls . . .* would appeal to a specialized audience, but it didn't. It played on Broadway for two years and toured all over the country.

ANDRE BISHOP: When I read something and like it, I do it. I don't test the play through umpteen readings or give the script to others for their opinions.

I read a play for what I think it *could* be as opposed to what it *is*. Everyone can find a million reasons for not doing a play. The script is just a blueprint for a production. A lot of people want to see everything "correct" on paper. I commit to doing the play and then go to work on it, instead of working on the play and then commiting to it.

GERALD SCHOENFELD: Authors whose work appeals to a limited audience, an audience that would not make the production economically feasible, are obviously not going to have their plays done on Broadway. Work that doesn't appeal to large numbers isn't deficient, but Broadway cannot force feed "culture" to an audience that does not want to be fed.

The idea that Off-Broadway or Off Off-Broadway, or regional theater, is doing "nobler" work than Broadway is absolute nonsense. Regional theaters are not surviving on Shakespeare, Chekhov, and Ibsen; they are surviving on tried-and-true American material, with a classic or two thrown in. What theaters produce reflects the audience's taste.

LLOYD RICHARDS: A subscription audience has an investment in the theater. They are investing in the personalities, in the product, and in the total life of a theater. For an audience, it's like going to dinner with good friends eight times a year. Occasionally, they aren't stimulating and the conversation is not always to one's liking, but that doesn't make these friends uninteresting people and it doesn't mean you shouldn't have dinner with them again.

Do you use readings or workshops to help you make a decision about doing a new play? To develop a new play?

LLOYD RICHARDS: There are no rules about doing workshops and there shouldn't be. The only valid question is: Does the play need it?

GERALD SCHOENFELD: The current glut of workshops reveals a lack of understanding of what workshops are supposed to accomplish. A lot of people use workshops as a means of raising money, as backers' auditions, or as an extension of the rehearsal period. A workshop should be for work—to rewrite, rework a play, so that by the end of the workshop the play is ready to go into rehearsal. If you come out of the workshop with the same play you went in with, you didn't need a workshop in the first place.

ANDRE BISHOP: A lot of the plays we do at Playwrights seem to give one impression on the page and another on the stage. I'm a great believer in developing a play on your feet in readings, in rehearsals, and in preview performances. We do a lot of readings—around-the-table, or with the actors sitting on stools.

GAIL MERRIFIELD: Some plays are too visual to put through readings. Some plays don't exist without the collaboration of the director, designer, performer, and even musicians. Some plays take imagination to visualize in production.

Our readings at the Public are always individually tailored to the project, but our objective is always the same: to get a script to the point where we can go into rehearsal. Sometimes we'll just sit around and read the play, with no one invited to hear it. We'll have readings of just one act; we have had plays that we've read over the course of a year, testing little sections along the way. We try to make the play as strong as possible before the final step, reading it for Mr. Papp's approval.

BERNARD B. JACOBS: Readings can fool you. I'm much happier if I'm given a script and can go home, read the play, and make my own judgment. My gut feeling after reading a play is pretty accurate.

FREDERICK M. ZOLLO: I don't do readings for myself. I do readings for directors and actors who are thinking of being involved in a play I'm producing.

LYNN HOLST: A reading doesn't tell you everything about a play. But it's the first time a writer hears the play outside of his own head. And that's important. The least successful readings are those that attempt to be productions. The less staged the reading is, the better. It serves the playwright better.

It's good to have an audience present at a reading. It helps the actors; it gives the playwright a more complete sense of what effect the play will ultimately have. I don't like audience discussions. I usually recommend a discussion the day after the reading, a discussion comprised of a couple literary managers from other organizations, a director, another playwright. The playwright can hear what pleased and what confused people who have a good theater sense.

BILL HEMMIG: Our theater's subscribers can come to see Circle Rep's staged readings. Marshall Mason or I will lead a discussion afterwards. If you hear enough people say, "I don't like this character," you know there is a problem, even though it might not really be that character but, rather, the direction or the performance. The playwright gets an idea of what to look at during the next round of rewrites.

LLOYD RICHARDS: The O'Neill National Playwrights Conference is based on the precepts of radio: You go in, get a script, read through it once, make cuts, read it through again, stand up, and act it. That system takes advantage of the honest, instinctive impulse of the actor. That impulse is sometimes closer to the emotional truth than anything you'll see again.

THOMAS G. DUNN: Staged readings are almost of no value. Frankly, you can get the same response from a sit-down reading. Many writers, after seeing a staged reading of their play, seem to think the play's finished—after all, they've seen the actors moving around "like" a performance.

New Dramatists' nonperformance workshops let the playwright sit around for a week to ten days with a director, dramaturg, and actors working on the script. Since there's no performance pressure, anything can be tried. For instance, if the playwright hasn't quite figured out the end of Act One, the director can have the actors improvise on that situation for an hour or so and the actor's work might help the playwright.

DAVID PARRISH: In a good staged reading the playwright gets to hear a reasonably accurate presentation of his play by actors who are reasonably well-cast and led by a director who has a reasonable understanding of the work. In a staged reading, the play is being tried out in a "performance" much closer to the final goal of the production process than if you used a sit-down reading.

PETER HAY: I do not think much of unrehearsed sit-down readings; sometimes they work by chance or because of the skills of the actors involved, but more often they are useless. Staged readings—with two or three rehearsals and done by experienced performers and a director—can be very helpful both for a theater company and for the playwright.

Most script development is done by the writer, alone or with the help of a dramaturg or director. But when a draft is completed, it is useful to hear it and have a discussion among knowledgeable and caring professionals about the play's strengths and weaknesses. An open discussion, although the playwright must be wary of which advice he takes, gives him access to a diversity of viewpoints, which he will not receive again until after the play is produced.

BILL HEMMIG: At Circle Rep sit-down readings are a forum for the company and staff to get together, listen to a new play, and discuss whether the play is a project our company should pursue.

On the basis of that sit-down reading we decide if the play is going on to a PIP, our play-in-progress series, which is essentially a rehearsed staged reading. A PIP is directed, fully cast, and gets two weeks of rehearsal. All together there are four performances: on the Monday and Tuesday of two successive weeks. After the first two performances, the playwright can rework the script, rehearse any revisions, cuts, or additions during the intervening week, and put up the changed script for the final two performances.

One example of our play development process, *As Is*, started as a thirty-minute one-act play, a series of scenes between two men, one of whom had AIDS. Marshall Mason decided to do a PIP of the play so that the playwright [William Hoffman] could work on it. Marshall gave the playwright some wonderful notes about enriching the relationships and bringing different kinds of people into the play to expand the play's world. The two of them did a lot of work, and what audiences finally saw on Broadway was a very different play from the PIP version, which had much more of a documentary feel to it. The great variety of secondary characters did not exist or were much smaller in importance. It was so exciting to watch the play grow.

So many theater companies have hired dramaturgs and literary managers. What are they and what are their responsibilities?

PETER HAY: A production is composed in part by a performance that lasts only a few hours and cannot be repeated, and in part by a text which is adapted to the performance but survives it. Almost everybody in the theater is exclusively concerned with performance; the dramaturg concentrates almost wholly on the text and how it is interpreted. The dramaturg is responsible for ensuring that the dramatist's intent is fully realized by the company and the play's meaning understood by the audience.

In advising the artistic director of a theater on both new and classic plays, the dramaturg will try to make a connection between the text and the concerns of the community: a production of *Othello* or *Ghosts* will be differently received in Mississippi than in San Francisco. This connection is achieved through a variety of means: textual research and analysis; discussions with the director and designers on the artistic concept, with the publicity department about promotion, and with audiences and teachers through program notes and special forums.

In rehearsal the dramaturg assists the director in translating the meaning of the text, as lucidly as possible, into the context of where it is being performed and for whom. This role of the in-house critic can only be performed in an atmosphere of collaboration and mutual respect.

The literary manager, whether the same or a separate person from the dramaturg, is in charge of the literary department of a theater. As a manager, he or she will solicit and receive scripts from agents and writers and ensure that these are read promptly, with critical feedback to the writer whenever possible. The literary manager is responsible for advising the artistic director on plays, especially those by local writers. The literary manager will also be informed about new plays that are being produced in other parts of the country and the world, and will evaluate whether they could be obtained and produced locally. A good literary manager will actively seek out local writers, encourage them to write for the specific needs of the theater company and work closely with them toward that end. The literary manager may champion their cause within the company, advocating commissions, residencies, and, above all, productions of their work.

What is your working relationship with the playwright?

ANDRE BISHOP: As a producer you have to be able to see what the writer is going for and help expand that impulse. I want to make sure the author and I are on the same track with the play. You only go crazy in the theater when each voice—playwright, director, producer—thinks the play should be something different.

DAVID PARRISH: Of course each play is completely different. When I see problems in a play while preparing a reading, I might *suggest* what they are to the writer, if I feel the writer is open. I prefer to wait until I feel a problem is completely evident—usually in a second read-through with actors. One needs simply to read, rehearse, and present the play open-mindedly.

LYNN HOLST: So often the playwright doesn't know what he or she has written. My role as dramaturg is not to impose my view of the play on the playwright. A playwright should be allowed to founder for a while.

PETER HAY: My first concern is to determine what the playwright has wrought. What is the intent of the play and has it been realized? The commonest mistake is to sweep aside or ignore what the writer wants to say and substitute what you—producer, director, or star—want to say. This fundamentally alters the relationship between you and the writer; it also detaches the writer from his or her original concept. It means that you will only be relating to the writer's skills, not to those deeper areas of his self where all genuinely creative work originates.

After I understand the intent of the play—by also asking the writer as many questions as necessary—I will focus on those areas where there are problems. I state the largest concerns first: It is a distraction to discuss what the butler wears or says, if the entire scene in which he appears needs to be cut. Examples of common problems include such things as lack of thematic clarity, uncertainty about genre or structure, no through-lines for characters, undramatic dialogue or monologues, and too much narrative or past tense rather than dramatized action.

Discussing such points, no matter how kindly or convincingly, is useless unless the writer feels I have really understood what he or she is trying to do and am essentially on his or her side. And only when he or she is really listening will the writer be able to integrate my criticism with the feelings and thoughts that went into the script in the first place. After all, it is the writer, not I, who will be doing the revisions.

LLOYD RICHARDS: You are working with the playwright from the moment you consider producing the play. Working with the playwright is like a marriage. You've got to be certain you are speaking the same language. Production is a very intense time for people who are not communicating. When you first meet with a playwright, you try to discover if you can communicate in a productive way about his material. You can't wait to ask the hard questions. Everything must be on the table before you make the commitment to producing a play.

What is your role in rehearsals?

GAIL MERRIFIELD: My job, director of play development, is really done once the play goes into rehearsal. If I'm asked, I will always go to rehearsal and tell them what I think.

FREDERICK M. ZOLLO: While we're in rehearsal I'll only talk to the director about the actors. I give specific notes. It's up to the director to take them or leave them.

GERALD SCHOENFELD: I know very few playwrights who would allow the producer to have the input of a dramaturg. I will read scripts and tell the author what I did and didn't like, but I will not tell him line by line what to rewrite. I might say that a particular character needs more development, or that a particular scene doesn't ring true.

ANDRE BISHOP: If the director is capable and the cast is good, and the design elements coalesce, I tend to leave rehearsals alone. I'll watch the first or second run-through of the play and then talk with the director and author. I'm basically going in to see if the production is coming together. Is it on the track we—playwright, director, producer—thought it would be? I never go into early rehearsals with a pad and take notes.

I'll go again to a later run-through, this time focusing more specifically on certain scenes or actors. I feel it's very bad to jump the gun and start rewriting the play before the production of the play is formed. From the tech rehearsals on I'm there all the time, urging everyone on. And, of course, I'm at all the previews. It's my favorite time, because it's a time of enormous terror and excitement. You have no idea how the play is going to be received. All these changes are being made as we see what works and what doesn't, what an audience will accept and what it won't. During previews I give very specific, detailed notes to the director about the staging, the acting, rewriting, and any minor adjustments that have to be made. As the production gets more polished there are more notes because you focus on details. It's a long process; you have to learn to be patient.

BERNARD B. JACOBS: The average producer doesn't get very involved in the creative work of a production. I get involved as little as I can. If I do get involved, it is in such a way that I am not perceived as exerting any force. What a producer says tends to have much more impact than it should have. It is essential that the director and the playwright feel comfortable.

FREDERICK M. ZOLLO: You find a new play you want to produce, a new playwright you want to work with. You attract the right director. Then the three of you sit down and do the work. We—producer, director, playwright—worked together for eight or nine months on the script of *Hurlyburly*.

What is your advice to theaters interested in producing new plays?

FREDERICK M. ZOLLO: Every theater's season should be balanced. Classics and new plays; comedies and dramas. If you have a season of two plays, one should be new. Doing a new play increases the community of playwrights by one. A playwright isn't a *real* playwright until he's had something produced.

LYNN HOLST: Once yours is known as a theater that does new work, you'll receive new scripts all the time. A theater should also encourage local writers.

BILL HEMMIG: Bring in playwrights who will excite your directors. Bring in directors and playwrights who already have working relationships. Instead of just looking for scripts, look for writers who are compelling. Developing writers is more exhilarating than developing a script and never hearing from the writer again.

THOMAS G. DUNN: There are many actors and directors running around trying to start theater companies, but so many begin without really thinking of what they're going to do. They should start by finding a playwright they want to work with. Instead of being like ninety other theater companies, you'll be distinctive; you'll be known as having a particular vision that you share with a particular playwright.

Also, an emerging theater company can make a much stronger case with the public and with granting organizations by having a particular playwright or two as a focus. You can add more resident playwrights to your roster as your company grows. It's much easier than opening your doors and inviting thousands of submissions.

For many young theater companies, one-acts are a good way to begin working with new plays. It's easier to evaluate the script, and by doing three plays in an evening you can present three different playwrights and not worry about putting all your eggs in one basket. If one of the three plays is a great success you might consider commissioning the playwright to do a full-length play for your next season.

What is your philosophy of producing new plays?

GAIL MERRIFIELD: I truly believe that the theater has the capability of making a powerful connection with an audience. That connection can be very beautiful, enriching, informative. I want to do plays that reach the greatest number of people, with a direct exchange of emotion between the actors and the audience. That's what theater is all about.

FREDERICK M. ZOLLO: I think we're in a renaissance of American playwriting. For the first time we have American voices we've not heard from this strongly before—especially women and blacks. Before, I could name only one major American woman playwright: Lillian Hellman. Now, currently writing, we have Wendy Wasserstein, Marsha Norman, Beth Henley, and others. Among blacks we have Charles Fuller, Samm-Art Williams, August Wilson. And these new voices are being produced on Broadway—that's very unusual and a very good sign for the theater.

ANDRE BISHOP: Theater remains a verbal medium. I find some*thing* new being said by some*one* new very satisfying. But no new play, no matter how wonderful it may be, can make it in the theater without a first-rate production. It's my responsibility to make sure the play—and the playwright—gets that production.

GERALD SCHOENFELD: If you have commercial success, terrific. If the play is also an artistic success, marvelous. If you have an artistic success and a commercial failure, that's terrible.

FREDERICK M. ZOLLO: The rewards of doing a new play are so enormous. It's uncharted territory; it's your territory. The new play goes into the literature with your imprint on it, whether you're an actor, director, producer, or designer. That's a huge responsibility, but it's the only way the theater can grow, develop, evolve.

CRITICS

Critics, for better or worse, are instrumental in the success or failure of a new play. A new play has litle chance of surviving without the critics' nod.

A critic has to be particularly perceptive about untested plays, open to new voices, new ideas, new forms of theatrical expression. Critics have to fight against a very human prejudice to dismiss anything unfamiliar, anything out of the ordinary.

Throughout the history of American theater, instances abound where the critics have almost single-handedly championed a new play or playwright. The Chicago critic Claudia Cassidy brought Tennessee Williams to the attention of the American theater public by literally dragging people to see the original production of *The Glass Menagerie*. On the other hand, any theater buff can tell you unhappy stories of reviews of the original productions of such plays as O'Neill's *The Iceman Cometh*, Sam Shepard's *True West*, or Lanford Wilson's *Fifth of July*. In these cases, the critics were confronted with a remarkable play, but because of an inability to differentiate the play from a less than perfect production, or an unwillingness to listen to a changed voice, a majority of the critics did not give the play its due.

With ticket prices soaring, the theater public has come to rely more and more on the critic to say what play is worth seeing, what performance worthy of applause. And with fewer and fewer newspapers publishing, the individual critic's influence has expanded.

The following eight critics offer their opinions on the underappreciated art of theater criticism. They discuss, among other topics, what attracted them to criticism, their backgrounds and training, what they feel are their responsibilities, and what for them makes compelling theater.

Michael Feingold, *The Village Voice*.
Mel Gussow, *The New York Times*.
Wayne Johnson, *The Seattle Times*.
Edith Oliver, *The New Yorker*.
Frank Rich, *The New York Times*.
John Simon, *New York*.
Mike Steele, *The Minneapolis Star and Tribune*.
Linda Winer, *USA Today*.

What attracted you to criticism? What is your training as a critic?

EDITH OLIVER: Despite my lack of training I have the basic requirement for a critic, which is that I am stagestruck and have been for life. You simply cannot do the job unless you are stagestruck.

Growing up, nothing in my family was considered an occasion unless it entailed taking us to the theater. I have been going to the theater for well over sixty years.

MICHAEL FEINGOLD: I'm only half a critic. The other half is playwright, translator, dramaturg, director. My "training" is that I've been interested in the theater all my life.

I majored in comparative literature at Columbia University, where I started writing reviews—of all the productions I wasn't cast in—for *The Spectator*. After Columbia I got an MFA in criticism at Yale. I spent seven more years there as literary manager of the Yale Repertory Theatre. I also translated about twenty plays and directed new play readings.

WAYNE JOHNSON: Theater has been a passion of mine for a long time. I've written plays, and I think that's an important part of how I look at new plays—from the point of view of somebody who has been there and has some notion of the kind of trauma and joy that is involved.

JOHN SIMON: I began as a poet and a teacher. I enjoyed both greatly, but when teaching became sour and poetry left me, the natural thing was to write criticism. If you combine poetry and teaching and apply them to works of art, you've got criticism.

MEL GUSSOW: My interest in the performing arts goes way back. Theater slowly became a specialty of mine. I cannot think of myself as a trained critic in the sense that some of the young critics today are, having studied dramaturgy and criticism as an academic course at Yale and other places. If I have any credential at all, it's having been a critic in excess of twenty years, having seen a lot of plays and having weighed them according to what I have seen before.

I've always been interested in literature, and I approach theater from the text rather than from the practical side. My background in the practical theater is rather limited, as is the case with most critics. Certainly critics could use much more knowledge of the practical side of theater.

FRANK RICH: I've always been interested in journalism and in the theater. Through an evolutionary process, drama criticism became the best way for me to combine both worlds. I don't think there is such a thing as formal training for a critic. There are very few professional drama critics in this country or in England who went to drama or journalism school.

LINDA WINER: I wanted to be a veterinarian. When I dropped out of pre-vet I got a degree in music. When I was almost through college, my uncle read an article on a Rockefeller Foundation program for the training of classical music critics. I wrote four dummy reviews and I ended up in the program.

When I was coming up, it was believed that critics were

either self-taught or that they just hatched. Up until very recently, no formal education for critics existed. There is still nothing like a degree in criticism, but most universities recognize the need for training, so there are at least courses.

Almost every critic fell into this business; virtually no one started out at age five saying, "I want to be a drama critic."

MIKE STEELE: I'm informed by my mother that I said I wanted to be a critic as early as age eleven. I used to paw through old *Theatre Arts* magazines and read the critics on the latest New York openings.

What do you feel are the responsibilities of the critic?

JOHN SIMON: A theater critic's responsibilities are to be three things: One, to be as good a writer as he possibly can. Two, to be as good a teacher as he possibly can. Three, to be as good a thinker, or, if one dares to be pretentious, as good a philosopher as he can.

As a writer you are responsible to yourself to write as well as exacting standards dictate. As a teacher, you reach out to everyone who is interested in the field you are writing about, whether it is architecture, fine arts, or theater. This includes those working in these fields, those interested in these fields, and even those not particularly interested in these fields. But perhaps those last readers become so hooked by the way you write about the particular art that you can drag them into becoming interested in these fields. As a thinker or a philosopher, you hope to be of interest to humanity at large because the theater deals with human problems. The playwright certainly is concerned with the quality of life, and the critic, in interpreting what the playwright and his fellow artists have done, is also concerned with the quality of life.

MIKE STEELE: I feel the critic has two chief responsibilities: One, to bring aid and comfort to audiences by giving them good descriptions of the theatrical event, interpretation and analysis to stimulate their perception of it, and as much other information as I can to enhance their experience; and, two, to bring a firm but sympathetic outsider's view to the theatrical experience, as someone with no vested interest in the event.

MEL GUSSOW: The main responsibility of the critic is to be as true to an event as he can not to color it with false emotions of one kind or another. One great danger—a pitfall that many critics fall into—is to feel pressed to decide firmly one way or another to say "This is good," or "This is bad," or "Go see it," or "Stay away from it."

In terms of making up one's mind, most things fall somewhere in the middle. It's rare that we'll see something amazing, magnificent. Almost as rare is something completely meretricious.

I don't feel I am here to instruct an audience about what they should or should not see. The main thing to get across is what the playwright is trying to do, how well he did it, and whether there is any value to what he did. Second, I make some judgment from my point of view about the play and the production. Third, I say whether this is something the audience might want to see. By writing a favorable review of a play I'm encouraging an audience to go see it.

EDITH OLIVER: Your only true responsibility is to tell the audience what you saw. If you do it well enough, you almost don't need an opinion. It's nice if you can be witty, but you must be truthful.

I see criticism primarily as reporting. I think when you do criticism properly, you see something in the work that nobody ever has seen before. You also have to be able—though I don't think any critic does it well enough—to celebrate when something wonderful happens.

WAYNE JOHNSON: The basic responsibility we critics have is to be as accurate as we can. A critic must be sufficiently informed, sufficiently charged, and sufficiently perceptive to be able to have a clear fix on what is happening and to be able to report that as clearly as possible.

LINDA WINER: I think the critic's only responsibility is to have credibility. I am not a part of the theater community and I'm not telling people how to write plays. I am a part of the audience talking to the audience, whether that audience is who-saw-it-last-night or someone who will see the show in five years. I share my reactions. If a playwright or someone else can get something out of the review, that's great, but that's not my job. I don't even presume to talk to them.

FRANK RICH: My major responsibility as a critic for the *Times* is to the readers of the paper more than to the theatrical community. The least important part of criticism is the judgment the critic renders. The most important part is the quality of the writing and the process by which the critic renders that judgment. The critic must serve a reportorial function by re-creating the excitement or lack of excitement of an event he saw take place on stage. If he does that job well enough, intelligent readers can often make their own judgment about the various qualities of a play and performance, regardless of the judgment the critic has made.

Too much of what passes for criticism these days is just unsubstantiated opinion, which is worthless. A "critic" who gives only an opinion is no more of a critic than someone who comes out of the theater saying, "I liked it," or "I hated it." The excitement and the responsibility of the critic's job are in describing a theatrical event as vibrantly as possible and in explaining *why* it succeeds or fails.

The critic also has a responsibility to be fair to the artists involved, not just to render flip judgments, but to explain the basis for those judgments. People can debate your reviews if you put the evidence on the table.

What do you look for when reviewing a play? What criteria and personal biases inform your criticism?

JOHN SIMON: I don't know what comes to me first, or second, or third. A production comes rushing at you in one bundle. I firmly believe a critic perceives a play the way any other human being does, with whatever heart, head, emotions, passions, prejudices, and hopes he or she may have. There is no such thing as looking at a play from a critic's perspective, as opposed to an ordinary theatergoer's perspective. The basic process, the production coming at you and your response, is the same. I don't go to the theater looking for this, that, or the other thing. I go looking for the whole experience, whatever it may be.

MEL GUSSOW: A great problem for the critic is the matter of deciding what the strong elements and the weak elements are. Criticism means weighing a lot of things, because you not only have to worry about the script, and the performances, but also about the lighting and the scenery (which are things that most critics are not really qualified to judge adequately).

LINDA WINER: What strikes you is a function of the particular play and production you're watching. Some productions are all about the acting. Some are all about the script, especially productions of new plays. I don't have a yardstick by which to measure all plays and all productions. You don't show up on opening night with a preset list of things to look for.

There are plays I don't particularly care for, but which I know certain of my readers would enjoy seeing—such as most light comedies. I have to remember not to give in to my personal prejudices when writing my review.

WAYNE JOHNSON: You have only your own eyes and ears, your prejudices, sensitivities, and insensitivities. You try to look at the play and describe it as accurately as possible. Opinions are implicit. I don't like reviews that begin with "I thought this."

I go into the theater saying, "What do you have to tell me about my world?" That approach affects the way I write. I don't see myself so much as a standard setter or king's taster, but as an enthusiast among enthusiasts.

The critic carries his own load of emotional and mental garbage when he goes to the theater. If you've got a headache or your stomach is aching, you're not really a good receptor of what's going on. A number of years ago, I went through a divorce and I was aware at the time that I was not being totally fair to the productions I was watching. I was so preoccupied with my own life that I found it difficult to get occupied with the life of anyone onstage.

MIKE STEELE: I have no checklist of what a play must have or not have. I do carry biases and intellectual baggage into a play with me, and will probably argue against certain types of plays, though I hope with the fairness to acknowledge whether or not the play is a good example of its genre.

My tendency is to work backwards on a new play, to have a gut reaction to it, and then figure out why it caused or didn't cause certain responses.

FRANK RICH: There is a delicate balance between the objective reporter and the subjective critic. Inevitably, what you choose to report is going to be refracted through your sensibility. If you are specific enough in your writing, I think the reader can judge if your review is fair or not by how the evidence is chosen and examined.

You must confess your biases and your blind spots to the reader. If you love *Measure for Measure*, a play a lot of people don't like and which is infrequently produced, that would be a prejudice worth stating to let people know that you might be more sympathetic to a production of that play by virtue of its very existence.

MICHAEL FEINGOLD: As critic you are a person who is going to the theater to see a play. You sit in the audience. You see the play. You respond. What is it? What effect does it have on you? What impression does it make on you? You have the experience the performers are giving you and, at the same time, in the back of your mind, you analyze the experience and take it apart as a critic. You have to disassemble the experience the production team has painstakingly assembled. You are dismantling your own experience as it occurs. It's a difficult juggle, but it is your obligation to your readers and to the artists.

The best thing to do as a critic is to state in the review what you have at stake. Let the reader know you have biases. I loathe critics who pretend that they are above it all. Everyone is prejudiced. Everyone has biases. Criticism is about your personal biases. That's the whole point: to give a perspective—your perspective. Criticism that doesn't have a personal commitment is not good criticism.

EDITH OLIVER: When I am reviewing a play, the playwright's intention is none of my business. I am concerned only with what he has done, not with what he is trying to do, which, for the most part, he himself doesn't know anyway.

My main prejudice? I hate monologues. With most monologues, I wonder who the character is talking to; he has not been introduced to me, so he can't be talking to me.

FRANK RICH: In writing a review, one does not enter a theater with a report card of categories to check off or grade. New plays are not graded against the theater of last year, or of antiquity; you take a new play on its author's own terms. I try to go to the theater open-minded, with no predisposition as to what the criteria of judgment are going to be, but, rather, to respond to what I am seeing. It is only later, when I am writing, that I work backwards from my visceral and emotional or intellectual response and figure out the whys and wherefores. Seeing a new play, I'm either moved, or bored, or irritated, or whatever, and the writing forces me to articulate the reasons for that reaction. I dig into myself and try to find out what those reasons may be.

Even within a specific genre there is much room for artistic variation and different critical criteria. *Hurlyburly* and *The Marriage of Bette and Boo*, both comedies by contemporary writers of roughly the same generation, with unique ends and stylistic means, are judged by different criteria. You couldn't fault *Hurlyburly* for not being like *Bette and Boo*. Their individual successes and failures have very little in common.

You go into the theater open-minded, but not as an idiot. If you go in weighed down with a checklist of what you are going to look for, you are probably foreclosing the possibility of having a real response.

How is reviewing a new play different from reviewing a revival?

MIKE STEELE: Increasingly, revivals are so extensively reinterpreted that they become much like new plays, which require immense concentration and close attention.

MICHAEL FEINGOLD: I don't think you approach new plays and revivals differently. I always find myself quoting film critic Robert Warshow's famous line about why he liked certain genre films, such as westerns, "A man watches a movie, and the critic must admit that he is that man." It reduces down to that.

EDITH OLIVER: I try, when dealing with revivals, to forget the original production as much as I can.

WAYNE JOHNSON: In the best of all possible worlds, the reviewer goes into the theater every time as a virgin. The critic may be seeing *Cherry Orchard* for the twenty-fifth time, but because there is no perfect *Cherry Orchard*, it's always like seeing a new play. There are resonances of previous productions, however, and you make comparisons to those productions whether you want to or not.

You have to give the new play the benefit of the doubt. The twenty-fifth time you see *Cherry Orchard*, if you don't believe the performances in the first ten minutes, you might as well leave. If the actors can't handle the first ten minutes of that play, they won't be able to handle the rest of it. If you go to a new play and the first ten minutes don't quite work, you don't dare walk out because the playwright may just not know how to write opening scenes, and the second act might knock your socks off.

Do you feel you can do justice to a new play after one viewing?

JOHN SIMON: If justice exists at all, it exists in heaven, and therefore probably does not exist. You do as well, as honestly, as enthusiastically, as dedicatedly as you possibly can. You can only bring an individual, original perception to the play—which is not quite the same thing as justice. It is one of the raw materials of justice. Only time can tell if you hit the nail on the head, or on the side, or not at all.

MEL GUSSOW: You really have to do justice to the play after that one viewing. One help for theater reviewers now is that we can go to previews, so we have more time to think about the production. The more time I have to think about it, the more justice the review would do to the work at hand.

WAYNE JOHNSON: No critic can do justice to a play on the basis of one viewing. I don't care how perceptive or articulate the critic is, there are going to be levels of things happening on the stage that the critic is not going to be able to get the first time through. Even if the critic gets them, he's not going to have the time to consider all the implications fully. Nor is he or she going to have the time or space in the review to express all those feelings.

MIKE STEELE: One obviously writes better about a new play after seeing it more than once. Frankly, most of the time this isn't necessary. Sometimes, given the realities in a busy theater town like Minneapolis, it isn't possible.

FRANK RICH: I feel complete justice cannot be done to a play after one viewing, but fairly full justice can. I believe strongly in seeing the play only once before writing my review. You may miss some details, but the responsible critic will absorb more than the casual theatergoer. It's the critic's job.

An audience, by and large, is not going to see a play more than once. That a critic only sees it once before writing his review puts him on a par with the reader. What a critic gets out of the play by seeing it once is roughly what an audience might get out of it—at least at the gut, if not the theoretical level.

If you see a show more than once before that initial review, you lose the spontaneity of response, which is very important to the writing of your review. When you see something for the second time, you have lost the first exciting blush of response.

I will often go back, again and again, to a play I like. I may write another piece about it. For instance, I wrote about *Fifth of July* at least three or four times. You keep getting more out of something that rich in subsequent viewings.

LINDA WINER: Most of the time, when I see a show again I get more details. The things that hit me the first time continue to be true each time I see it.

How do you separate the play from the production? Have you ever re-reviewed a play and found your opinion changed on subsequent viewings?

JOHN SIMON: In terms of separating the playscript from the production, each group—playwrights and critics—is eager to believe that it knows, or that the other one does not know, the difference. As always, the truth is somewhere in the middle. It is very hard to separate the production from the play.

How this separation is reached is based on two things. Experience: if you have seen enough work by many or most of the people involved in the production, then you really have something to go on. You can see how one actor's work is better in this play than it was in another play. You begin to wonder if the director perhaps elicited this change.

Some insight can be achieved by mere experience, but experience alone isn't sufficient if there isn't also memory. I am shocked by myself, but also, *a fortiori*, by some of my colleagues, who seem to forget what someone did in the past, and how well it was done. Consequently, unless you also have a good memory to go along with the experience, the experience isn't going to be worth much. If you can put together a lot of experience and a good deal of memory, then you have one possible way of judging which is to credit, and which is to blame, the production or the play.

WAYNE JOHNSON: I'm damned if I can tell—even after as much experience as I've had on both sides of the footlights, as a critic and as a playwright—who's doing what when. I don't think any critic, no matter how experienced or sensitive, is able on one viewing to separate the play from the production. How do you know the dancer from the dance?

MIKE STEELE: Separating the production from the play is difficult, but becomes easier with experience. The playwright obviously is at a disadvantage here because his play can look very, very bad in a bad production, whereas a dazzling, slick production makes one suspect that it's a cover-up for mediocre writing.

LINDA WINER: There's no way to pretend that you know what the playwright *wanted*, as opposed to what the director *suggested*, as opposed to what the actor *did*. It's not that critics are stupid, but that art is complicated.

MICHAEL FEINGOLD: You can never know how much of what you're experiencing is the contribution of the playwright, the director, the actor, or the designer. If you could separate the elements easily, then, by definition, there would be something wrong with the experience; it would mean that the artists were not working in collaboration.

MEL GUSSOW: I like to think that I can separate the production from the script, but I've been proven wrong enough times. I felt that *True West* was not a good play, didn't succeed in doing what Shepard wanted to do, had no roles for the actors. Several years later, when I saw the Steppenwolf production, I realized *True West* was one of Shepard's best plays; the production changed my mind. I suppose if I'd read the script at some point, it might have made the difference, but I'm not sure it would have.

JOHN SIMON: We all have made mistakes: overvalued, which isn't so bad, and undervalued, which is bad. Sometimes a play comes back in a different version, it's better and I realize I was wrong. I might think something a terrific play and the production a disaster, and then a good production comes along and, by God, it *is* a terrific play. I say, "Ah ha, I was right." It also can happen that I was wrong.

EDITH OLIVER: The first time around, I, who am not of the theater, tend to swallow the production whole or not at all. Sure I can make some distinctions, but I think that, unless you've been attending rehearsals, it's awfully hard to know what is performance and what is playwriting.

WAYNE JOHNSON: If the play is worthy and you have the time, you go back and take another look. The second time around it looks a whole lot clearer. I haven't yet changed my mind about whether a play works, but have about the relative degrees to which it works.

FRANK RICH: Of course you cannot separate the production from the text one hundred percent. This is where the sheer bulk of theatergoing the critic has under his belt comes very importantly into play.

If you've seen the work of a director over a period of years, you tend to notice his or her artistic signature—similarly with a playwright, and actors and designers. You recognize certain consistent traits. You pull information together and you can make an educated guess—which is the best you can hope for—about who is responsible for what.

If there is ever a problem in assigning credit or blame, you must articulate that in your review. There is nothing wrong with writing a sentence that goes, "It's hard to know whether the director or the author is responsible for the fact that *x* happens in Act Two." There are lots of times when you can't know.

I don't think I've ever really changed my mind completely about a play. Certainly my opinions have changed to a degree over time. I've never felt a play was great and later decided it was terrible, or vice versa. But I'd like to think my taste does evolve and isn't set in concrete. My opinion changes in degrees that are gradual rather than radical. I've never felt I should recant my beliefs. I'm suspicious of that, of not sticking to your guns.

Does the history of the playwright, or the other artists involved in a production, influence you?

WAYNE JOHNSON: Of course a critic is influenced by the previous work of a playwright, director, or actor. If you have liked their work in the past, you expect more and that can be very dangerous. Those expectations are inescapable. You want their past successes to be repeated.

MEL GUSSOW: I suppose I have stricter standards for the playwright I'm familiar with. I expect something more from Lanford Wilson or Sam Shepard the next time around, whereas I greet the first-time playwright absolutely cold, with no expectations to fulfill. This doesn't mean a playwright is going to get by me with a work that shouldn't have been onstage in the first place. On the other hand, because of my fondness for Shepard and Wilson, perhaps I am willing to go a little bit further toward trying to understand what they are up to.

EDITH OLIVER: Even if you closed your eyes you'd know that it was Sam Shepard two words out.

LINDA WINER: You can't ignore the fact that some artists have a context. You have some expectations of them, yet you can't pretend you've seen something you haven't. You still have to deal with what's on the stage.

MIKE STEELE: The only trap is if you've liked a writer's previous work and try to keep him repeating it. This causes stasis in the writer, or at least paranoia, and puts the wrong kind of creative pressure on him.

JOHN SIMON: Experience and intelligence tells us that there is no such thing as infallibility in human conduct, whether it be ethical conduct, business conduct, or artistic conduct. Just because someone has been good as a director, an actor, or a set designer four times in a row, or even eight times in a row, it doesn't mean he or she won't bomb out the next time. This is not the end of the world, but it is the end of the world if a critic thinks that Mike Nichols can do no wrong, or that somebody else can do no right. That simply isn't true. People can turn out turkeys for years and then suddenly something really gets to them and they do something wonderful. The critic has to be open to that possibility.

Because I like what Circle Rep has done over the years, it may make me more hopeful, but, at the same time, while the hopefulness may work in their favor, the fact is that from greater hope may spring greater disappointment.

When is a new playwright interesting to you? What can a critic do to encourage new playwrights?

MEL GUSSOW: A new play has to stir my imagination. Quite often I will come out of something saying I enjoyed it, but begin to wonder if it was really new and good. Certainly with new plays the freshness of the experience matters a lot. You don't want to see someone going over the same old ground again, especially if it is that same playwright going over that same ground. Each time out I expect something new, some variation.

If there is any way to encourage new voices, it is through the enthusiastic embracing of a work of quality, wherever it is—from Broadway to farthest Off-Broadway. If I see a play in a dingy workshop, with hardly anyone else in the audience, but I think it's a play of merit, I will say so and say it in the same terms I'd use if it were on Broadway. Talent has to be recognized wherever it is.

EDITH OLIVER: I hope that my enthusiasm for a good play will come across to the reader.

WAYNE JOHNSON: A critic has an obligation to encourage new playwrights and to encourage theater companies to do the work of new playwrights. Any art that is not consciously and continuously renewing itself is moribund.

The thing that tells me if attention must be paid to a new playwright is whether he catches and keeps my attention. I'm a sucker for plays that shed light on what it means to be alive today.

JOHN SIMON: What attracts me to a new play is a sense that it evolves from a tradition and strives toward something new. It either does something that has been done before, or does something, informed by what went before, that is different, significant, communicative, and moving.

Dürrenmatt has said that the playwright should be able to write with the stage, which is to say, with theatrical image. An image, I think, is both visual and verbal, both action and language. If the new playwright can do that, then he commands my respect, admiration, involvement, and my sincerest commendation. There have been people who have been able to achieve things in lesser ways. For example, some people are just brilliant at dialogue. Other people come up with tremendously good plots, and just enough characterization to support their plays.

MICHAEL FEINGOLD: You can always tell if a playwright's work is original. You can hear it. It is possible to train yourself to hear it. I've found it in the most extraordinary and unexpected places. You can always tell a hack. The problem is that most people prefer hacks. Hacks are obedient, don't get anyone upset, meet expectations instead of altering them, don't challenge anybody, are easy to digest, and you can lure stars into playing in their work.

The important thing is, as Diaghilev said to Cocteau, "Surprise me." It doesn't mean twist yourself into knots. It may mean to take the old pattern and work a very conscious, albeit small, change on it.

MIKE STEELE: I like theatrical, imaginative, textured theater. I do not like realistic theater for the most part. I wince at the number of one, two, and three character plays being written and long for writers who can deal with more spacious relationships and larger ideas.

FRANK RICH: What most interests me about a new writer is his voice—if it is original and striking. Beyond that, there are so many different kinds of writers that there is not one common denominator that unites all writers I find interesting. Writers I will go back to see again and again might have never written a play I completely liked, but if I hear a voice that is original or unique, I will seek that writer's work out.

The writer who doesn't interest me is a writer who might write a play that is technically proficient but empty, unoriginal, and derivative. I'm looking for that original twist of mind. Playwrights with fresh voices I would follow to the ends of the earth.

JOHN SIMON: There are all kinds of critics. There are those avant-garde, on-the-barricades critics who go out there and discover wonderful new talents. I perceive my role as being the one who prevents this playwright, after he's been discovered, from getting a swelled head. These are two different critical functions.

Do you prefer to read a new play before reviewing a production?

MIKE STEELE: I will always try to read new plays. I will even try to talk with the playwright or director. There's no particular nobility in missing the point of a new work in an unfamiliar style. When we go to see *Waiting for Godot* now, we go knowing a lot about it and that knowledge only enhances the depth of our perception. Even sportswriters know the quarterback's game plan before a game. Only in theater is there a tradition of critical ignorance going into the theater game.

MEL GUSSOW: Hardly ever will I read a script before seeing a new play. With a classic, quite often I will read it again if it is something I haven't encountered in a long time. Reading a new play first will only distort my initial reaction to that production.

The increasing fashion of docu-dramas—*In the Belly of the Beast, The Execution of Justice*—poses a problem: One cannot review plays like that cold, in a vacuum. They are not just plays, they are events of contemporary history. One has to know as much as one can about the incident that provoked the story, and other works that might have been written about it. That's essential. I'm not sure a lot of critics are willing to do that; they look to see if a play works or doesn't work. That's just not enough.

LINDA WINER: A brand new play is often difficult to read because, often, it has changed quite drastically during rehearsals and previews, so reading a draft before reviewing it is pretty useless. Sometimes, if the playwright or the theater insists, I will read the first act to get a sense of the world of the play, the vision of the playwright.

EDITH OLIVER: I won't read scripts before going to see the production. A lot of critics like to read the scripts before they go, and we critics can get scripts easily enough. I've always said that if the producers pass out scripts to every member of the audience, I'll take one also. I don't want what I see on the stage to conflict with the production formed in my mind when I read the play.

WAYNE JOHNSON: I prefer not to read the play. It's important to go into the theater as a tabula rasa, like the rest of the audience. Frequently, I will ask for a script to be given me after I've seen the performance. This way I can watch the production and later search through the script to accurately quote the dialogue in my review.

FRANK RICH: I don't read new plays before I see them. I would much rather know as little as possible. I like to have that fresh response. If you lose that ability to have an open mind and a fresh response, you lose the excitement of going to the theater. The job would then become a very onerous chore.

Describe the mechanics of reviewing a play. Do you take notes during the performance? Do you prefer to attend a preview or opening night?

EDITH OLIVER: I never stop taking notes, but I can never read a word of them after the performance. Notetaking is just to remind me I'm at the theater to work, not to laugh and cry and applaud and sob. After the play I come home,

I put a yellow sheet in my typewriter, and I write everything that comes into my mind. I call that the "battle sheet." I set the alarm for very early in the morning, go over my notes, and pretty much rerun the play in my mind. Then I know if I've seen anything worth writing about the night before.

WAYNE JOHNSON: I rarely take notes. I don't think that's what a critic ought to be doing. My philosophy of writing a review is based on the Wordsworthian edict of "intense emotion recollected in solitude." You go out and get whatever it is a production has to say to you. You experience the production as fully as possible and then you go back and try to re-create that experience as accurately and completely as you can.

Sometimes it's necessary to take notes. Especially when you're seeing a new play and you're not really sure if a certain character is the brother or the lover of another character.

MICHAEL FEINGOLD: I do not take a lot of notes while a performance is going on. I will sometimes scribble down a word or half a line that I might want to quote. I might ask the press agent or someone in the company for a script afterwards in order to look up the exact line. I will put down a key word that will remind me of an expression on an actor's face or how something looked. I know some prominent critics who spend all their time in the theater with their noses buried in their notebooks. I wonder when they ever have time to see the play. They tend to review the concept of the play rather than the actual performance and its effect on the audience.

LINDA WINER: I take a lot of notes—in shorthand—but I don't take my eyes off the performance, which accounts for all the inkspots on my clothing. I do look at my notes later on. What I scribbled down in the theater reminds me of the production and it is a chance to relive the experience.

When I wrote for a daily newspaper, my deadline made me responsible for a review seemingly minutes after seeing a performance. There is something to be said for that pressure, but I do love writing the next morning having slept on it and mulled over the experience. With the wonderful invention of press previews I'm able to write the next morning. I think it makes for saner critics than having to write immediately. It allows us to have the same rhythms as other people.

When writing a review, I take as much time as I am allowed. If I have five hours I take five hours. If I have twenty minutes I take twenty-five.

JOHN SIMON: I don't sit there in stony silence not discussing the production with whomever I'm with, not talking to other critics, rushing out of the theater so somebody won't talk to me about the play and influence my judgment. I think one should be as open as one can be to every reaction that comes one's way. Then, when one sits down to write, one must be as individual, no nonsense, and hardheaded as possible.

This has been attributed to several critics, and I don't know who first said it, but when some critic was asked what he thought of a play, he said, "I don't know, I haven't written my review yet." It's true. You don't really know until you start writing the review.

I do take notes when I think notes are called for—usually of bits of dialogue I think I might need. Some plays are so good that I just can't afford to write anything down because I'll miss something wonderful while I'm writing. There are other plays that are so bad I won't need to quote anything. What's the point of quoting the dialogue when the problem is something else?

I write extremely fast, and I correct very, very little. I write in longhand and then I type slowly and make changes. When the review is typed I make a few more corrections and that's it. If I don't have the review due the following day, I procrastinate as passionately as anybody. I tend to write not quite at the last moment, but certainly at the next-to-last moment.

Opinions, half-finished notions, are obviously forming and germinating all the while. The big thing is to have an opening, to have a first line or a first paragraph. That first line or paragraph can come at any time. Sometimes it comes during the play, sometimes on the way home, and sometimes you have to stare at the blank page for a few minutes before it comes, but it does come, and the rest sort of follows from that.

Does the audience reaction ever affect your perception of the production?

WAYNE JOHNSON: Sure. Theater is a communal art. The critic is part of the audience, and their response affects you. But if the audience response affects you in such a way that all you do is report that response, then you're not doing your job as a critic.

FRANK RICH: A professional critic is always surrounded by people who are enthusiastic. Whether critics go during previews, as is now the practice, or on opening night, as in the old days, everyone is cheering. If the play is a comedy they're in the aisle laughing. There is always a standing ovation.

You're not a critic if you are not secure in your own

tastes; when you know what you find funny or not you don't need the response of the people around you to reassure you. I usually don't notice the audience response pro or con. Being in the audience is some of the fun of going to the theater, but it really doesn't have an effect on the critic's judgment. At some of the shows I've loved I've seen people fall asleep or walk out.

LINDA WINER: When the entire audience is laughing and I'm not, it's what I call the Martian syndrome—are all of these people from another planet? You cannot be influenced by the audience at a press preview or at an opening night because the house is papered with friends of the production, people who have a personal stake in the show. Our job isn't to take the temperature of the audience.

MEL GUSSOW: I'm certainly aware of the audience, but in no case would it influence what I write. When I hear loud laughter from an audience and I'm not enjoying the performance as much, my tendency is to think something is really wrong with the play and with the audience.

EDITH OLIVER: I'm not aware of the audience at all. I realize that most are friends or backers.

JOHN SIMON: To be with the kind of opening night audiences that you get today is just a circus. It probably makes it harder to evaluate the play fairly. The producers load these previews with close friends who feel obliged to laugh at every stupid joke they hear—maybe they're not obliged, maybe they are idiots. This can sway you toward harshness rather than kindness.

What advice would you have for a young critic reviewing new plays? What is the ideal training for a critic?

EDITH OLIVER: Go to the theater. See what you think and write it in as forthright a manner as possible. I hate advice. "What he should do" is my least favorite phrase in the English language. You report what you see. If you happen by nature to be funny, hooray. If you happen by nature to be very smart, hooray. If you stop enjoying going to the theater, quit.

MIKE STEELE: My advice is not to go to drama school, but instead study humanities generally, read theory and talk, argue, fight with practitioners in the field. Then write honestly without pulling punches and try to write interestingly and passionately. You should have a passion for theater, enough so that you will constantly challenge, cajole, and argue with it when it lets you down.

MEL GUSSOW: I've always felt that Harold Clurman was as close to an ideal theater critic as I've known and read, because of his comprehensive background in the theater and in other arts. When he saw a play he would never greet it coldly as an object onstage, but would bring with him a vast knowledge of acting, directing, and stagecraft.

Whenever anyone would ask Harold what credentials you need to be a critic, you would expect him to say that you should know everything possible about the theater, but the theater would come about tenth on his list. He would say to know everything you can about music, literature, history, current affairs, and all the areas that comprise the liberal arts or humanities. Obviously you have to know the form itself, but you cannot approach it in isolation.

WAYNE JOHNSON: You know a whole lot more about what's happening if you've been directly involved in theater in some way or other. You have to see a lot of plays, know the literature, the history of theater—anything you can learn about theater. If you don't know how to write, even if you know all about theater, you're not going to be worth a damn as a critic. You must have enough skill with the language to express yourself and share with the reader what you saw and thought.

FRANK RICH: You can only be a critic of an art form if you know the form and know how to write. There is no substitute for going to the theater a lot. Theater is an ephemeral art. It isn't like movies; if you want to be a film critic and have never seen a film in your life, you can essentially make up that loss by seeing the films you've missed. Theatrical productions, once over, are gone forever—even if the text remains.

No one should be a critic who doesn't have a deep knowledge of and consuming passion for the theater. But a critic must have a broad intellectual background, not just a background in the art he is reviewing. Any serious criticism takes into account all of the arts, literature, history, current affairs—you name it. Without that background you'd be a terribly parochial, not very interesting critic.

LINDA WINER: You need to know as much as you possibly can. There is no excuse for ignorance. If I had one gripe it would be that critics go to the theater too much; they become overspecialized. Their world view becomes smaller and smaller. They end up comparing theater to theater instead of theater to life.

JOHN SIMON: Dance, music, fine arts, movies, architecture, you name it, there is no art that doesn't have some bearing on the theater. I think the best thing a body could do would be to have a genuine love, interest, and concern for all the arts. Beyond that, an interest in just about everything that pertains to life, because the worst thing that art can do, and therefore the worst thing that criticism can do, is not to have a bearing on life.

What is your philosophy of criticism? What makes for good criticism?

JOHN SIMON: The difference between a reviewer and a critic has been defined in many different ways. I think the main difference is that the reviewer is preponderantly a journalist or a reporter. Whereas a critic, I think, is an artist. Maybe a secondary artist, maybe a lesser artist—I'm perfectly willing to grant that—but ultimately an artist, doing all the things an artist does in a somewhat different, perhaps less important, perhaps less original, perhaps less creative, way. But when I say "less," I don't mean not at all, I mean less. Perhaps it is an art the way that ceramics is an art compared to the way sculpture is an art.

EDITH OLIVER: Gertrude Stein used to say that a bell would go off when she saw a painting she liked. It seems to me that is true for plays. The top of my head comes off.

MEL GUSSOW: We really should enjoy ourselves in the theater. It is live entertainment. I'm always amazed at critic-scholars who can write entire books without mentioning performance. Performance is so involved with theater that it is essential to any observation.

There is judgment going on in every sentence of a piece, even in terms of a plot summary. Anyone can say "I liked it," or "I didn't like it." You don't have to be a drama critic to do that. A critic has to think more deeply than that. You have to try to analyze what's going on both on the stage and in the playwright's mind. Criticism is analysis, not just giving one's opinions.

LINDA WINER: For criticism to be vital, we need a lot of critics, a lot of voices. Each voice should be just one ingredient in a stew of people talking about the theater.

Live performance attracts me. I review anything that sweats. To have the experience and to analyze it in a limited space and time is almost a performance. When it's good, it's great. The combination of a spontaneous reaction, a certain amount of analysis, plus a sense of reporting keeps reviewing from becoming boring for me.

Sometimes when I'm having trouble getting a handle on a show I remind myself of those three little questions: What were they trying to do? How well did they do it? Was it worth doing? So often critics go directly to the third question, to "No, I don't like it because I don't like it."

MEL GUSSOW: There is something about the live theatrical experience that has never paled, even though I've spent many of the most boring nights of my life in the theater.

WAYNE JOHNSON: Anyone who reads a critic over time is going to have a pretty good fix on what the critic's prejudices and "philosophy" are.

FRANK RICH: Too many people are led by the nose by critics. I'm not saying people shouldn't read criticism, but people should know their own minds, have their own responses, and not be burdened by any kind of conformity, whether it is imposed on them by fellow audience members or by critics.

If people went to theater more as an adventure, and

less as a reason to sit in a cushioned chair and relax, they'd get more fun out of it. They'd be able to take in the excitement that is going on in today's theater. Critics must help spread the news of that excitement and explain what it's about.

JOHN SIMON: If there was such a thing as the most wonderful, ideal critic in the world, who would please everyone from Aristotle to Bertolt Brecht, even *he* should not be taken as holy writ. Every critic is just an instrument the reader can use to help develop his or her own taste and judgment. If critics have proved themselves useful to you at times, then certainly read them, but never substitute their opinions for your own thinking.

When the price of the ticket is fifty dollars, people will almost have to depend on critics. What the critic could do by thinking out loud—without actually sending someone to this play or not sending him to that play—is to get the public to do their own thinking, their own discriminating, their own weighing, measuring, evaluating, comparing, and contrasting.

What I hope for from a theatrical experience is that it will make me aware of something I've not been aware of before; that it will deepen my understanding of something I may have understood, but not as clearly, as sharply, or as deeply; that it will couch some experience in a form, a shape, an expression, an impact that is new, different; that it will reach me in a more startling, thought-provoking, rich way. I hope to have my awareness extended, whether in height, breadth, or depth, and to come out of the theater—speaking almost metaphorically—a better person than when I went in.

God knows it's never been proven that theater really improves people. What is demonstrable is that if you go to theater, and if you are open, you can in some intangible way improve yourself as a human being. One of the benefits will be reaped by the person you love, whom you will love more sensitively, another will be reaped by humanity at large, with whom you will become more concerned. Whether you will become a more honest businessman, I don't know. There is a moral value in beauty, and a beautiful piece of theater will stimulate those moral juices to flow. Even if it isn't true, it's a beautiful hope, a beautiful assumption, a beautiful hypothesis toward which one can work. Finally, whether or not it becomes real in the fullest sense doesn't matter.

LEE ALAN MORROW is a writer, director, and teacher. His feature articles and interviews have appeared in such publications as *Playbill* and *Back Stage*. He has directed over seventy-five musicals, plays, and operas in professional and university theaters across the country. Morrow did his graduate studies at Northwestern University and was on the faculty of Moorhead State University. He is the author of a forthcoming book on the history of Broadway (Abbeville Press, 1987).

FRANK PIKE is a writer and teacher. His plays have been produced in New York, Boston, Los Angeles, and Minneapolis. Pike received his Ph.D. in theater from the University of Minnesota in 1980 and has been on the faculty of the University of Minnesota and Middlebury College. He has conducted playwriting workshops in schools, theaters, and writing groups across the country. He is co-author of *The Playwrights' Handbook* (NAL/Plume) and the co-editor of *Scenes and Monologues from the New American Theatre* (NAL/Mentor, Winter 1987). Pike has received writing grants from the Andrew Mellon Foundation, the Bush Foundation, and the Jerome Foundation.